Acknowledgments

We acknowledge the financial support of the many agencies for research that is incorporated in this book. George Lin for support from the Research Grants Council of the Hong Kong Special Administrative Region (China) (HKU7666/05H), the Faculty of Arts Research Supporting Scheme 2006–07, the University Research Committee (Grant # 10204022) and the Committee for Research and Conference Grants (CRGC) in the University of Hong Kong University. Terry McGee for assistance from the Institute of Asian Research, University of British Columbia and the Faculty of the Built-Environment, University of New South Wales, Australia. Mark Wang for support from Melbourne Research Grants Scheme and the University of Melbourne. Andrew Marton for support from the School of Contemporary Chinese Studies and the University of Nottingham Research Committee Small Grants Scheme.

Personal acknowledgments

The writing of this book as with much of the academic life relies upon the ongoing support and patience of our families, close friends and colleagues. T. G. McGee dedicates this book to Lori, Katrina, Tyler and Belinda and the next generation, Dylan and Holly, who will have to grapple with the reality of China's emergence as a major actor in the world system. George Lin wishes to thank Professors Hu Zhaoliang and Wang Enyong of Peking University for their help for undertaking field work in China and to Stacey and Jimmy for their understanding, tolerance and support during the three summers when the manuscript was written at UBC away from home. Mark Wang is grateful to his family members Lucy, Sherry and Dennis for their understanding and support. Andrew Marton wishes to acknowledge the prodigious personal and intellectual support of Liu Junde, Professor of Geography and Director of the Administrative Divisions Research Centre at East China Normal University and Mr Zhu Hongcai, now retired Deputy Director of the Land Resource Management Bureau in Kunshan, Jiangsu Province. Jiaping Wu wishes to thank Fu Ping and Chelsea for their support and he dedicates this book to his newly born son – Brendan.

Permissions

In synthesizing a book such as this, which utilizes original research by the authors carried out over the last 15 years, it is inevitable that some sections of this book will have appeared in the authors' previous publications. We are therefore grateful to the following publishers for permission to use material from the following sources.

Elsevier, for Tables 3–5, Figure 5 and related text in Lin, G. C. S. (2002) The growth and structural change of Chinese cities: a contextual and geographic analysis. *Cities* 19 (5), pp. 99–316; Carfax Publishing, Taylor and Francis Ltd., for Tables 4–6, Figure 1 and related text in Lin, G. C. S. (2001) Metropolitan development in a transitional socialist economy: spatial restructuring in the Pearl River Delta, China. *Urban Studies* 38 (3), pp. 383–406; V.H. Winston & Son Inc. for Tables 6 and 8 as well as selected sections in Lin, G. C. S. (2004) Towards a post-Socialist City? Economic tertiarization and urban reformation in the Guangzhou metropolis, China. *Eurasian Geography and Economics* 45 (1), pp. 18–44, and for Tables 1–4 and Figures 3 and 8 in Lin, G. C. S (2006) Peri-urbanism in globalizing China: a study of new urbanism in Dongguan. *Eurasian Geography and Economics* 47 (1), pp. 28–53; Blackwell Publishing Ltd. for Figure 3 in Lin, G. C. S. and Ho, S. P. S. (2005) The state, land system, and land development processes in contemporary China. *Annals of the Association of American Geographers* 95 (2), pp. 411–36, and Tables 8.3 and 8.4 and some of the related text in Chapter 8, which are adapted and revised from Tables 2 and 1 (pp. 32, 31) respectively in Marton, A. M. (2002) Local geographies of globalization: rural agglomeration in the Chinese countryside. *Asia Pacific Viewpoint* 43 (1), pp. 23–42; Routledge, for Tables 8.1 and 8.2 and Figures 8.1, 8.3 and 8.4 and some of the related text, which are adapted and revised from Tables 1.1 (p. 7) and 3.5 (p. 88) and Maps 1.1 (p. 4) and 5.4 (p. 152) respectively in Marton, A. M. (2000) *China's Spatial Economic Development: Restless Landscapes in the Lower Yangzi Delta*.

Abbreviations

CBD	central business district
EMR	extended metropolitan region
ETDZ	Economic and Technology Development Zone
LYRD	lower Yangzi River delta
IMR	interlocking metropolitan region
PRD	Pearl River Delta
RMB	*Renminbi* (unit of currency in China)
SAR	Special Administrative Region
S–D	Shenyang–Dalian
SEZ	Special Economic Zone
SOE	state-owned Enterprise
TVE	town and village enterprise
NBSC	National Bureau of Statistics of China

Pinyin terms

Chinese rural and urban spaces

cheng – city (traditionally means a walled place)
chengshi – city
chengshi fu zhongxing – ancillary urban center
chengshi ci zhongxing – sub-urban center
chengxiang yitihua – urban rural integration
chengzhongcun – village within a city
cun – village
diji shi – prefectural level city (formerly prefecture)
huying gouxiang – urban echo
kaifaqu – development zone
shequ de shi – city with districts
bu shequ de shi – city without districts
shi – municipality (traditionally refers to a market)
shiqu – urban districts
xian cheng – county seat
xianji shi – county level city
xianshu zhen – towns under county administration
xiang – township
zhen – town
zhixia shi – centrally administered city

Chinese urban planning

chengshi yongdi – urban land
jianzhishi – designated cities
jianzhizhen – designated towns
jiben jianshe touzi – capital construction investment
leixingxing – local typicality
peiqu – branch zone (adjacent to, but not part of the main zone)'branch' development zone
shequ – community or literally "social area" – administratively part of a built-up area of cities and towns

shi guan xian – city administering counties
teshu zhengce – special policies
tudi churang – land conveyance
tudi huabo – administrative allocation of land
yi tian zhi – unified (rural) land system
zao cheng – city building

Chinese population

fei nongye renkou – non-agricultural population
gang'ao tongbao – Hong Kong and Macau compatriots
Huaqiao – overseas Chinese
Hukou – household registration system
liudong renkou – floating population
wailai renkou – outsiders (or migrant population)
yigong yinong renkou – people engaged in both industrial and agricultural work
zanzhu renkou – temporary residents
zanzhu zheng – ID lodging card for temporary residents
zili kouliang renkou – people who look after their own needs for food, housing, medical care and other urban services when moving to cities

Chinese economic activities

buchang maoyi – compensation trade
danwei – work unit
duzi jingying – wholly foreign-owned ventures
gaige kaifang – market-oriented economic reform and the adoption of a open door policy
getihu – street traders and household enterprisers
hezi jingying – equity joint ventures
hezuo jingying – cooperative ventures
jiagongfei – processing fee
lailiao jiagong – export processing
nong-gong-mao lianhe qiye–agricultural–industrial–trade cooperative enterprise combines
sanjiaozhai – triangular debt
sanlai yibu – three supplies with one compensation
shangren – businessman or small enterprise owners
siying qiye – private enterprises
xiangzhen qiye – township and village enterprises

Chinese history and culture

jiu Zhongguo – "old China," usually means China before 1949
tianming – the Heavenly Mandate

tianxia – all under Heaven
tianzi – the son of Heaven
zili gengsheng – self-reliance
Zhongguo – Middle Kingdom

Chinese sayings

mantian xingdou queshao yilun mingyue – a spread of numerous stars in the sky without a large shining moon in the center
cun cun dianhuo, chu chu maoyan – in every village fires stir, and everywhere is belching smoke
chengshi taidale, buhao – it's no good if cities are too big
gongye jinyuan, minzhai jinqu, chengzhen jinquan – group industries into parks, merge individual housing estates into urban districts, and link scattered towns to form urbanized regions
nongmin jizi jiancheng – peasants raise funds for town building
xiao kang shui ping – a moderately well-off level of living standard
yinian yixiao bian, sannian yizhong bian, wunian yida bian – a minor change in one year, medium-scaled change in three years and major change in five years.

1 Introduction

Moreover – and more importantly – groups, classes or fractions of classes cannot constitute themselves, or recognize one another, as "subjects" unless they generate (or produce) a space.

Henri Lefebvre (1991)[1]

This book is an exploration of urban changes occurring in the coastal region of China in the period since its "opening-up" after the end of the Maoist era in 1976. These changes have been brought about as a consequence of both China's economic and political reform and its increasing integration into the global economy. Geographically the book focuses on the coastal provinces that were the first areas opened up to foreign investment in the period after 1979. The term coastal areas is the same as the Chinese government's designation of the eastern region consisting of the provinces of Liaoning, Hebei, Shandong, Jiangsu, Zhejiang, Fujian, Guangdong, Guangxi and Hainan, and the provincial level cities of Beijing, Tianjin and Shanghai. For our purposes it also includes the Special Administrative Regions (SARs) of Hong Kong and Macao.[2] In the early stages of reform the formation of the Special Economic Zones (SEZs), such as Shenzhen, Zhuhai, Xiamen and Shantou that were created in 1979 and Hainan island in 1988, allowed special economic policies, new systems of management and experiments with land markets that encouraged foreign investment. The policy was expanded in 1984 with the establishment of 14 "open coastal cities" that were given considerable autonomy in fiscal and management matters. This policy initiative was directed towards fulfilling Deng's vision that these cities would become catalysts for international trade and investment that would flow outwards to the surrounding regions. This action was quickly followed by the extension of these incentives to "Open Economic Regions" in the Yangzi River Delta, Pearl River (*zhujiang*) Delta and coastal Fujian to be followed by the inclusion of other parts of the coastal zone including parts of Shandong and Liaoning provinces. In the early 1990s Pudong was created as a New Zone in metropolitan Shanghai. It became the focus of major national and municipal initiatives and investment. At the same time many provincial capital cities and five cities along the Yangzi River were granted open city status (see Figure 1.1).

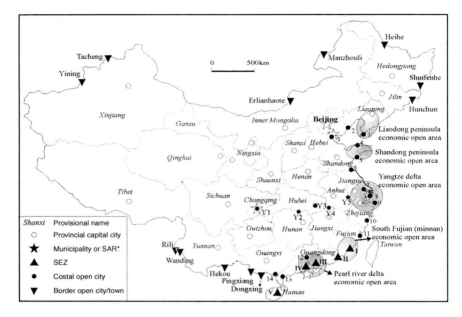

Figure 1.1 Spatial sequence of China's opening-up since 1978 (sources: Hu, Zhaoliang, Wang E. Y. and Han M. L. 2000, China Socioeconomic Development and its geographic background, Beijing: *Renmin Jiaoyu* (people's education) Press, pp. 135; Liu, Peiqiong (ed.) 1994, Mega trends of China economic development, Guangzhou: *Guangdong Jiaoyu* (Guangdong education) Press, pp. 52–109.

Notes

I – Xiamen SEZ, II – Shantou SEZ, III – Shenzhen SEZ, IV – Zhuhai SEZ, V – Hainan SEZ.

Fourteen coast open cities: 1 – Dalian, 2 – Qinhuangdao, 3 – Tianjin, 4 – Yantai, 5 – Qingdao, 6 – Lianyunguang, 7 – Nautong, 8 – Shanghai, 9 – Ningbo, 10 – Wenzhou, 11 – Fuzhou, 12 – Guangzhou, 13 – Zhanjiang, 14 – Beihai.

Five Yangzi River open cities: Y1 – Chongqing, Y2 – Yueyang, Y3 – Wuhan, Y4 – Jiujiang, Y5 – Wuhu)

1980: Four SEZs were established (Shenzhen, Xiamen, Shantou and Zhuhai).

1984: Fourteen coast open cities were open.

1985: Five coast economic open areas.

1988: Hainan SEZ was established.

1990: Shanghai Pudong new area was established.

1991: Thirteen border open cities/towns and five open cities along Yangzi river (cities of Chongqing, Yueyang, Wuhan, Jiujiang, Wuhu).

All provincial capital cities were listed as open cities.

2000: Large scale inland development began.

* Municipality directly under the jurisdiction of the central government.

SAR – Special Administrative Regions of Hong Kong and Macao.

Overall the spatial dimensions of the Chinese "modernization" followed the same principle as was applied to the general economic reform program, i.e. gradualism. Wang *et al.* (2002) show the spatial sequence of the opening-up of China to the world economy from the late 1970s.[3]

These economic reforms are also important to understanding the Chinese urbanization processes. First and perhaps most important from the point of view of the formation of "urban spaces" were the development of urban and rural land markets that are discussed in Chapter 2. Cities in the coastal zones were also encouraged to set-up Economic and Technological Development Zones[4] where the focus was on the new high-technology industries that would be the leading edge of the technological revolution in Chinese industry that have proved so important in the city-building process of Kunshan discussed in Chapter 8. Undoubtedly the most dramatic example of this process was the case of Shenzhen Municipality that saw the transformation of Baoan County adjacent to Hong Kong from a population of 30,000 in 1980 into a metropolis of seven million by 2000.[5]

However, in the 1980s when these city forming activities were begun, the more significant process of creating urban space associated with rural reforms has been labeled "rural urbanization."[6] Central to the reforms in the countryside was the abolition of the socialist collective systems administratively centered on the commune and the adoption of a form of contracted "household responsibility system" that gave farmers more freedom in decision-making and incentives to increase production. Many of these changes occurred spontaneously at the local level to be sanctioned later by the state. Another consequence of the relaxation of state control over the rural economy was that it provided a trigger for increased commercialization and industrialization that led to a surge in small industrial enterprises located in the towns and villages of rural areas that was a form of "in-situ urbanization."[7] This tremendous surge in rural industry was initially fueled largely by domestic investment and produced consumer goods for Chinese markets although in south China much of this town (or township) and village enterprises (TVE) development was funded by investment from Hong Kong and Taiwan producing products for global market.[8] There has been an ongoing debate concerning the relative importance of these endogenous and external factors in influencing the modernization of China but this study supports the view put forward by some commentators that operation of these two forces created a "two-track" process of urbanization that initially lead to the spread of urban activity into the countryside as well as slower growth in the large urban centers. Thus for a short moment in global history it seemed as if China might be embarked upon an ad hoc process of creating "urban space" in the early phases of the urban transition that was almost unique to world history: one in which the problems of surging rural–urban migration, inadequate urban infrastructure and unemployment that characterized so many developing countries in the early phases of their urban transition might be avoided.

But in the 15 years since Deng's tour of south China in 1992 the pace of economic and political change has accelerated particularly in the coastal zones as China has become more integrated into the global economy and the forces of globalization became an important driver of a repositioning of urban space in large cities and the political centers of provinces and counties that are discussed in Chapters 3 and 4. This is not to ignore the fact that many other parts of China have also been opened up because they have importance in the strategic vision of the Chinese government. For example China has been following a policy that is dedicated to reducing regional inequality between the coastal and central and western region. However, it is the coastal zones that are the "vanguard" of the "New China" and the areas in which the most rapid economic growth, urbanization and social change are occurring. They have become a major destination of rural migrants especially since the relaxation of its *Hukou* system.[9] The coastal region has also been the major focus of the first policy "experiments" in opening-up the Chinese economy. This dynamic economic growth in the coastal zones of China has been the subject of voluminous research by investigators from both within and outside China. It may be argued that this research forms part of a "global fascination" with one the world's largest country's development experiences in an era of increasing globalization. Part of this fascination is the interest in the question of whether, or not, China will eventually move to become a fully developed capitalist society.

It is, therefore, reasonable to ask what new perspective this book brings to understanding of urban change in China. The answer to this question involves consideration of the perspectives that have been used in earlier studies to explain Chinese urbanization. Examples of these approaches include "globalization," "global–local interactions," "growth coalitions," the growth of extended metropolitan regions and the special trajectory of socialism with distinct Chinese characteristics that are discussed in the next three chapters. Despite the difference in these approaches they are in one way or another concerned with exploring the interaction between "space" as an abstract category and "place" as some form of bounded conception of localities that may be physically and culturally demarcated. As Stephan Feuchtwang points out these two intersect in the process of territorial place-making.[10] Our choice of the title of the book is very deliberate. We seek to see the production of China's urban space as a form of modernizing the Chinese state. The construction of urban China is firmly focused on territorial places that in a hybrid way can be both urban and rural space at the same time. This enables us to adopt an approach to study of the Chinese urbanization process as a multi-scaled phenomenon utilizing a more holistic approach that attempts a more comprehensive capture of its political and social dimensions. Laurence Ma captures this process as follows: "Viewed spatially this strategy of nation-building represents a downward shift in state power from a single unitary national scale to multiple local scales, giving rise to a new power matrix in geographic space since the 1980's."[11] There is another dimension to this argument that should be surfaced. There is an ongoing shift in the study of China that is emphasizing an interdisciplinary and disciplinary as well as an area studies approach to China.[12]

Our project adopts a perspective that attempts a more holistic approach to the study of Chinese urbanization. Namely it seeks to position Chinese urbanization in the context of global urbanization. In this manner the special features of the Chinese urban experience can be delineated and contribute to a richer analytical portrayal. Of course we realize there are dangers in this approach. The spatial diversity and rapid change of China in the last 28 years means that it is easy to reject broader theoretical paradigms as having only momentary relevance and regional irrelevance. But we are not convinced that these arguments are valid because we would want to argue that there is a national urbanization process in China that can be better understood in its spatial and global context.

The special contribution of this book is that it approaches the study of urban China from the perspective of the overall urbanization process, by which we mean the increase in the numbers of people who live in places defined as urban (although in China this is a very weak measure of urbanization because of the over-bounding of urban areas), the increase in the number of people engaged in non-agriculture (this too is a slippery measure because of multiple income sources not being captured in censuses) and the growth in the value of the non-agricultural production in an urban–rural space. Thus we suggest that the urbanization process, which has often been conventionally defined in terms of the demographic components of urban increase including rural–urban migration and urban natural increase, is too narrow to elucidate all the aspects of the urbanization process. In our view the urbanization process in China is best seen as an integral part of the general processes of development, political, social and economic change that have assumed distinctive configurations in China in the post-1978 era. Within the statistical framing of the urbanization process that the narrow demographic interpretation utilizes there are spatial, political, economic and social changes that cannot be separated from the demographic components of this process. Indeed some writers would argue that urbanization in this broader sense is the way the state enters a new accumulation mode.[13] The urbanization process thus becomes a central component of economic growth. In the Chinese context some commentators would argue that this is a central manner by which the state overcomes the contradictions that emerged in the state regulated economy.

Much of the research and writing about Chinese urbanization has been about Chinese cities not about the broader urbanization process.[14] The titles and contents of many recent books on urban aspects of China invariably use the word "city" or "cities."[15] But the urbanization process affects other parts of space than spaces defined as cities. As "urban populations" grow they spread outwards and usurp space that is defined as "non-urban" and there is constant ambiguity as to the meaning of this expanding urban space. As urban centers grow economically they attract migrants from non-urban areas that create both positive and negative effects on rural areas. On the positive side the flows of remittances from urban to rural areas provides capital and income to the countryside. A major negative aspect is the decline in rural populations and rural life. Thus rural and urban areas are enmeshed in networks of transactions that make the concept of rural–urban differences outmoded. Therefore the study of the urbanization process requires an approach that sees urbanization as one way of reorganizing nations or, as we choose to label it, the production of urban space. The use of the term "production" is intended to suggest many aspects of the process of urbanization including the physical construction of urban infrastructure, the administrative construction of urban units and the ideological construction of urbanization as a part of the development process.

From our perspective the entry point into this investigation is through an exploration of the "spatiality" of urbanization. Whatever the current fads of post-modernism it is an incontestable fact is that "things urban" must eventually be grounded in territory although academic discourses on urbanization often engage theory rather than the grounded reality of the urbanization process. This does not mean that we want to deny the post-modern insight that the interpretation of the urbanization process involves generating "constructed knowledge" about the process but hopefully our project is informed by an understanding of the empirical facts of the "grounding process" as crucial to any investigation of the urbanization process. Thus one of the important features of Chinese urbanization in the reform era since 1978 has been the political and administrative redefinition of non-urban space, as urban space has become of major importance. In the Western context this has often been explained in terms of processes such as "suburbanization" and outward spread of economic activity from the city core that has not always been associated with the redefinition of the non-urban as urban.

In the Chinese context this process has, until the 1990s been dominated by "in-situ" urbanization in which local agencies have been the prime "developers" of urbanization within an institutional framework that has "allowed" this process of "locally driven" urbanism to develop. This is often described as "urbanization from below." But in more recent years there has been an emergence of what we describe as "city-centering urbanization" that has been driven by "bureaucratic entrepreneurial elites" based in the administrative cores of the sub-regions of the coastal zone. This response was driven by policies of administrative decentralization, economic reform, the accelerated integration of China into the global economy and the surge of foreign investment. This process has involved a repositioning of individual cities in relation to one another to make them more competitive. This repositioning often involves vigorous "place-making strategies" designed to improve the individual competitiveness of each city. In many cases this involves investment in transportation infrastructure (e.g. airports) and the creation of branded public buildings (often designed by foreign architects) that are built to give the city identity.[16]

While recognizing the importance of this economic restructuring we are also concerned to emphasize the repositioning of urban space that occurs as a consequence of both political and economic restructuring. This has occurred not only through the internal reorganization of the internal space of core cities (which is not the focus of this book) but primarily through the expansion of urban administration into areas that have previously been defined as non-urban land that are located on the margins of the city cores. We argue that it is in the margins of the core cities that the major challenges of Chinese urbanization are emerging and for this reason they are the focus of this book. Thus the vectors of the repositioning of Chinese urban space need some theoretical framework that goes further than the usual "city-bound" conception of the urbanization process. Instead we focus upon the creation of multiple "urban spaces" in which territorial place making is occurring and the forces that drive this process rather than limiting our discussion to the statistical interpretation of the urbanization process that is the prevailing paradigm. This book adopts a more holistic version of the urbanization process that sees it as one of the important processes shaping the spatial economy of China. But in order to understand this we need focus our attention on the most rapidly urbanizing part of China – the coastal zone – in the post-reform era. This is not to deny the importance of the urbanization process that is occurring in other parts of China where the process of the production of urban space has many parallels. We also recognize that the Maoist era and previous dynasties have played a significant role in shaping contemporary Chinese urbanization, but we are more concerned with the manner in which historical paths have positioned and differentiated the coastal regions in the current phase of urbanization.

How do we propose to navigate our way through the complexities of the production of urban space in China in the period since 1978? In a broad conceptual sense the approach suggests a threefold division. In the first four chapters we explore the issue of theoretical approaches and issues relating to the role of the State and other "drivers" in the urbanization project in China. This involves a discussion of the historical framing of urban and rural development in China as a State project. Thus State driven fiscal reforms, administrative redefinition of rural to urban, redefinition of urban space and other drivers of urbanization, such as foreign direct investment and the urban place-making strategies of local and national governments, are seen as important. This leads to a discussion of the spatial pattern of Chinese urbanization, regional variations in national urbanization and the changing urban system with particular attention to the emergence of mega-urban regions in the coastal zones and their internal spatial differentiation.

Second, we explore the actual experiences of urbanization in a number of "places of representation" in which the "spatial practices" of urbanization are being carried out. These case studies are drawn from three distinctive regions of the coastal zone. First, the Pearl River Delta in Guangdong Province, that includes the SARs of Hong Kong and Macao and the Special Zones of Zhuhai and Shenzhen. Second, the lower Yangzi River delta that incorporates the three provincial level administrative areas of provinces of Jiangsu and Zhejiang, and Shanghai Municipality, and finally the old industrial heartland of the northern province of Liaoning. Each of these areas has been the subject of ongoing research by four of the book's authors, Wang, Marton, Lin and Wu who have been researching these areas for many years. Some may argue that an additional chapter should have been included on Beijing–Tianjin extended metropolitan region but this has been the focus of accelerating commentary that can be easily accessed.[17]

In the final section, Chapter 10 incorporates the results of the case studies into a synthesis to explicate the current repositioning of Chinese urbanization. The chapter shows the manner in which changes in urbanization at the case study level enable a more fine grained analysis of the changes in Chinese urbanization particularly in terms of the role of "drivers" and the emergence of functionally different trajectories that represent various degrees of "hybridity" in the inter-action between the various driving forces of urbanization. The book concludes with a final chapter entitled "Conclusion: rewriting China's urban future." This summarizes the main conclusions of the preceding chapters arguing that these developments in Chinese urbanization are important to an understanding of global issues of urbanization such as sustainability and livability and the policy implications of these developments. This chapter addresses these major issues from a Chinese perspective including the challenges that the current urbanization transition in China poses for national and global sustainability.

2 The political economy of Chinese urbanization

> In scripting the contemporary Chinese city, a critical question is what are the major, political, cultural/historical systems and institutions that are specific to China and that have affected the (re)configuration of urban space.
>
> Ma and Wu (2005b)[1]

Introduction

The study of the urbanization process has been carried out from many theoretical perspectives including the theory of rural–urban differences, economic development theory and theories of urban behavior that have been primarily formulated out of the study of urbanization in developed Western countries.[2] But from our perspective, these theories while offering insights into the urbanization process are inadequate because the historical, ecological and political–economic contexts of China are so different from the Western experience. Central to this assertion is the fact that China's situation as a former socialist state engaged in a process of opening-up its economy to market conditions and international transfers of capital and technology is not yet exhibiting all the features of a developed market economy such as the United States. At this point China seems embarked upon a developmental process that is proceeding in an incremental manner designed to avoid the rapid institutional change that occurred in other socialist countries such as the former Soviet Union. For example, as we illustrate in this chapter, land markets in China are operating in a very different manner from those of market societies in the early phases of the urban transition and this has an important influence on the growth of urban activities in Chinese space. We therefore suggest that the theoretical approaches that emphasize the role of institutions in social, economic and political change within a broader framework of political–economy theory offer the most valuable theoretical insights. In this approach we draw heavily on the ideas of theorists such as Victor Nee (1991, 1992), Nee and Cao (2000), Nee and Swedburg (2005), Henri Lefebvre (1991), David Harvey (1982) and the more recent approaches of "critical economic geography."[3] In this respect the studies in the sociology and economy of the post-Mao China have undergone similar theoretical shifts.[4] We also recognize that there are different approaches to China practiced by scholars from "inside" and "outside" China. In this book we try to blend the insights of China specialists with the broader theories of societal change in the comparative global context. The case for this approach has been made by Yeung and Lin (2003) who have persuasively argued that the study of China's institutional and economic change offers the opportunity to revise the ideas about industrialization and economic change that have grown out of the Western experience.[5] These arguments echo earlier efforts to formulate such positions by McGee (1991a and 1991b), Zhou (1991), Lin (1994 and 1997), Wang (1998), and Marton (2000).[6]

But the assumption that the Chinese developmental experience offers the opportunity to reevaluate Western theory is insufficient to offer a theoretical framework of the urbanization process in China. For this purpose we find the ideas of Henri Lefebvre quoted in Chapter 1 that emphasize the importance of political and economic processes in the "production of space" most helpful in delineating the urbanization process in China. Lefebvre argues that the "production of space" is carried out within a triad of "spatial practices" (human activities), "spaces of representation" (lived spaces) and "representations of space" (conceived and abstract spaces). It can be argued that this approach helps in the understanding of changing urban spaces at a variety of geographic scales: international, national, regional and local. In the Chinese context we also suggest that it is helpful to see the national urbanization policy as being filtered through a series of administrative scales from national to local. We agree with Ma (2002) that the urbanization of China is best seen as a project of state formation (this involves negotiation, resistance and compromise by all scales of government and quasi-government agencies and non-government institutions such as firms and foreign companies) that is driven by various developmental, political and social goals.[7] The process of activating this urban project involves the state in defining urban and rural space, regulating urban and rural space and implementing these regulations through surveillance and enforcement in an attempt to bring conformity to governmental representations of rural and urban space. For example the central government of China has begun to use remote sensing, Geographic Information Systems (GIS) and aerial photographs to find cases of illegal land use in cities and their margins.

But the same urbanization project is actually being encountered and experienced by people engaged in the urbanization process who may operate as individuals, households and economic and social groupings engaged in everyday life (spatial practices). There is also a process of interaction between the state (at various levels) and people engaged in everyday spatial practices that involves negotiation, resistance and compromise. The lived spaces (spaces of representation) are hugely diverse in a country such as China reflecting different linguistic, cultural, ecological and historical experiences.

To further complicate this theoretical model of the urbanization project in China the boundaries between these various components of the production of space have become increasingly porous in the period since 1978. Thus the insights of the new economic geography emphasize the social networks that transcend this triad of Lefebvre's categories. Capitalists in Hong Kong use kinship networks to facilitate their investment in the Pearl River Delta.[8] Local government bureaucrats from the coastal zones use personal networks with former government officials from their place of birth, who are now in central government, to gain the approval of government for local entrepreneurial ventures. Migrants from rural areas flood into the coastal zones despite the efforts of the central government to try and control their movements that are increasingly being discarded.

Globalization and China's transforming urban space

In this section it is also necessary to interrogate the issue of *globalization as it is affecting the Chinese urbanization process*. Simply put the task is to work out how globalization's "signature" is affecting Chinese urbanization. If studies in the social sciences of the 1990s were to be identified by one single word, there are really few better choices than "globalization," a concept that has influenced so powerfully and pervasively almost all documentations and interpretations of changes in the human society of our time.[9] Despite continuing debates over the precise meaning and nature of such a "chaotic concept" as globalization,[10] the prevailing intellectual trend has been to emphasize the explanatory power of globalization in understanding our rapidly changing economy, society and urban spaces. Whereas earlier scholarly interests in "urbanism as a way of life" were intertwined with theories of modernization, recent studies of urbanism in different world regions have been invariably empowered by the concept of globalization and accompanied understandably by a curiosity about global convergence.

For the cities in the global north, it has been extensively documented that, as a consequence of globalization, a system of "world cities" or "global cities" has emerged in which "world cities" such as New York and London no longer function simply as the centers of their respective country but have become command and control centers of the global economy.[11] The increased spatial mobility of capital and labor at the global scale is believed to have given rise to both the (re)agglomeration of metropolitan centers on a regional level and greater segmentation and segregation of the intra-urban space based on occupation, race, ethnicity, income and other socio-economic identities.[12] The globalization of Western consumerism, which was central to the notion of a "borderless world,"[13] has been linked to the proliferation of "global metropolitanism."[14] The result is "a cultural homogenization and synchronization that makes for increasingly convergent but fast-changing urban architecture and metropolitan lifestyles throughout the developed world."[15]

For the countries in the former Soviet Union and Eastern Europe, the "unique" characteristics of "the socialist city" identified by Szelenyi and others[16] that include under-urbanization, less urbanism (less urban diversity, less inner-city urban density and less urban marginality), and a relatively uniform urban space, are believed to be undergoing profound transition. As the socialist economy is exposed to the forces of global capitalism, many of the features of Western urbanism appear to be emerging in "cities after socialism"[17] although under-urbanization continues to be reproduced in countries such as Hungary, Poland and Czechoslovakia fueled by expanding rural housing (weak push) in the countryside and limited employment opportunities in cities (weak pull). In these cities increasing urbanism is marked by greater ethnic diversity, growing commercial sectors, higher urban marginality and emerging urban problems such as prostitution, homeless, crime and deviance.[18] Moreover, suburbanization and inner urban decay, the two popular trends of urban growth existing in the Western world for decades, are now replicating themselves in the post-socialist countries to accommodate and segregate the new rich from the poor.[19]

For the developing countries, the operation of global forces has effectively brought the town and country of the less developed nations into the orbit of capital accumulation and "global metropolitanism" although the breath and depth of global penetration remain in debate.[20] In their provocative study of urban change in Southeast Asia under globalization, Dick and Rimmer identified a trend in which Southeast Asian cities are "showing clear evidence of converging with Western patterns of urbanization."[21] They observed that rising real income and a rapidly expanding urban middle class in Southeast Asia since the 1980s had created a huge market demand for social comfort and public security which have, in turn, "given rise to market opportunities for well-funded entrepreneurs to borrow urban elements from the US."[22] Consequently, many of the American urban elements such as gated communities, patrolled shopping malls and entertainment complexes, air-conditioned offices, freeways and edge cities are all taking place in Southeast Asia. Because of this process of convergence, cities in Southeast Asia, they argue, can no longer be seen as a discrete from the developed world. To Dick and Rimmer, "Any attempt to explain either the historical or contemporary urbanization of south-east Asia as a unique phenomenon is therefore doomed to absurdity."[23] The logic of "globalization has made the paradigm of the Third World City obsolete" and "there should now be a single urban discourse indifferent to regional partition."[24] We would argue that while this argument has validity in the context of some Southeast Asian cities such as Singapore and perhaps Bangkok, many of the cities of Southeast Asia such as Phnom Penh and Manila still maintain many Third World city characteristics. There arguments also show no understanding of the processes of urban transformation in former socialist economies such as Vietnam and Laos that are part of Southeast Asia.

The transforming power of globalization is also believed to be extending into contemporary China where an urban transition of a tremendous scale is quickly unfolding. For decades, urban growth in China has been understood as having demonstrated some unique Chinese characteristics distinct from the cities of the Western world.[25] In recent years, however, important questions have been raised over whether or not Chinese urban change should continue to be seen as a unique phenomenon subject to special and separate interpretation even after China reintegrated itself into the global economy. A recent critical evaluation of the status of the field of study on urban China expressed dissatisfaction with the fact that "in China geography has remained under the shadow of the area-studies tradition and that China geographers need to move beyond their self-confined circle of empirical studies and become actively engaged with major theoretical debates in the disciplines of geography and urban studies."[26] Another commentary on the recent growth of "transitional cities" with special reference to China contends that these cities "are not themselves a prototype of something qualitatively different from the emerging neo-liberal city" and therefore "should not be excluded from being treated in the same way as the city is treated in the West."[27] The commentary goes on, "[B]y overly emphasizing the uniqueness, the regional specialists slip into a self-imposed intellectual exile. By overly emphasizing the otherness, the Western gaze may exclude these variants as important laboratories to observe contemporary urban changes."[28] Similar critiques are made by Yeung and Lin (2003) who call for a common ground to be made in line with "the globalization of knowledge and theories."[29]

The new trends of urban growth identified in major world regions raise serious questions concerning not only the way in which urbanism within different regional contexts should be reinterpreted but also the changing essence of urbanism under globalization. This situation is particularly relevant to the case of China – one of the largest and rapidly globalizing nations that has been reintegrated with the world since 1979 after decade-long isolation. Under the seemingly irresistible and irreversible tendencies of globalization, can we still see Chinese urbanism as something unique and incomparable with that in other world regions? Is the convergence made by Dick and Rimmer for globalizing Southeast Asia also applicable to globalizing China? Put it simply, is Chinese urbanism converging with "global metropolitanism" in the Western fashion, or is it still a unique phenomenon extending from what it has been for decades even after the intrusion of the powerful forces of global capitalism? These are some of the legitimate questions that need to be raised and answered in order to understand better the complexity of globalization and urban change.

Bringing the local into Chinese urbanization: an actor-centered approach

Perhaps the most practical way to approach this discussion is to introduce the idea of "drivers," which Douglas Webster (2002) uses in his work in terms of a four-fold division between external, national, regional and local forces.[30] The investigation of these drivers raises significant questions as to the way the drivers operate at these different levels and how they interact in the formation of urban space:

- external forces (e.g. foreign direct investment, WTO, World Bank, etc.) that are driving Chinese globalization;
- national (e.g. the national state): national forces working with globalization and sub-national partners to advance of the goals of national development;
- regional (e.g. provincial): at these levels provincial authorities are vigorously competing to attract global forces particularly in the coastal zones that are accelerating the processes of urbanization;

- local activities of entrepreneurial bureaucrats at the scale of the cities and their immediate margins and the outer margins of cities that are attempting to capture global investment through vigorous strategies of "place-making."

Another way in which the urbanization project is being modified by everyday practice is the increasing competition that is occurring between local urban governments to position their urban locality to capture more economic benefits of development than other urban areas. This has been very variously described through models of local state corporatism and growth coalitions. These models provide analytical insights into the behavior of local governments at various scales that are fulfilling the growth-oriented developmental goals of the central state but at the same time creating fiscal and management problems for higher levels of government.[31] Other consequences of this process are the various land-use and environmental problems that emerge as urban activity spreads into adjacent areas. This has forced the national state to respond with policies designed to reduce the number of political administered spaces through centralization, annexation and amalgamation of units of political administration as well as the decision to allow private entrepreneurs to join the Communist Party announced by Jiang Zemin in 2001. Indeed Jae Ho Chung (1999) has argued that sub-provincial governments, particularly sub-provincial cities:

> perform an indispensable role in the complex process of economic reform. Most importantly, they spread "developmental ideologies" and distribute opportunities of reform both intra- and inter-provincially. Vertically they work as agents of the center, not without a considerable degree of discretion, in carrying out policies of reform and opening. Horizontally, they constitute "corridors" of development by linking with domestic businesses.[32]

The growth of urbanization in China is thus often portrayed as being driven by the strategies of "entrepreneurial bureaucrats" that in various capacities administer the urban places and other political areas (e.g. counties) in which urban activity is occurring as well as influence the operation of capital and labor markets. As we will show later this term "entrepreneurial bureaucrats" in the Chinese context actually encompasses three "bureaucratic groups" within the cities. First, local government officials and their leaders such as local mayors whom because of their local power can dominate the leasing and development of urban land. Second, there are a group of "entrepreneurial bureaucrats" that carry on the work in the various "quasi" governmental organizations that city governments have set up to facilitate the city development process. Examples of this kind of organization are the many city development and investment corporations that have been set up by municipalities. They are particularly significant in infrastructure and development projects. Third, there are those "bureaucrats" that belong to vertically organized national units such as the army and national departments, who previously occupied administratively allocated land. During the Maoist era they occupied large areas within municipalities that were in effect "gated communities" and, as urban land markets have developed, they have used their claim to this land as a basis for negotiating compensation and have used the capital acquired for developmental initiatives.

Private entrepreneurs make up a separate category but they are quite diverse including small scale retailers of goods and services such as street traders and household enterprises (*getihu*), private entrepreneurs that owned medium sized enterprises (*shangren*) and large scale entrepreneurs who own bigger businesses (*siying qiye*). Finally there were a small but important group of very large private entrepreneurs (market entrepreneurs) that have developed in the internet business and retailing franchises, etc. There is also an increasing number of foreign educated and overseas Chinese who are involved in the processes of economic development and play an important role in overseas investment. The task of disentangling the contributions of these various groups to urban development is complex but not impossible.[33]

Since our concern in this volume is with the production of urban space we consider that the manner in which the various actors involved in urban formation shape urban space through changes in land use, land status and land value to be of crucial importance. The process of land acquisition is central to this creation of urban space and is often characterized by conflicting claims on land that are a cause of much competition and confusion They often prove an institutional blockage to attempts of the city administrations, in particular City Planning Departments, to try and create city plans that are aimed at making cities more efficient, livable and sustainable. But at the same time it is the "entrepreneurial bureaucrats" who we argue are the major drivers of economic growth in urban growth and transformation of the built-environment. In making this argument we do not want to downgrade the role that is played in this process by Chinese "corporate enterprises" and market entrepreneurs that have increased dramatically in the 1990s. But we argue that the two sectors of state and market are so interpenetrated that it often impossible to distinguish the differences between "entrepreneurial bureaucrats" and "market entrepreneurs."[34] While there are often differences between these two entrepreneurial groups they work in close liaison to promote urban development. As several researchers have shown with respect to the strategies of China's city governments, superficially these driving forces would seem to lead to risk taking and profit motivated, place-making and development projects that are typical of capitalist developed countries. These have been variously labeled "entrepreneurial" (Harvey, 1989), "new urban politics" (Cox, 1995), "growth machines" (Logan and Molatch, 1987) and "urban regimes" (Stoter, 1995). The adoption of various growth oriented strategies through "place marketing or promotion" (Kotler *et al.*, 1990), "city boosterism" (Ashworth and Voog, 1990), "prestige projects" (Loftman and Nevin, 1996) or mega-events (Hiller, 2000) has also drawn much attention.[35]

The political economy of urbanization in China

Thus urban development in China must be seen within a wider theory of the political economy of urbanization in the period since 1978. First the national policies have shifted dramatically to the encouragement of urbanization as the prime catalyst of economic growth. Second fiscal decentralization policies that began to impact from the early 1980s have greatly encouraged the city formation activities of city governments. Third, the increased commodification of land markets that had been occurring unofficially from the early 1980s in rural areas but was sanctioned by the central government in 1988 for both rural and urban areas has facilitated urban growth. Finally the acceleration of China's economy, of which an important part is the increased integration into the global economy, has led to rapid urban change particularly in the coastal cities. From the early 1990s these various macro-components have coalesced to drive the huge surge of urbanization and increase in urban land values focused on the municipalities.

The reaction of "entrepreneurial bureaucrats" to these macro-changes was to develop particular strategies that were designed to "position" their "urban spaces" so as to achieve rapid economic development.[36] It is important to understand that this repositioning is essentially carried out as a collaborative venture with the national state that is setting in place policies of rationalizing political space particularly focused on the coastal zones that are the main impact areas of globalization. This is seen by the central state as an essential component of the reorganization of political space to enable China to develop more rapidly and make it more attractive to global forces. Such initiatives were rewarded at the national level by recognition of these achievements through promotion of individual leaders (e.g. the case of the Mayor of Dalian). There are four main components of these strategies. First, the expansion of the control of land by municipalities that was brought about by the reclassification of rural counties adjacent to the existing municipal areas (e.g. the case of Panyu and Huadu in Guangzhou discussed in Chapter 5). Second, the encouragement of land leasing and land development that became an increasing source of revenue as the land market developed. This is actively facilitated by the reclassification of land from collective to urban that is occurring when adjacent counties were redefined as urban districts in which the creation of industrial estates of various types has been significant. Third, the need to create competitive cities in reaction to the increasingly competitive structure of the Chinese economy that accelerated with increasing globalization. This has led to an increasing emphasis upon infrastructure development (international airports) and property development (shopping malls etc.) that are designed to increase the cities' administration income and to attract increasing capital. Finally these strategies increasingly have to be packaged in the language of "global urbanization" with an emphasis upon creating sustainable, livable and "clean" cities (e.g. Dalian case in Chapter 9).

A second facet of this process relates to fiscal restructuring in the political system that allowed the market system to emerge. The increased role of entrepreneurs of all types (at all levels of the urban system) in the recent growth of urbanization has been the result of a socialist political economy undergoing transformation.[37] Traditionally, the city in a socialist economy has been established, financed and managed by the central state essentially as a functional node of the centrally planned economic system that is linked together through vertical linkages. Once a city has been established, the municipal government could rely on state budgetary allocation for capital investment for the maintenance and improvement of urban infrastructure. Prior to the fiscal rearrangement between central and local (provincial and municipal) states in the 1980s, state budgetary allocation took the lion's share of capital input in China's urban construction, accounting for over 80 percent of all capital construction investment (*jiben jianshe touzi*) (see Figure 2.1). This is by no means to suggest that urban construction was very well looked after by the central state. On the contrary, the city was basically treated as a "cash cow," to borrow the words from Barry Naughton (1995),[38] from which output and revenue were to be drawn and to which little input was channeled. However, there was a relatively stable source of capital for the maintenance of the urban infrastructure at a minimum level. More importantly, the number of cities was relatively small under the state strategy of urban containment and these cities relied mainly on vertical linkages with the central state. Competition among cities and between cities and the rural economy was internalized and controlled by the central state and was therefore not a major concern to individual municipal governments at the local level.

The institutional changes since the 1980s have brought about profound changes to not only urban capital formation but also to urban politics. To arouse local developmental enthusiasm, the central state has relaxed its control over local developmental affairs and allowed municipal government greater flexibility in handling issues of urban development. In 1984, the central government relaxed its criteria for the designation of cities turning away from the previous practice of urban containment. A direct consequence of the relaxation of state control over city designation was the dramatic growth of the number of cities from 193 in 1978 to 668 in 1998, an increase of 475 new cities in 20 years, which was far greater than the 61 new cities established over the previous three decades.[39] The growth of such a large number of cities means that it is no longer realistic for the central state to look after the financial needs of all municipal

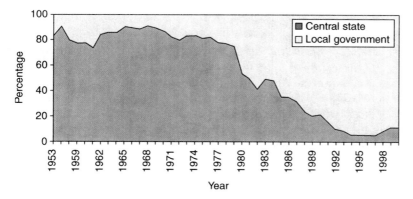

Figure 2.1 Capital investment in urban construction, China, 1953–2000 (source: China State Statistical Bureau (2001), p. 163).

developmental affairs. The approach adopted has been to decentralize the power of decision-making from the central to local (provincial and municipal) governments. As Figure 2.1 shows, state budgetary allocation has been reduced substantially from 80 percent to only 10 percent during over the past five decades. Although state budgetary allocation of funds for local urban construction has been reduced, local (provincial and municipal) governments are given greater autonomy in financing urban developments, particularly in the use of the surplus revenues after the agreed quota of remittance to the central government has been met. However, municipal governments are also held responsible for the profits and loss from municipal financing. Under this situation, individual municipal governments have to find their own way of fund raising or capital formation to finance the maintenance and upgrading of the urban infrastructure. In other words, municipal governments have to change themselves from being simply managerial into entrepreneurial.

The reformulation of central–local relations has also brought about changes to the way in which cities interact with one another. As the vertical linkages are loosened in the national urban economic system, horizontal linkages and interaction among cities as well as between cities and countryside have become increasingly important. Since the central state can no longer be counted on for the provision of capital, municipal governments have to turn to alternative sources such as foreign investment and the domestic private sector. This has given rise to strong competition among cities for foreign and domestic capital. Cities are no longer friendly partners of the same centrally planned socialist economy. In the most recent period of rapid economic growth that has accelerated since 1995 municipalities constantly reposition themselves in order to lure and spatially "fix" capital that is becoming more mobile. Since the location of foreign investment and private enterprises is often based on the minimization of transaction costs and maximization of profits, many municipal governments have endeavored to create a new favorable transactional urban built-environment attractive to foreign investors and the private sectors. Innovative local strategies of "place-making" and "place-promotion" have been adopted by municipal entrepreneurial bureaucrats to expand, upgrade and restructure the existing urban space as a means to reposition and reassert themselves in the endless process of competition among cities and between the urban and rural economies. Very often, such strategies are featured by the development of mega-projects, creation of definitive and signature building, the formation of new urban skylines and distinctive cityscapes, and above all the acquisition of a new and impressive symbol or identity of urbanism reserved for that particular city. Examples included the newly created cityscape of the Pudong New Area in Shanghai (in which there has been a major investment of national capital), the 63-story-high tower of the China International Trust and Investment Corporation (CITIC) in Guangzhou and the Landmark Building in Shenzhen. Many cities in China are also inspired to upgrade themselves into the class of "world cities" or "international cities." This ambition in the "representation of space" has necessitated the creation of new "spaces of representation" including international convention centers, public squares, new city hall, museums and opera houses, sports stadiums of the Olympic standards, theme parks, gigantic shopping malls, high-speed trains with cutting-edge technology, pedestrian streets and new central business districts with a water front location. These newly created "spaces of globalization" may not necessarily suit the actual needs as many of them have actually never been fully used, but they are believed to be essential to the upgrading of the city into the prestige of a "world city" or "international city."[40]

The reconstruction of new urban spaces naturally entails a huge amount of capital input. Given the fact that the central state is no longer solely responsible for financing urban construction at the local level, how then do municipal governments handle capital formation in the current era of decentralization, marketization and globalization? As Figure 2.2 shows, there are four main sources of capital input for urban construction in the Chinese context, namely state budgetary allocation, foreign investment, bank loans and local fund raising. State budgetary allocation accounted for a negligible share and foreign capital took up only 20 percent of the total capital input. The largest sources of capital are local fund raising and bank loans, which accounted for over 60 percent of all capital input in urban construction. These two sources of capital formation require close scrutiny.

When a municipal government in China realizes that it can on longer count on the central government for state budgetary allocation to finance urban construction projects, it naturally has to explore all possibilities of capital mobilization.

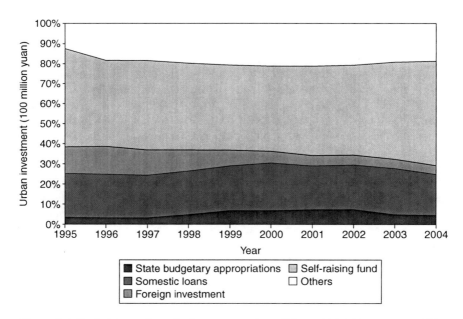

Figure 2.2 Capital formation of urban construction, China, 1995–2004 (sources: China State Statistical Bureau (2005), p. 197).

Apart from foreign capital, which is often mobile, uncertain and unstable, there are only two valuable assets that are under the firm grip of the municipal government; namely land and credit. In the current land system, land within the city is owned by the state. Although state ownership rests ultimately in the National People's Congress and executed by the State Council, it is the municipal government that is entrusted to claim the ownership of the urban land, which includes land within the urban districts as well as the land in the suburbs.[41] Prior to economic reforms, land was treated as a means of production for the socialist economy rather than a commodity for exchange and circulation. It was allocated to users who are usually state units (*danwei*) free of charge and with no terms. Since the introduction of the Land Management Law in 1988, the rights to use state-owned land in the city and the suburbs can be conveyed to commercial users at a conveyance fee and for a fixed term depending on the uses of the land. Municipal governments are now entrusted by the state to claim landownership, to be responsible for conveyance of the urban land and most importantly the collection of the conveyance fees. This had never been the case in the pre-reform era and it has become a new and reliable source of revenue for the municipal government. By leasing out land to commercial users in all sorts of entrepreneurial ways (i.e. requisition of existing administratively allocated land for paid conveyance to commercial users, expropriation of collectively owned rural land at lost cost and then converting it into land for conveyance to commercial users, etc.), municipal governments can collect substantial amounts of land conveyance fees. Incomplete statistics showed that in 1998 alone China collected conveyance fees of 24.35 billion yuan from domestic users and another US$65.27 million from foreign commercial land users.[42] By law, 30 percent of the conveyance fee should be remitted to the central government (i.e. the Ministry of Finance of the State Council) and 70 percent could be retained by local governments of various levels. In reality, however, little of the conveyance fee has ever been remitted to the central government and the bulk has always been retained by municipal governments.[43] Land leasing has therefore become a main source of local revenue generation and naturally capital formation for urban development. It was estimated that at the early stage of urban development, the income generated from land leasing accounted for nearly 70 percent of the municipal revenue in Shenzhen Special Economic Zone.[44]

When a municipal government has exhausted its existing land stock and run into the difficulty of negotiation with its surrounding counties for the expropriation of rural land, a common approach adopted is to incorporate or annex the rural counties into its urban administration so that its land will be firmly under the control of the municipality. Shenzhen Municipality has managed to incorporate its rural neighbor of Bao'an County into its jurisdiction. The most typical case has been Guangzhou, which incorporated Huadu County to its north and Panyu Municipality to its south and turned them both into urban districts of Guangzhou in June 2000 expanding the land area of the Guangzhou Municipality by more than twice (see Chapter 5). Clearly, under the current situation of a socialist political economy undergoing transformation, land has become a crucial asset of strategic importance to municipal financing, capital formation for urban development and above all the pursuit of the strategy of "place-making." The continuing expropriation and development of urban and rural land has thus been one of the most important driving forces explaining the booming and dramatic expansion of Chinese cities since the 1990s.

If land is an immobile and fixed asset firmly under the control of a municipal government, credit is a seemingly inexhaustible and renewable asset that can be claimed, (ab)used and manipulated by the municipal government for fund raising and capital mobilization. In a manner similar to the land-centered strategy of capital formation, the importance of credit to municipal financing in contemporary China is also a by-product of the ongoing transformation of the socialist political economy in which market forces have not yet fully operated and the socialist legacy remains very much in action. Here, the concept of "soft budget constraint" introduced by the political scientist Kornai (1986)[45] is instrumental to understanding how a Chinese municipal government engaged in capital mobilization on the basis of the credit commonly accepted and sometimes misconceived. Originally, the concept of soft budget constraint was introduced to explain the fact that in a socialist economy a firm does not have the incentive to look after capital investment in an effective and efficient manner because over-expenditure or investment failure would never lead to bankruptcy. Bad investment decisions or poor business performance can be taken care of by the state through the transfer of credits, subsidies and other refinancing bailouts. In other words, the outcome of over-investment or business failure under the available hard budget can be softened by the financial institution of the socialist state. This concept helps explain the poor performance of the state-owned enterprises in many socialist economies including those in the former Soviet Union, Eastern European economies and China in the Mao era. The recent reforms of China's state-owned enterprises have introduced new market forces designed to hold individual firms responsible for their own profits and losses. It is thus questionable to what extent the concept of soft budget constraint is still relevant to the performance and behavior of China's state-owned enterprises. Interestingly, the concept can help explain the recent involvement of Chinese municipal governments in credit-based capital formation. A Chinese municipality is commonly believed to have good credit and would never declare bankruptcy. Credits can therefore be used by a municipal government for borrowing from the public and private sectors and the issue of paying back has not been a major concern because of the belief that the hard outcome of over-investment or bad debt would eventually be "softened" by the Chinese state through various bailouts.

There are at least two major ways in which credits are used by municipal governments for fund raising. The first is to obtain loans from the local branches of the Bank of China for the purposes of urban development. Since the municipal government is not allowed to act directly as a developer, the approach adopted by the municipal government is to set up a seemingly independent company responsible for the development of a large project. The municipal government will then serve as a guarantor for the company to obtain bank loans. With the strong support of the municipal government, local branches of the Bank of China and even foreign financial institutions have no strong reasons to question the credits needed and are therefore likely to cooperate. This process of fund raising has been facilitated by the fact that many banks in China are not purely financial institutions but are often under the control of the local administration. In other words, they are not in a good position to reject the proposal of the developers setup by the municipal government. On the contrary, there has been a huge surplus capital in China in recent years due to the increase of personal income and bank savings. For the year 2004, for instance, personal bank savings in China reached RMB11,955.5 billion, which was 87 percent of GDP. By March 2006 China's foreign currency reserves rose to US$853 billion and became the world's largest ahead of Japan. With such a huge amount of bank savings, all banks in China are eager to lend so that a profit margin can be made between savings and lending. Since China's state-owned enterprises are still under reform with great uncertainty and the private sector is still only just beginning lending to the developers sponsored by municipal governments, bank loans have become a viable and logical solution. This situation explains why bank loans have become a major component of capital formation for urban construction as revealed in Figure 2.2. It should be noted, however, that many of these bank loans have ended up with bad debts because of over-investment and poor management. These bad debts are usually referred to by the Chinese as "triangular debt" (*sanjiaozhai*) because they involved at least three parties, which are all state-owned or state-run organizations or economic entities. Consequently, no one knows who should take the ultimate responsibility because they all belong to and work for the socialist state. Obviously, such an economic synergy or financial partnership formed between municipal governments and local branches of Chinese banks has been a peculiar by-product of the socialist political economy undergoing structural changes. It has been another major driving force explaining the recent dramatic expansion and restructuring of Chinese cities and the process of city-forming urbanization process.

In addition to seeking bank loans, another way in which municipal governments mobilize capital for urban development has been the establishment of various local trust institutions in a manner similar to CITIC. The financial institutions are run independently but they are commonly understood as being formed by municipal governments for the purposes of fund raising from all sources including foreign investors, banks and the private sectors. They have become another major channel through which capital can be mobilized to finance large urban development projects. These institutions have been operated essentially on the basis of the credits associated with the municipal governments. However, there have been occasions when some of these trust corporations ran into bad debts that the central and local governments have taken a hands-off approach and refused to rescue them. A prime example that has attracted considerable international attention was the case of Guangdong International Trust and Investment Corporation (GITIC) that ran into the red during the Asian financial crisis in 1998. Neither the central nor the provincial government agreed to honor the bills resulting in great disappointments among the many overseas investors who were involved in lending funds. Nevertheless, these trust corporations have remained one of the important sources of fund raising for many municipal governments and therefore help explain why the process of city-forming urbanization could carry on despite the decline in state budgetary allocation in urban construction and the reduced direct involvement of the central state in urban development.

The above analysis of how capital has been mobilized and used demonstrates the operating mechanism and peculiar nature of the city-forming process that has been taking place most noticeably since the early 1990s. It should be noted that this process has found its spatial manifestations not only in the phenomenal expansion and restructuring of the urban space of existing cities but also in the restructuring of urban–rural relations. Among many other things, this process has allowed Chinese cities to reassert themselves in the rapidly growing national economy undergoing structural change and globalization. However, the reassertion of cities has often come at the expense of the outer urban margins and the rural periphery. Initially these sources of capital mobilization described above were only available to cities particularly large cities on the eastern coast but recently many large cities such Chongqing, Wuhan and Xian have had similar access to national capital. The outer urban margins often do not have the privilege of gaining access to either state-owned urban land or the credits necessary for borrowing until their land system is reclassified as urban. Moreover, the expropriation of land by the city core has generally been undertaken at the expense of the interests of the outer urban margins. The current repositioning of Chinese cities and the restructuring of their urban spaces have therefore led to a financial disarticulation of the urban core and the outer urban margins. This process of disarticulation is demonstrated in the case studies presented later in the book.

This preceding description of the political economy of capital formation for "urban space" forming projects has emphasized the important role of the land and capital markets that have developed in the urban areas and their rural margins. Central to this assertion is the understanding of the radical change that has occurred since the era of state socialism under Mao when land was treated as the means of production and allocated administratively by the state free of charge. To accommodate the interests of foreign investors the state has since the 1980s separated land-use rights from landownership and openedup a new market track for the conveyance of land-use rights to commercial users. The result has been a distinct two-track land-use system that is central to the understanding of the urbanization process, which is most advanced in the coastal zones where foreign investment is most prominent. In dealing with land management the state makes three main distinctions as follows: (1) the distinction between urban and rural land, with the former referring to the land in officially recognized cities, county seats, designated towns and industrial and mining areas; (2) the distinction between state-owned and collective land – the Chinese Constitution stipulates that "(L)and in urban areas is owned by the State. Land in rural and sub-urban areas, except for those stipulated by laws as being owned by the state is collectively owned by rural residents" and (3) finally all other land is classified according to its use as "agricultural land," "construction land" and "unused land" (the rest). This land classification has existed since 1988 (actually 1987 where it was first applied in Shenzhen in order to experiment with these new systems) when the Chinese government introduced constitutional amendments that enabled them to separate landownership from land rights, which enabled urban land to be still owned by the state but its use rights can now be transferred to commercial users. The issue of transfer of land in rural areas characterized by collective ownership is more complicated because while the state has attempted to limit the conversion of agricultural land (for reasons of food security) it has allowed the institutional units of the rural collective (villagers' committee, village economic cooperative, or township collective economic entity) to allocate rural construction land for other uses subject to approval by the Land Bureau at the county level or above. In the coastal provinces where the growth of TVEs and numerous "development zones" (*kaifaqu*) was very rapid in the early 1980s, this was in effect closing the gate after the horse had escaped (see Figure 2.3).

It is important to our understanding of the manner in which urbanization in the coastal provinces has occurred to realize that in the period since 1988 the conversion of land particularly in "rural areas" to non-rural uses has been driven by state institutions at various levels. In many cases the leasers of this land may be described as "firms" and be regarded as part of the "private sector." In some cases they are simply reinvented out of existing public sector agencies. Thus there is a broad coalition between "public and private sectors" that drives this conversion. From the local government point of view this is advantageous because the change in land use to higher valued commercial and industrial uses becomes a major source of local revenue and an important source of loan capital for these agencies. This process is also enhanced by the ability of the local authority (counties, communes, etc.) to have their administrative areas reclassified as urban. Thus in the period since 1980 the number of counties, and other administrative units at lower levels that have become urban, have increased massively (see Chapter 4). This also occurred in the case of larger municipalities such as Shanghai that took over adjacent counties, illustrated in Chapter 7. This gave the reclassified units the power not only to have greater control of their finances but also to make land conversions of a certain size without having to refer to higher administrative units for approval. Thus Naughton's reference to the idea of cities as "cash cows" becomes a central element of the urbanization process.[46] This process of "land conversion" also offered the opportunity for the acquisition of much illegal capital through bribery and illegal land conversion.

Ultimately the understanding of the political economy of Chinese urbanization involves not only an understanding of the actual creation of urban space but also that it is a process of capital accumulation. If we use Harvey's (1982)[47] theoretical framework for this purpose, in market economies capital can be said to operating in three circuits. First, the circuit of "primary capital" that involves the appropriation of surplus value from labor. Second there is the circuit of

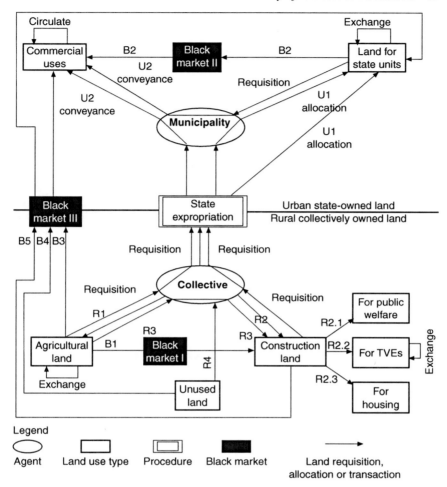

Legend

| | | | | |
| Agent | Land use type | Procedure | Black market | Land requisition, allocation or transaction |

Figure 2.3 China's land system in transition (source: Lin and Ho (2005), p. 421, Figure 3).

"secondary capital" that is characterized by the flow of capital into fixed assets that can either be in the production process, or in a consumption fund that functions as an aid to consumption (e.g. services). Finally there is a tertiary sector of capital that involves investment in capacity development such as education or research. These circuits of capital operate through networks that are constantly circulating this capital between and within circuits. During the phase between 1978 and 1992 when rural urbanization was dominant "production capital" was invested in the "rural counties" mostly in the coastal region while in the period since 1992 "production capital" has been largely focused on municipalities and their expanded areas. In the Chinese context locally derived capital through revenue earned from leasing and development fees and loans from local banks has been the major source of capital. This latter has been aided by the existence of so-called "soft budget" conditions that have enabled city administrator borrowers to gain loans that were risky because of inadequate business plans etc., which is an ongoing problem. By contrast the "rural urbanizing areas" on the city margins have generally had smaller amounts of "production capital" to enable them to engage in city-forming investments.

Conclusion: towards a model of spatial and urban transformation in China

This chapter has attempted to provide a frame for the theoretical understanding of the urbanization project in China in terms of the three developing phases that are summarized in Figure 2.4.

The figure highlights the different political economies of the three phases of urbanization. First, in the Maoist period when the emphasis was placed on trying to reduce rural and urban differences (1950–76); second in a phase of rural urbanization that led to the growth of small towns in the countryside that reached its peak in the 1980s but has continued until today, and third a phase of city-centered urbanization that assumed growing importance in the period since 1992. It should be emphasized that the model presented here represents a simplified conceptual framework to help in the understanding of the relationship of the national economy to spatial change but it still remains useful in elucidating the urbanization process. In particular in this book we focus on the two later phases of urbanization. Judged from both the political and fiscal perspectives, the process of urbanization in China since 1978 has been largely a result of the uneven withdrawal of the central state accompanied by macro-policies after the mid-1990s that have accepted and encouraged the inevitability of Chinese urbanization. While the spontaneous expansion of production space based on small towns that fueled the "rural urbanization" in the period 1978 to 1992 was facilitated by the relaxation of control over developmental affairs at the local level, the creation of the Special Economic Zones and the Open Cities in 1984 actually laid the foundations for the phase of city-centered urbanization that accelerated in the 1990s. However the general disregard of migration restrictions, reform of the grain-rationing system and acceptance of local capital formation were also important in encouraging rural urbanization. This first phase of growing out of the plan thus involved a mixture of official and unofficial activities that were ideally suited to the small towns of the Chinese countryside. The third phase of city-centered urbanization has led to the growing importance of the larger cities in which "bureaucratic entrepreneurs" and private entrepreneurs are transforming the built-environment of these cities through large infrastructure projects and project developments that are aimed to position their cities competitively within the rapidly transforming spatial economy of China and the global system. This has not meant that "rural urbanization" has ceased but that "city building" (*zao cheng*) has become a major feature of the processes of urbanization in the coastal zones. It is tempting to argue that this growth of "city-centered urbanization" is predominantly influenced by the

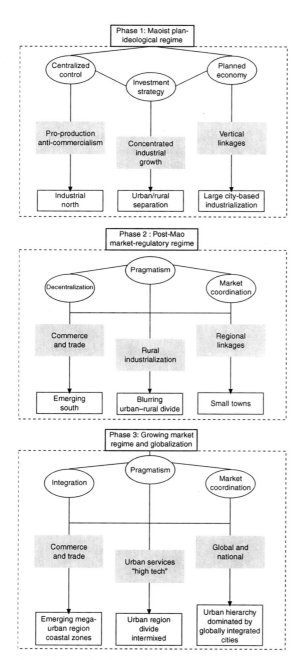

Figure 2.4 Main phases of urban development in China, 1949–2006.

Notes
(1) Maoist period 1949–76, (2) initial phase of market/regulatory regime, (3) 1995– growing market regime, globalization.

increased integration of China into the global economy (globalization) but it is also a response to local economic restructuring and reshaping of the national economy, which is a project still in progress. It also often involves a locally led response that is facilitated by national policy.

A final advantage of this model is that it is not tied to some unilinear assumption that China's urbanization is following some trajectory that will lead to the duplication of the model of urban transition from socialism to capitalism but rather that it is evolving to use Deng's metaphor "like a man crossing the river who has to feel for the stepping stones." Chinese urbanization is a process of experimentation constantly changing and adapting to the realities of the immediate situation at all scales from international to local. Nee's description of the supposed transition from socialism to a market economy captures this reality. "Rather than conceive of market transitions as a linear progression to capitalism, we may analyze the departures from state socialism as likely to produce hybrid market economies that reflect the position of institutional centricity of their parent institutional form. The deep structures of the reform period are likely to reproduce important features of the state socialist redistributive economy."[48]

3   "Seeing like a state"
The urbanization project in post-1978 China

> There was to put it mildly, an elective affinity between high modernism and the interests of many state officials.
>
> Scott (1988)[1]

Introduction

In this chapter we turn to the analysis of the state's urbanization project in China. This idea of the state's urbanization project is drawn from James Scott's perceptive study entitled *Seeing Like a State: How Certain Schemes to Improve the Human Condition Have Failed* (1988). This book is basically about the efforts that states make to create development through preferred "forms of planning and social organization (such as huge dams, centralized communications and transportation hubs, large factories and farms and grid cities) because those forms fit snugly into a high-modernist view and also answered their political interests as state officials."[2] Scott identifies four main elements of these state-initiated projects. First the "administrative ordering of nature and society"; second, the reliance upon on a "high modernist ideology" that includes the "acceptance of the idea of scientific and technological progress, the expansion of production, the growing satisfaction of human needs, the mastery of nature (including human nature) and, above all, the rational design of social order commensurate with the scientific understanding of natural laws"; third, the existence of an authoritarian state that has the power to bring the project into being; and fourth "a prostrate civil society that lacks the capacity to resist these plans."[3] Much of Scott's book is devoted to a historical examination of such schemes and the reasons for their failure. To summarize, at great risk to a complex argument, Scott's explanation of the failure of these schemes is that they paid insufficient attention to the knowledge, views and understandings of people on the ground. In our language this means that the voices emanating from local spaces were given limited input even though the intentions of the state policy-makers were often directed to improving the overall condition of people in their nations.

In contemporary China we would argue the particular context of the development represents a more complex mix of state "high modernism" and local reactions. This position essentially supports the arguments put forward by Jae Ho Chung that "'Unpacking' the state has indeed become a crucial approach to the study of development" reflecting the fact that "China's developmental reform was from the outset accompanied by the delegation of central authority and the promotion of local initiatives." This "unpacking" involves the recognition "that the state is a multi-layered structure of authority with its own complex intra- and inter-governmental dynamics."[4] At this time of rapid development, in the coastal provinces (where urbanization is in high flood) there appears broad agreement between the different levels of the state and its administrative agencies (provincial, municipality, county and township) and the local people on the developmental role of the state. This does not mean that civil society is prostrate; there are many examples where resistance is occurring but they are insufficient to derail the state development project. Sometimes this resistance occurs outside the state surveillance and is supported by "benign neglect at lower levels of the state." In this chapter we have tried to tease out the various components of the state's urbanization project in China by (1) looking at the broad historical context of China's urbanization; (2) analyzing the main components of the state urbanization project, definition, policy and implementation; and (3) interrogating the manner in which these national processes interact with globalization and the local situation in the production of urban space.

Historical emergence of rural and urban differences in China

While we recognize that the main thrust of this book is concerned with urbanization in the reform period it is necessary to engage the relationship between the state and urban and rural space within China over a longer period if the post-1978 patterns of urbanization are to be understood. During the Republican period in the first few decades of the twentieth century cities were usually placed under "rural-based administration entities," which reflected administrative practices developed in the Imperial period. In the Maoist period this practice generally continued with cities having control of limited territory that reinforced the rural–urban dichotomy typified by Naughton's image of the "hard" and "soft" edges of cities.[5] But in the Reform period there has been a steady expansion of the administrative role of urban places indicated by the proliferation in their number, the expansion of their territory and the urban population they control. This has led to a softening of the rural–urban divide and the ascendancy of urban administrative units in the local administration systems. It is now popularly believed that "as many as 70 percent of China's administrative jurisdictions now come under the rule of urban governments."[6] Within these urban jurisdictions there are of course many people who still engage in rural activities, or in the case of rural migrants, keep close contacts with the rural households from which they have come in other parts of China. This raises intriguing questions concerning the nature of the Chinese urban transformation particularly when it is compared with urbanization transformation in Western countries, which we will explore in the conclusion to this chapter. What will become clear from the Chinese experience is that it is necessary to understand how the ideologies and practices of the Chinese state shape the nature of the urbanization project, which is not always understood from outside China.

In this respect it is useful to return to the ideas of Henri Lefebvre to contrast the state's creations of the "represented spaces" (political space) of the "urban" with the "spaces of representation" (urban form, cityscapes, etc.) and study how "spatial practices" (human behavior, investment decisions, spatial mobility, etc.) reshape these other spaces. In the next section we look at the way the state has created "urban and rural space" in three periods during Chinese history.

Urban–rural interdependence in Imperial China

China has had an extensive record of civilization and urbanism that originated in the North China Plain during the Shang Dynasty (1766–1122 BC). From its inception, Chinese urbanism has always been intertwined with the state's ideologies, practices and exercises of power for social control. The word city in Chinese is *chengshi*: *Cheng* means a walled place (for military and defense purpose) and *Shi* means a place for commodity exchange (market and commercial purpose). However, early Chinese cities were built by the state as "the pivot of the universe" or the axis of the "middle-kingdom" (*zhongkuo*) where the emperor as "the son of heaven" (*tianzi*) or holder of "the Heavenly Mandate" (*tianming*) could worship Heaven, the God on High, and seek counsel and intercession from their ancestors so that he could preside over "all under heaven" (*tianxia*).[7] These cities were primarily intended to perform ceremonial functions and served as administrative and military foundations for the monarchy.[8] In contrast with medieval European urbanism in which cities emerged as a fusion of fortress and market as identified by Max Weber, early Chinese urbanism was distinguished by a lack of political autonomy, a great dependence upon and extensive interchange with the rural hinterland, and a commercial sector that played only an insignificant role.[9] There were places for market exchange within the city, but these markets could only occupy a location of secondary importance under the "hall of audience in front with markets behind and ancestral hall on the left with altar of the god of the soil on the right" principle.[10] There were walls encircling cities, but these walls were primarily for security and defense considerations and not for the separation of cities from the countryside.[11] In his masterly documentation of early Chinese urbanism, Paul Wheatley noted that

> the vast majority of city dwellers, not only in Chou times but even in Han and later periods, were cultivators who, in summer at any rate, went out daily through the city gates to work in their fields. In this mass of agrarian labor which constituted the urban population, the craftsmen and merchants generated only a small leavening influence and, more important for urban theory,

never constituted an autonomous group able to undertake the collective exercise of power.[12]

Clearly, early Chinese urbanism was characterized by a great spatial mobility of the urban population (many of them who were also agrarian labor) and a "daily" interchange between town and country, and this was logically connected with the state's engagement in the "representations of space" at the time. As cities were conceived spaces primarily for the ceremonial and symbolic functioning of state power, they relied on the extensive support of their immediate hinterlands and frequent exchange with the rural economy.

Commercial activities began to flourish during the late Tang (AD 618–907) and the Song (960–1279) periods when the growth of urbanism and extravagance reached the climax. The interchange between urban and rural societies had been further strengthened and extended geographically as major cities such as Kaifeng and Hanzhou experienced suburbanization and a large number of small commercial towns grew all over the country.[13] Suburbanization as a part of growing urbanism was clearly described by Sen-dou Chang.

[The suburbs] were favored sites for markets and businesses serving the rural populace. Inns and other services catering to travelers and traders were established outside the particular gates that gave access to long-distance routes. Many of the cities whose walls were built in the Ming period or earlier could not contain the absolute growth in urban population that occurred during the Qing. By the nineteenth century, few walled cities lacked sub-urban development outside at least one gate, and in many cities, particularly those in Guangdong, built-up areas in the suburbs exceeded those within the walls.[14]

Suburbanization and the proliferation of small urban centers continued in the late Ming (1368–1644) and Qing (1644–1911), contributing to a "bottom-heavy" economic system and an "urban involution" in which large urban centers did not grow so rapidly whereas small market towns flourished in some economically advanced regions.[15] After the Opium War, the arrival of foreigners and the growth of treaty port cities created an alienated elite urban class closely affiliated with the colonists.[16] However, Chinese cities continued to rely upon their immediate rural hinterlands and the urbanites maintained free and extensive interchange with their rural counterparts. Traditional Chinese cities were therefore "soft edged," to borrow the words from Barry Naughton despite the existence of walls that encircled them for security reasons. Under this context of a "soft" rural–urban interface, peri-urban regions in the immediate outskirts of the cities became the loci where intensive rural–urban interaction occurred and spatial mobility of the urban population took place. In other words, the state project of "representations of space"–which Arthur Wright[17] believed to be "the longest tradition of city cosmology the world has ever known"–was one in which cities were conceived as administrative, ceremonial and symbolic foundations that created "soft edged" urban "spaces of representation" which in turn accommodated the "spatial practices" of intense urban–rural interaction and spatial mobility of the people who lived in these areas.

Anti-urbanism and the urban–rural divide in socialist China under Mao

Traditional Chinese urbanism was then subject to profound transformation after the Communists took power in 1949. In the era of state socialism under Mao, the role played by state ideologies and practices in the growth and transformation of urbanism was as important as, if not greater than, it was in the pre-socialist era. Chinese cities continued to function as major administrative centers for the state to exercise its power of social and political control. However, they were profoundly transformed by the socialist state at least in two major ways.

First, the Communists' ideological commitments to the elimination of inequality, exploitation and class stratification meant that most, if not all, of the defining features of classic urbanism (bigger size, higher density, class and ethnic heterogeneity, social stratification, inequality, neighborhood decay, impersonality, anonymity, alienation, a conspicuously consuming urban elite, crime and prostitution etc.) found in "old China" (*jiu zhongguo*) and other capitalist societies had to be abandoned and replaced by a new way of life suitable for the "socialist man."

For urban size and density, Mao reportedly told Chinese urban planners that "It's no good if cities are too big [*Chengshi taidale, buhao!*]" partly because many of the urban ills tended to occur when "cities are too big" and partly because excessive urban concentration would exacerbate the devastating effects of nuclear attacks from the US. Mao instructed Chinese urban planners that "we must disperse the residents of the big cities to the rural areas and construct numerous small cities, for under the conditions of atomic war this would be comparatively beneficial."[18] This policy was reinforced by the *hukou* system (household registration system) introduced in 1958 that limited residential transfers from the communes to the cities. Despite these efforts to prevent large scale urbanization in the first ten years of the People's Republic of China (PRC), all cities expanded dramatically. The urbanization pace in the 1950s was without parallel in the history of China driven by the development of city-centered heavy industrialization; a rapid increase of urban population resulting from famine in the countryside and the need to concentrate industrial activity in certain areas in order to strengthen China militarily in the cold war situation of the 1950s. From a Maoist perspective service activities and consumption were considered to be "non-productive" activities and even "exploitative" because they appropriated, or exploited the surplus value already yielded by the productive (industrial) capital and created no new wealth for society.[19] As such, urban commercial activities had to be restrained and Chinese cities had to be transformed from the centers of consumption ("consumer cities") into the centers of production ("producer cities").[20] For the layout of cities, residential segregation was unacceptable to the socialist regime and a neighborhood concept was introduced to arrange the city into uniformly self-contained units (*danwei*) in which the workers lived and worked. These were often housing compounds attached to factories in which workers from the same work unit lived.[21] Housing was arranged and built in a standardized manner. There was no central business district and the city center was a ceremonial public space for political gatherings such as those found in Beijing's Tiananmen Square during the Great Proletarian Cultural Revolution in the late 1960s.

After three decades of ongoing ideological indoctrination and political campaigns, Mao's radical and ideal regime managed to develop a distinct model of urbanism characterized by, among many other things, a system of cities whose size was determined not by free market forces but by the ratio of the productive labor force to the total population; an urban economy focused on production rather than consumption; an urban space arranged according to the principles of uniformity, standardization and classlessness; a highly developed bureaucratic system for the allocation of jobs and residences with high security and stability, population mobility with a monitor and control system using the *hukou* system, an all persuasive residential work unit organization system that ensured neighborhood familiarity, conformity and citizen involvement in public affairs; minimal differentiation in income, consumption patterns, religious customs and life styles, and rigid taboos on alternate forms of dress, expression, ritual life and communication that did not conform to the socialist convention.[22] While these features bore significant resemblance to those of "less urbanism" (i.e. lower urban density, less internal urban diversity and less marginality) found in other former socialist countries, they "arose not from a special Chinese historical and cultural tradition, but from changes introduced after 1949."[23] One may be cynical about the effectiveness of Mao's utopian rhetoric in transforming Chinese cities, but one can never fully understand the distinctive features of Chinese urbanism identified above without making reference to the state's egalitarian ideological conviction and the institutional changes introduced, although ambiguity and discrepancy existed between ideal goals and actual practices.[24]

Second, the socialist state under Mao followed the Soviet model of industrialization for a period and adopted an approach that aimed at optimum industrialization by "squeezing agriculture" and minimizing the cost of urban service provision. Known as "economizing on urbanization" or "industrialization with controlled urbanization,"[25] this approach essentially involved a restriction over both urban expansion and rural to urban migration on the understanding that uncontrolled urban growth may increase the burden of the state in the provision of "non-productive" urban services, absorb too much of the capital that should be reserved for industrial production and therefore jeopardize the state's ambition of rapid industrialization designed "to overtake the UK and catch up with the US." It remains a topic for careful investigation as to how this strategy of "economizing on urbanization" had affected the multiple facets of contemporary urbanism. It appears quite certain, however, that the institutional setting put in place by the state to ensure an optimum industrialization with minimum urbanization costs led to the separation of the urban from the rural sector, limited population mobility and reduced urban–rural interaction in the sub-urban and peri-urban regions. In particularly, the *hukou* introduced since 1958 had classified all people as either agricultural or non-agricultural population.[26] Non-agricultural population was officially recognized as "urban" and was entitled to state provision of rationed food grain, cooking oils, employment, housing, education, medical care and other welfare benefits. On the other hand, agricultural populations were regarded as "rural" and largely excluded from the state's welfare provision. The *hukou* system had functioned as an invisible yet effective "wall" separating the urban from the rural society and prohibiting rural–urban migration because any unauthorized migrants in the city could hardly survive without the supply of food, job, housing, health care and other urban services that were all firmly controlled by the state.[27] Ironically, traditional Chinese cities with visible walls had "soft edges" to allow free urban–rural interaction and suburbanization. By contrast, socialist cities under Mao had their visible walls removed and replaced by many "invisible walls" and "hard edges" that separated them from the rural society for the state imperative of robust industrialization and urban manageability. With these "invisible walls" and "hard edges" in place, most Chinese cities were relatively compact and few ever experienced sprawl into the countryside. There was limited urban–rural interaction in either the sub-urban or peri-urban regions. As Naughton observed:

> Indeed, the average urban dweller, even in Shanghai, the largest metropolis, could easily ride a bicycle to the edge of the city, and then continue out into a countryside that was markedly different from the city itself. The sharp distinction between urban and rural lives was visible in the abrupt end, the "hard edges" of cities. ... it was the direct physical expression of policies that concentrated economic opportunities in cities and then sharply limited access to those opportunities.[28]

Obviously, the ideologies and practices of the socialist state under Mao had found their "physical expression" and created new "spaces of representation" characterized by a sharp urban–rural divide, and this had in turn affected the spatial mobility as well as other "spatial practices" of the population at the time.

Renewed urbanism and revitalized urbanization in the era of market reforms and globalization

The death of Mao in September 1976 and the subsequent change in leadership ushered in new state ideologies and practices that began to transform Chinese urbanism. Whereas the Maoist regime emphasized ideological correctness in line with the Marxist doctrine, the new regime under the late Deng Xiaoping favored pragmatism and valued materialism, efficiency, comparative advantage and openness more than ideological indoctrination, equity, communal interests and self-reliance. This new pragmatic regime has since late 1978 made significant institutional changes to "reform and open" (*gaige kaifang*) the Chinese economy.

Specifically, the central state relaxed its control over local economic affairs by decentralizing the power of production decision-making to local governments, firms and individual farm households on one hand and reducing the scope of central planning to allow "a socialist market economy" to grow out of the plan. In the countryside, an agricultural production responsibility system linked to output was introduced to give material rewards to better production efforts, giving rise to a substantial increase in productivity. This was associated with a process that reduced demand for rural agricultural labor and created greater unemployment and underemployment in the countryside. As a result, a large number of surplus rural laborers emerged awaiting transfer into non-agricultural sectors and employment in urban settlements. In the city, the private sector and individual economy including those financed by foreign investment started to flourish at a pace unprecedented in the history of the People's Republic. In addition, cities were not just viewed as heavy industry dominated producer cities but consumption and service sectors were encouraged. These "non-state sectors" and "non-productive sectors" operated largely outside the state plan and created a phenomenal demand for labor to be met through channels out of the state control.

In recognition of the supply of a surplus rural labor force in the countryside and its growing demand in the city, the pragmatic central leadership eventually relaxed its control over labor mobility and the labor market. In 1984, the state allowed peasants to move to towns for permanent settlement and to carry out non-agricultural jobs provided that they could look after their own needs for food, housing, medical care and other urban services (*zili kouliang renkou*). In 1985, the state further relaxed its control over rural to urban migration by permitting migrants to become "temporary urban residents" (*zanzhu renkou*). Although these migrants were officially treated as "agricultural population" and excluded from the provision of the benefits reserved for the urban "non-agricultural households," they were now allowed to enter the city and find their own living, which was not possible in Mao's era. At the same time, the growth of the private sector and market economy opened up many market channels through which foodstuffs, employment, housing, medical care and other urban services could be obtained (at a higher price, of course) out of the control of the state. As a result, the *hukou* system could no longer effectively prevent rural–urban migration although the system still had a role to play in the segmentation of the labor market and differentiation of citizenship rights.[29] In other words, the "invisible walls" and "hard edges" previously set up by the Maoist regime to separate urban and rural sectors had become increasingly permeable.

The relaxation of state control over population mobility has had profound effects on the growth and diffusion of urbanism. As the institutional "walls" collapsed and the city "edges" softened, millions of urbanites were moving out of the urban centers to the peri-urban areas and an even greater volume of rural migrants were moving into cities and towns. It was estimated that about three million urban people were working in "rural" firms in 1993.[30] As for rural to urban migration or what the Chinese called "floating population" (*liudong renkou*), the latest national population census in 2000 revealed that China's total "floating population" (defined as those who have resided out of their place of *hukou* registration for six months or more) had reached 145 million (79 million inter-county and 66 million intra-county migrants).[31] Of this total floating population, 86 million took up residence in cities, 28 million migrated into towns and another 31 million moved around in the countryside. In other words, a total of 114 million migrants, whether defined as "floating" or "temporary" had moved into Chinese cities and towns by the year 2000. The bulk of these migrants were found in the economically advanced regions on the eastern coast particularly in such large cities as Shanghai, Beijing and Guangzhou. At the same time, the urban population with officially recognized urban or "non-agricultural" status has also increased steadily as the central state relaxed its control and local governments started to sell urban resident registration for revenue generation.[32] During the years 1984–96, for instance, urban population in the urban districts (*shiqu*) of the 286 officially designated cities increased from 109 to 154 million or 42 percent.[33] The influx of the "floating" people and the increased urban population have combined to reshape nearly all facets of Chinese urbanism in the new era of market reforms and globalization.

The growth of the "urban" is manifested also in the dramatic expansion and reorganization of the urban built-environment. After three decades of practicing urban containment or compact urbanism, Chinese cities are now expanding both vertically and horizontally. During the years of 1984–96, for which comparable data are available, the urban built-up area in China's 286 officially designated cities expanded from 870,000 to 1.4 million hectares, an increase of 62 percent. Using Landsat images taken in 1986, 1991 and 1996, Chinese authorities found that the urban land occupied by 27 extra-large cities with an urban population of over one million in size had expanded from 3,267 square kilometers in 1986 to 4,907 square kilometers in 1996, or by over 50 percent. The most spectacular expansion occurred in three large cities in the economically advanced region of the eastern coast. Dalian expanded its urban land by an incredible 214 percent, Shijianzhuang 110 percent and Guangzhou 109 percent.[34] At the same time, the number of officially designated cities rose from 295 to 666, their urban population (non-agricultural population in urban districts) grew from 110 to 207 million (88 percent), and their built-up area expanded from 8,816 to 20,532 square kilometers (133 percent) during 1984–96.[35] The addition of new cities in China is not, of course, entirely natural, spontaneous and market-driven because it could be the result of administrative changes or official reclassification. Suffice to say that many of the cities previously denied of an urban status by Mao's regime have finally received their due official recognition and made themselves a part of new Chinese urbanism.

There are at least three distinctive but interlocking driving forces facilitating Chinese urbanization in the post-Mao era. First, relaxed state control over the spatial mobility of people has allowed both the peasant migrants and urban population to take up residence out of the inner city. For the "floating population" or peasant migrants, it is usually difficult and expensive to find housing in the inner-city. A more affordable and realistic solution is to find rental housing either in the urban fringe or in some less favorable loci of the city. For the existing urbanites, increased income has brought with it a growing desire to move to new and bigger houses that are often built also in the urban fringe simply because land in the sub-urban area could be obtained more easily and cheaply than in the inner-city.[36] The combined result of the influx of "floating population" and outward movement of urban residents has been a continuing expansion of urban built-up areas into adjacent areas. Second, the earlier socialist practice of urban containment, described by Kirby[37] as "a stubborn unwillingness to invest in non-productive urban infrastructure" created a "bottleneck" that has been opened up through massive investment in and expansion of the urban infrastructure. Almost all of the large cities have engaged in the construction of "ring roads" as a means to reduce traffic congestion and improve transport accessibility. As the ring roads expanded outward continuously, so did the urban built-up area. Guangzhou *shiqu*, for instance, spent RMB190 billion on its urban infrastructure during 1979–2000 and dramatically expanded the area covered by paved road from 342 to 2,805 hectares. Its urban land subsequently doubled its size from 35,000 to nearly 70,000 hectares.[38] Finally, as a result of the implementation of the open-door policy, many Chinese cities have established "development zones" (*kaifaqu*) to attract foreign investments. It was estimated that by 1997 a total of 4,210 development zones had been created covering a land area of 232,200 hectares.[39] Many of these zones were located in the economically advanced coastal region, particularly in the outskirts of large cities.

Chinese cities are no longer compact, clean, spartan, orderly, uniform and safe. As the market economy starts to grow out of the plan, commercial activities and urban consumption have returned to the city. In fact, the previous antagonism towards urban consumption under Mao had created a huge pent-up demand for service activities and this has now given rise to an explosive growth of the service economy.[40] Whereas Mao's regime sought to transform Chinese cities from "consumers" to "producers," the post-reform leadership now sees the growth of the tertiary sector as a critical means to maintain urban economic vitality and social stability because it could provide employment to accommodate massive layoffs from the profit-losing state-owned enterprises (SOEs) and rural unemployment.[41] As a result, traditional commercial centers have been revitalized and new central business districts are taking shape in many large Chinese cities.[42] Many of the factories previously built in the inner-city have been relocated to the outskirts of the city to make space for more valuable commercial activities[43] and/or to keep the urban environment clean (rural areas have less tough environmental regulations than urban). The reform of housing provision from tenure allocation by the state unit (*danwei*) into a long-term lease has led many new housing estates and villas to develop at the edge of the city. In the meantime, peasant migrants have clustered in enclaves scattered around the city that often are characterized by concentrations of migrants from the same place.[44] The cityscape and skyline have also been quickly changing as skyscrapers and high-rise buildings started to replace the four to five story buildings that characterized the Chinese cities under Mao. To Chinese urban planners, building height has increasingly become a key marker of identity and a symbol of modernity, success and a world city status.[45] Under this new skyline of modernity is of course growing economic polarization, social stratification and inequality. For the existing urban population, marketization and privatization of the state-owned enterprises have contributed to massive layoffs and rising urban poverty.[46] For the newcomers, the city has now become a space for the migrants and the local people to contest citizenship.[47] Although residential segregation in the Western style is still limited in Chinese cities, it is quite obvious that contemporary Chinese cities have become increasingly diverse and multi-nucleated with perhaps many different kinds of space juxtaposed. Indeed, the spatiality of Chinese urbanism in the current era of market reforms and globalization is characterized by an overlapping of many "spaces of representation" such as those identified by Ma and Wu,[48] as "the spaces of globalization" (development zones, industrial parks, convention centers, etc.), "the spaces of elitist consumption" (shopping malls, supermarkets, hotels, restaurants, golf course, etc.) and the "spaces of differentiation and marginalization" (gated communities, urban villages, migrant enclaves, etc.). The new Chinese urbanism is thus characterized by growing diversity, heterogeneity, inequality, marginality and irregularity as well as illegality. In the next section we want to evaluate how the state urbanization project since 1978 has played a major role in producing this situation.

Urbanization as a national state project post 1978: creating the spaces of representation

In China the state's approaches to urbanization consist of three main components. First it is necessary to define urban units for both administrative and statistical purposes. Second broad policies concerning urbanization have to be developed and at the macro-level are put forward as part of Five Year Plans. Third the state creates ministries, departments and agencies that are concerned with the monitoring and implementing of macro-policy laid out in the Five Year Plans and managing the state. These implementing units are organized in a hierarchical manner at central government, provincial, prefectural municipality, county and township levels. The next section describes the main features of this system that drives the state directed component of the urbanization project.

Defining urbanization

The state needs to define urban areas for two purposes (a) administratively for management and fiscal purposes, which reflects government power and responsibility, and (b) statistically, which is a territorial measure for the purposes of measurement of trends and the assessment of performance. Thus the administration distinction between urban and rural in China may be seen both as an administrative function and a form of spatial surveillance of urban and rural populations because it frames entitlements to residence, jobs, education, housing, birth control, etc., as well as fiscal allocation.[49]

Administrative definition

The first requirement of urbanization as a national state project involves the definition of urban areas and rural areas that Ma describes as the creation of "political space." Lin comments that

> The city in socialist China was not merely a human habitat but an official establishment required to perform political and economic functions. All cities needed to obtain official designated urban status to guarantee themselves a state budgetary allocation and given necessary state capital investment for the development and maintenance of urban facilities. By the designation of new cities or elimination of existing ones the socialist state could constantly re-shape the existing urban system according to the state's ideological and strategic considerations.[50]

In the period since 1978 China has engaged in a radical restructuring of its administrative and economic power as reflected in political space. We summarize some of Ma's excellent descriptions of these changes. First he points out that

> The rescaling of nation-building downward in the post-1978 era represents not so much the retreat and disarticulation of the central state as a rearticulation of state power with different form of state intervention at lower spatial scales. Basic decisions on the general directions of national development, national institutional changes, key industrial, transportation and energy projects and financial institutions remain centrally controlled. Sub-national administrative/spatial units such as provinces and cities now enjoy greatly expanded powers to develop their own economies.[51]

The complex political landscape is best understood as being divided between six levels of national political space as reported in the *China Statistical Yearbook* (China State Statistical Bureau, 2004). First is the national level. Second is the provincial level, consisting of 22 provinces, five autonomous regions and four centrally administered municipalities. Third there are prefectures (333). Most provinces are subdivided entirely into prefectures whose government administers large areas often rural in character divided into counties as well as city districts. Fourth the county level that consisted of 2,861 units comprising 1,642 counties, 374 county level cities and 845 districts in higher level cities. Fifth the township level that has about 44,000 units including 18,100 mostly rural townships, 20,200 towns and 5,750 street communities. Finally at the grassroots level there are some 680,000 villages that are officially not part of the administrative system.[52] The other type of administrative units is city-type units that "refer mainly to *Shi* of different morphological types and different administrative levels and, by extension to officially designated towns."[53] Ma points out that *shi* can be classified in terms of legal and administrative status of which there are three categories: (1) provincial-level cities (*zhixia shi*) (Beijing, Tianjin, Shanghai and Chongqing); (2) cities with districts (*shequ de shi*) referring largely to cities at, and above, the prefecture level (*diji shi*); and (3) cities without districts (*bu shequ de shi*) mainly made up of county level cities (*xianji shi*). In terms of administrative ranking they fall into four levels: (1) provincial level cities; (2) sub-provincial level cities of which half are a level lower than provinces; (3) prefecture level cities; and (4) county-level cities. In addition there are many different types of special administrative status for selected cities including provincial cities, special economic zones, open coastal cities etc. In some cases this can occur with the limits of a city as in the case of the Pudong Special Administrative area.

Thus in the Chinese system, cities of different levels have varying degrees of decision-making responsibilities in such areas as domestic and foreign investment. The end product of this system of classification is that there is much confusion in the meaning of "*shi*" that can apply to many different urban administrative units.[54] But for most Chinese bureaucrats *shi* has a clear connotation of "urban" and thus the process of expansion of the spatial area of *shi* that began with the "city administering county" (*shi guan xian*) policies that were introduced in the 1950s have now been implemented on large scale in the period since the sixth five year plan (1981–85) that began to create city-centered regions. These measures have greatly accelerated in the post-1998 period. Thus in the period 2000–03 the Chinese Ministry of Civil Affairs adjusted 130 administrative divisions to above the level of county.[55]

There are three main ways of creating these city-centered regions. First, by cities annexing adjacent counties as is the case in the expansion of Guangzhou with the annexation of Panyu and Huadu in 2000. Second as explained by Ma (2005b) "a number of prefecture-level cities have been merged with prefectures in which the cities are located and the counties that used to be under a prefecture are placed under the newly established prefecture-level city."[56] Jianfa Shen neatly encapsulates this process with the distinction between vertical rescaling (change in administrative status) and horizontal territorialization (expansion of administrative area).[57] The end result is that the number of urban places has proliferated since 1978 leading to an expansion of urban administrative control. Third by the reclassification of counties as municipalities as is the case with Dongguan.

Statistical definition

China has a long history of collecting statistics about its society that has continued until the present day. National statistics are used by governments as measures of demographic economic and social trends that can provide information on the success of national policies. They thus can have a positive informational role in influencing national policy. They also represent a form of surveillance that can be used to establish the degree of conformity to regulations in a given society. Thus they are an important part of the state apparatus of measurement and control. There are also great problems in establishing uniformity of definition at national levels and monitoring the effectiveness of local statistical agencies.

Within China there are two main statistical series that are used to measure urbanization: first, the national population census that has been administered since 1953; second, statistics that are gathered by national departments such as the Ministry of Civil Affairs and provincial and urban authorities. In this section we analyze the role of population censuses since they are most important at the national level. This provincial and municipal statistical data is analyzed in the case study chapters. The national population census is the most internationally recognized source of information on the demographic features of urbanization. Data from the national census is used in international data such as the United Nations' biannual *World Urbanization Prospects* (United Nations Population Division, 2002) that provide the most comprehensive data base on global urbanization.[58] Within China there have been five official censuses since 1953, which are administered on an approximate decadal basis and there have been frequent changes in the definition of urban population during this period. Prior to 1982 the urban population was defined as the total population within the administrative jurisdiction of designated cities (*jianzhishi*) and designated towns (*jianzhishen*), making the total population of cities and towns. Thus the level of urbanization reflected the fluctuations in the number of designated cities and towns whose numbers fell dramatically during the Cultural Revolution from 1956–66. Thus levels of urbanization fell significantly during this period. The 1982 census adopted a definition that widened the definition of cities and towns. The 1990 census used two criteria. First, the same criteria as 1982 that resulted in an urban level of China of 52 percent that overestimated the number of urban population by incorporating substantial numbers of rural population). Second new criteria that were much more administratively and spatially limited, which yielded an urban level of 26 percent. In the 2000 census the rapid growth of urban places led to the adoption of new criteria that were designed to accommodate this expansion. Zhou and Ma describe these differences in this way.

> First the new census uses population density to separate the "cities with districts" into two types. For city districts with more than 1,500 persons per square kilometer, which generally refer to the urban core and sub-urban districts, their entire population is counted as urban. For city districts with less than 1500 people per square kilometer which mainly refer to outer sub-urban districts only the population in the built-up areas of the city districts is counted as urban.[59]

A more rigorous definition was adopted for county level cities and designated towns based on residence that excluded agricultural populations in adjacent parts of the counties that had been included in the 1990 census. These changes resulted in a much more realistic urbanization level of 36.9 percent. There are two further complications in this changing statistical picture. The first relates to the use of the non-agricultural proportion of the population of cities and towns, a criteria based on employment that has been adopted since 1964 and is used in certain statistical series of what is now the State Statistical Bureau. Second until 2000 the National Census did not include information of the number of migrants in cities and towns, which led to an underestimation of the urban population.

National urbanization policies

The overarching urbanization policy is put forward in the National Five Year Plans. For most of the post-1978 period the plans have not dealt explicitly with urbanization although for example the encouragement of the growth of smaller towns was emphasized in the 1978 Five Year Plan. However, rapid economic growth that is driving the growth of urban areas particularly in the coastal provinces has been a major factor in producing changes in the plans from the 1980s designed to promote cities as "catalysts of development." At the same time the Chinese government has been concerned with ongoing regional inequality between the coastal zone and the interior and has attempted to be addressed in the plans. There is thus ideological ambiguity to China's urbanization project that is an overarching theme of policy formation. This is particularly marked in the duality of policy approaches that emphasize small town development and the growth of larger city regions.[60] This has been further accentuated in the last ten years when rapid growth has also increased social and economic inequality between urban and rural populations throughout China and is a major concern of the most recent Eleventh Five Year Plan (2005–10).

While government policies in the post-1978 period clearly understood that urbanization policy was part of a broader strategy of economic reform that was necessary for the modernization of China they were also driven by equity and efficiency concerns. In the initial period the urban policies up to 1992 included the following measures:

- promotion of towns and small and medium-sized cities particularly in the non-coastal provinces;
- selective growth of the large and medium-sized cities particularly emphasizing their role as central places with the ability to stimulate economic growth with the hope that economic regions of different scales would be developed;
- creation of new cities oriented to the international economy such as Shenzhen;
- the opening-up of cities in the coastal region to foreign investment;
- development of satellite towns serving larger cities;
- relocation of heavy industries out of urban areas;
- promotion of the tertiary sector in larger cities;
- improvements in all forms of urban infrastructure;
- improved management of peri-urban areas surrounding large cities;
- improvement in the financial and administrative management of urban areas;
- restructuring of urban enterprises, labor markets and social security systems;

- encouragement of urban growth in central and western regions in order to reduce economic disparities with the coastal zone.

However the Tenth Five Year Plan (2001–05) shows a much greater commitment to the ongoing urbanization of China as part of the modernization process. The Tenth Five Year Plan makes this emphasis on urban development much more explicit as is clear from the following statement: "the conditions are ripe for China to push urbanization forward and it should lose no time in implementing its strategy along this line."[61] The Tenth Five Year Plan spells this out as follows:

- "Reasonable systems of cities" should be fostered;
- the growth of large, medium and small cities should be coordinated to make regional relationships more efficient;
- economic growth must be encouraged to absorb surplus rural labor;
- small cities and towns should be developed on a selective basis with emphasis on county seats and towns with good foundation and good potential;
- the system and policy blocks to urbanization should be eliminated (this refers to the *hukou* system and its associated policies such as the employment system, schooling);
- mechanisms should be established for the orderly shift of population from rural to urban areas;
- the land-use systems in cities and towns should be reformed including land being reserved for agriculture;
- the investment and fund collection channels for the construction of cities and towns should be improved by pursuing multiple systems of investment;
- standards for the establishment of cities and towns should be stipulated in a scientific manner;
- an administrative system conforming to the demands of the market economy and urbanization should be established; and
- policy coordination should be strengthened and macro-control of urbanization improved.

An analysis of the semantic content of the Tenth Five Year Plan captures the ideology of the National Urbanization project. Key words and phrases that recur in this statement emphasize this thrust: "push urbanization forward," "reasonable," "orderly," "scientific" and "macro-control" that echo Scott's formulation of "high modernism." These form part of the semantic lexicon that emphasizes the central government desire to gain greater control and more efficient "management" of the urbanization project. "Push forward" suggests that the central government accepts the inevitability of urbanization.

The most recent Eleventh Five Year Plan (2006–10) while continuing the policy thrust of encouraging urbanization is much more focused on reducing rural–urban income inequalities that have been growing rapidly over the last decade and have been associated with growing protests from farmers. The plan called "The New Socialist Countryside" puts forward a number of measures including the abolition of agricultural taxes, regulation to prevent the conversion of farmland to industrial and other uses (a particular problem in the peri-urban areas), incentives to lift grain production and massive infrastructure spending on new roads and other transport links. There is also increased investment for education and health services. Whether this policy, which involves increasing rural subsidies, will be successful in raising incomes and defusing political discontent in rural areas, and in stemming the flow of rural migrants to urban areas, is unclear. Some Chinese economists believe that policies should be directed to accelerating the movement of migrants to the urban areas thus forcing technological innovations in agriculture as labor becomes more expensive. This is what is happening to agriculture in peri-urban areas of the Pearl River Delta and lower Yangzi delta. The issue of allowing peasants to sell rural land has been left in abeyance as the government is deeply concerned that this would accelerate the rate of rural–urban migration. In the rapidly urbanizing coastal region this issue has in effect been resolved by the reclassification of rural as urban areas that we have discussed in Chapter 2. But the issue of how to manage the more than 700 million rural population as Chinese urbanization proceeds is a central policy issue in the rural–urban transition.

State administration units responsible for the development and implementation of urban policy

These policies that are developed at the national level are implemented by a myriad of national, provincial, municipal, county and township administrative departments through which national urban policy is carried out. This is complex to explain and at the risk of greatly oversimplifying the picture we have divided this administrative structure into three main components.

Overall urbanization project

This is the responsibility of the State Council and National People's Congress. Basically it involves the presentation of broad goals in the formation of five year plans and other policy initiatives developed by the central government and approved by the People's Assembly. It also has the responsibility for defining urban administrative units.

Implementation

At the national level, many different ministries are involved but the following are important. Since the early 1980s, the most important government body is the Ministry of Construction of the State Council (it used to be called Urban and Rural Construction Commission), especially its Urban and Rural Planning Bureau, which is responsible for overall urbanization strategy and policies, organizing development plans for all cities and monitoring the implementation of these plans. The second most important government body is the Ministry of

Land and Resources set up in April 1998.[62] It has ongoing responsibility for verification of the overall plan submitted to the State Council, the supervision and inspection of the law enforcement of those responsible for land resources management at various levels. The ongoing loss of agricultural land in the urban margins has been a major concern to the Chinese government and the new Ministry of Land and Resources is particularly focused on developing policies concerning cultivated land, land revitalization and reclamation. The National Development and Reform Commission (formerly the State Development and Planning Commission) is also involved in urbanization strategy and policies' development. It is the line agency responsible for provincial planning. The Ministry of Civil Affairs has considerable influence on urbanization, through its Bureau of Administration Areas Planning and Place Names is responsible for approval of new cities or new administrative regions and standardization of place names. This has become of increasing importance in the period since 1998. The State Environmental Protection Administration of China (SEPA) has no direct involvement in urbanization policy but its responsibilities are important to urban policy because many of the environmental problems of China are the result of rapid urban expansion. There are of course many other ministries such as the Ministry of Finance that influenced urbanization but as yet China has not established a ministry that is directly responsible for urban affairs unlike, for example, Brazil that has created a Ministry of Cities.

Relationships between the various spatial scales of government

The manner in which national policies on urbanization work their way down the various administrative scales in China is not dealt with in detail in this chapter but is closely analyzed in the case study chapters. In order to clarify this process it is important to understand that the administrative hierarchy of China is basically organized into five tiers: central government, province, prefecture, municipality and townships. While there are clear responsibilities for each administrative level there is also cooperation, negotiation and resistance between the various levels that reflect the powerful role of the local in Chinese polity. There are many examples in the case studies in this book that illustrate the complexity of this relationship.

Interrogating global/domestic processes impacting upon the urbanization process in China

The earlier sections of this chapter have discussed how the urbanization process in China has been framed by the state. But the urbanization process is basically shaped by the processes of change that occur at the sub-national level. In our judgment the best way to look at these processes is to divide them between domestic and international impacts. In fact this division between domestic and international is quite arbitrary and does not allow for the fact that the interaction between domestic and international is constantly occurring. One way to think about this problem is to imagine that these processes are in fact circuits that are constantly overlapping, interacting and creating new and synthesized processes.

In this section we will not discuss the domestic changes that are discussed in the earlier chapters and the case studies. A comprehensive list of these domestic changes that have impacted upon urbanization have been provided by Ma and Wu[63] that includes such domestic developments as changes in the production structure including decentralization, restructuring SOEs and reintroduction of the market system, which have all contributed to China's development internally and its increasing participation in international markets. Similarly, the increasing commodification of land, housing and retail markets have also provide increased domestic capital for urban development.

In contrast, the international impacts are often presented much more starkly as a one-way process of globalization that the Chinese are embracing with enthusiasm. We think that it is important to deconstruct globalization. First, it is often represented in a hegemonic sense (often the term "Westernization" is used) as being disseminated from the major centers of capitalism (USA etc.), which ignores the effects of sub-regional globalization (if this is not a contradiction in terms) from other parts of Asia. Second, the standard interpretation portrays globalization as a universal process that is a type of "steam roller" flattening the local into global homogeneity that ignores the interaction between the local forces.

It is therefore necessary to interrogate this homogeneous portrayal of globalization that emphasizes three components of the process. First, a technological component that emphasizes the role of changes in communications and transport technology as underpinning this new era of globalization of which "the space of flows" argument (Castells, 1996) is most persuasive.[64] Second, an economic component that argues the global economy is becoming more integrated and, with the "collapse" of socialism, becoming more homogeneous (i.e. capitalist). A sub-part of this argument is the emphasis upon the role of globally organized firms. Another aspect is the increasing structural change that comes about as the consequence of globalization that has urban impacts in for example the increase of the service sector in the largest cities. Finally, there is an ideological component of globalization that can be described as the "neo-liberal ideology" that legitimizes the activities of globalization. International agencies such as the World Trade Organization (WTO) that create the rules for free trade are both a result of this ideology and an implementing agency (see Figure 3.1).

A basic premise of the ideology is that globalization leads to economic growth and greater world wealth. It is argued that countries that resist globalization such as Iran are anti-growth and will increase in poverty. Another part of the ideology relates to the idea of "increasing consumption" and the creation of universal consumption needs that go beyond the "local" or indeed national needs. Thus the creation of consumption desires at the household level for privately owned houses, automobiles etc., has important consequences to urban space. Appadurai with his idea of "scapes" that emerge in the urban landscape of globalization captures the consequences of this more general view of globalization very well.[65]

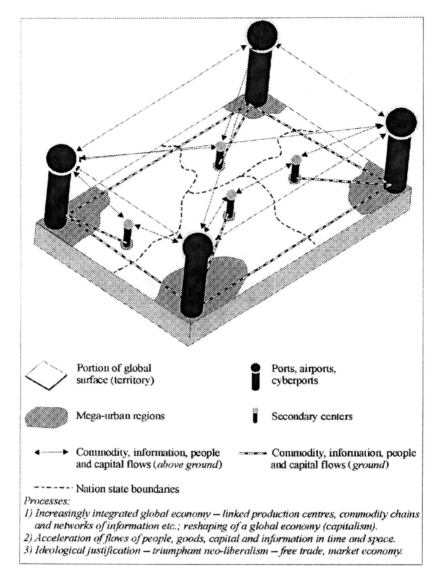

Portion of global
surface (territory)

Ports, airports,
cyberports

Mega-urban regions

Secondary centers

Commodity, information, people
and capital flows (*above ground*)

Commodity, information, people
and capital flows (*ground*)

- - - - - - Nation state boundaries

Processes:
1) Increasingly integrated global economy – linked production centres, commodity chains
*   and networks of information etc.; reshaping of a global economy (capitalism).*
2) Acceleration of flows of people, goods, capital and information in time and space.
3) Ideological justification – triumphant neo-liberalism – free trade, market economy.

Figure 3.1 Schematic representation of globalization processes and spatial formation.

In the Chinese context, however, we think there is a need to deconstruct the concept of globalization from a Chinese point of view. We would suggest that there are several themes to this deconstruction of "globalization." First the historical perception of the Chinese of the "outer world" that has been put forward by many historians, and, as is suggested by some, still affects their views of the "outside."[66] Second there is the need to distinguish between "internationalization" and "Westernization." Internationalization reflects a willingness to accept "outside technological advances" and what might be described as "material aspects of globalization." This process of internationalization also involves a desire to learn about these material aspects of globalization in other parts of the world through international education. It appears that China has enthusiastically embraced this aspect of globalization. "Westernization," however, assumes a process whereby the "internal culture" i.e. of "being Chinese" is changed to "being Western." We are struck by the parallels with Japan in the case of China as important. As many writers have pointed out, Japan achieved development, at least up to the end of the Second World War, by embracing "internationalization" while at the same time protecting its "internal culture" thus creating a kind of dualistic society that was reflected (and still is for that matter) in the internal organization of space in Japanese, middle and upper income homes that have "Western" and "Japanese" rooms;[67] the former with carpets and Western furniture, the latter with *tatami* and Japanese adornments (minimal). It is also reflected in the urban landscapes of Japan. The interesting question, however, is what happens over time? One interpretation is that over time "Westernization" begins to overwhelm the "internal culture." Marxists would say that because of the creation of consumption needs associated with Westernization, this leads to practices that appear to be Western. For example living in suburbs and commuting to work is part of the consequence of the commodification of land, housing and transport.

But there is another interpretation that suggests there are other ways of interpreting this process. For example writers such as Piertse and Hannerz have suggested that the end product of the globalizing era may be some form of "global mélange" in which all cultures will become hybrid.[68] This view is not shared by all researchers. This is well illustrated in a recent article about Japan by Goldstein-Godoni who argues that neither the "homogenization" argument (Westernization) nor the "heterogenization" (hybridity) nor the reciprocal relations between global and local (glocalization) explanations are adequate because there is a need to understand how Western and Japanese cultures interact.[69] She suggests that many Japanese in fact manage this process by role playing at being Western, which they position in relation to behavior that may be described as Japanese. Appadurai sums up this ambivalence in globalization as creating a tension between cultural homogenization and cultural heterogenization that creates "disjuncture and difference."[70] Goldstein-Godini argues that these processes need to be analyzed as ongoing interplay of cultural constructs that in her case are described as a difference between "Japanese" and "Western." She tests this approach by studying Japanese weddings and shows the manner in which elements of the Shinto ceremony are held first followed by the Western "chapel" wedding. Indeed, during the ceremony the bride changes her dress from Japanese to Western at various times in the wedding. Other aspects are the combination of Japanese and Western food on menus etc.

Goldstein-Gofini explains this as "cultural production" by which she means "the production of Western as made in Japan" that breaks down the passive image of non-Western societies accepting Westernization. Thus China's urbanization process while influenced by "internationalization" is nationally and "subnationally" a constructed process, built upon different historical paths. If one accepts this kind of argument then we have for example not one central business district in Chinese cities but several "Chinese central business districts" in Chinese cities. How else do we explain the fact that research on Chinese central business districts suggests that they are very different in their locations and organizational features than those in the USA for example? It is helpful to explain that this is a consequence of the historical paths and urban land markets but that does not make them the same as central business districts in the USA.

Conclusion

Many of the salient features of urbanization and urbanism identified above signify a clear departure from those found in socialist China under Mao. Are they then illustrative of a trend toward convergence in urbanism between a globalizing China and the Western societies? It remains to be seen whether or not the thesis of convergence can be proven correct in a very long run. Certainly the idea of "cultural production" of Chinese urbanism has affinities with and, indeed, is part of the "production of urban space" in China that suggests a form of hybridity in Chinese urbanization that is neither convergence nor divergence. Thus the available evidence suggests that it is still too early to reach a conclusion of convergence. Although Chinese urbanism has shown certain forms similar to those found in the West, its underlining processes remain distinctive with some important "Chinese characteristics." It is important to recognize that the growth of urbanization in China in the post-socialist era has been deeply influenced by the socialist legacy. Despite marketization and globalization, the Chinese economy and society are still under the control of a party-state that possesses the power to make decisive changes in the growth and diffusion of urbanism.[71] As we have argued in this chapter the institutional changes that the Chinese state has implemented are fundamental to the urban transformation. Chung and Lam emphasize the main dimensions to these changes[72] that have been already discussed. But they also stress that these urban changes were driven by efforts of organizational streamlining designed to reduce the numbers of administrative units that were aimed at producing more effective management of urban areas. This is also guided by the use of land-use planning that attempts to create a more efficient and rational land use in urban areas.

As this chapter has emphasized urbanization in China must be centrally understood as part of the overall urbanization strategy of the Chinese government designed to create an urban-led modernization of China but at the same time manage the rural–urban transition so as to avoid the destructive impacts of uncontrolled rural–urban migration that characterize many developing countries. More specifically the growth of commercial and service activities in Chinese cities, for instance, has owed a great deal to the state policy introduced in June 1992 to promote the tertiary sector as a means to create employment and maintain social stability. Urban sprawl and massive urban land development since the reforms cannot be fully explained without making reference to the fact that state organizations of various levels have acted as both regulators and users of land with vested interests in land development.[73] The process of labor market segmentation and urban social stratification has also been the result of the persistent influence of the household registration system (*hukou*), a legacy of Mao's socialist society, as it continues to differentiate the urbanites into "the elites, natives, and outsiders" and affect their occupation, income and social welfare entitlements.[74]

Thus, in contrast with the "paradigmatic shift" from modern to "postmodern urbanism" identified in America,[75] changes in Chinese urbanism are characterized by an overlapping or juxtaposition of multiple spaces from both the past and the present of socialism and reformed socialism. A new market economy is growing out of the plan, but the planned economy remains in place. The new Chinese urban system, for instance, has been a result of a juxtaposition in which a new track of town-based and market-driven urbanization added upon the earlier track of city-based and planned urbanization.[76] In a similar manner, the (re)organization of the urban built-environment has been the outcome of a dual-track land market—a planned track of administrative allocation of land (*huabo*) in the inner-city coexisting with a new market track of conveyance (*churang*) or paid transfer of land-use rights in the outskirts of the city.[77] In all cases, the new market track does not totally replace the planned track but, instead, they stand side by side making it more complicated than before to sort out the exact nature of the new urbanism.

To conclude the urbanization process in China in the post-1978 period, while it has been deeply influenced by forces of globalization and by the increased market forces in China, has fundamentally occurred with the framework of state policy and implementation. Thus, any understanding of the Chinese urbanization process involves careful attention to the relationship between the state, the emerging market and international forces that recognizes the constant process of negotiation that is at the core of the urbanization process.

Finally, the origin and diffusion of urbanism have not been limited to cities in the recent two decades in the case of China. The fact that market reforms started earlier in the countryside than in the city and because state control over the economy and society has been relatively relaxed in the rural than in the urban sector means that urbanization has leap-frogged into rural spaces. If Chinese urbanism is characterized by the juxtaposition of multiple spaces, then there must be intense negotiation, contestation and reconciliation of the interests and forces coming from all social and political scales (e.g. global, national, local and individual households; urban and rural; local and outsiders; plan and market). Nowhere else can such negotiation, contesting and reconciliation be more intense than in the urban margins that are the focus of this book. To foreign investors, the urban margins are particularly attractive because land and labor can be obtained at a price lower than in the city, whereas its accessibility is not far behind that of the city. To municipal governments, the peri-urban region serves as the locale for many new land development projects including building up new housing estates to accommodate the urban new rich and setting up "development zones" (*kaifaqu*) either to attract foreign investment or to house the old industries relocated from the city center. To the migrant workers, the margin regions are probably the only place they could afford to live and work. To the *in situ* populations and the local entrepreneur bureaucrats, the urban margin regions offer opportunities for increased income from land transfers, employment and the development of small enterprise. Thus the urban margins are an ideal locale for industrial, commercial and urban developments because of their proximity to the urban market. But as we have emphasized developments in these areas offer many challenges of social justice, environmental deterioration and governance. The urban margin regions are therefore one of the most dynamic and important places for studying how the forms and processes of Chinese urbanism have changed in the context discussed above that is historically contingent and place specific. The emergence of these urban margins is discussed in detail in the next chapter and illustrated by the case studies that make up Chapters 5 to 9.

4 Representing urbanization in China

Official and unofficial readings of the urban process

There is increasing appreciation in the social sciences that context is important in understanding social, economic, cultural, political and demographic processes. An important element in context is the type of place in which people live and work, hence it is important to be able to categorise them according to their situation within the human settlement system. Unfortunately, at present the only such contextual element that is widely captured in standard population data collections is a characterization of areas into either rural or urban.

Champion and Hugo (2004)[1]

The urban landscape no longer grows in harmonic concentric layers separated by time, united by space, but consists of atonal fragments pressed into one another like felt, the generic city. Only gravity makes it stick, an urban form that lacks urbanity, that neglects traditional differences between the city and the countryside, that thickens the body of earth with a plaque of urbanity more and more organized by time, less and less by space.

Dolphijn (2005)[2]

Introduction

The analysis of the preceding chapters suggests that there is a need to evaluate critically the manner in which the urbanization process in China is being represented. One of the important facets of this deconstruction involves analyzing the spatial consequences of the accelerated growth of urbanization. At present urbanization is being monitored largely through the lens of "official" definitions of urban. This emphasis begins with a national state development project that accepts the inevitability of the growth of urban places as central to the task of making China into a modern state. Cities are seen as the "institutional engines" that facilitate increases in productivity and national and international competitiveness. Cities are also important because they are huge "consumption islands" that will play a crucial role in the development of the national consumption market. In order to accomplish this task cities will have to be made more efficient "distribution nodes" in the national and international transportation systems. Thus the internationalization of cities becomes an important part of urbanization policy improving the infrastructure for business and tourism. To facilitate this policy cities have to be made more livable with improved public facilities and environments. This means that the main emphasis on monitoring the urbanization process at the state level is in generating data that will enable the role of the city to be evaluated in terms of its contribution to national development. But urban activity is not confined to these "monitored units" of political urban space. Urban activities are spreading out from the urban areas and developing within non-urban areas in "extended urban regions" that include both units of "urban political space" and "rural space." While the state is well aware of these processes and has been engaged in an ongoing administrative reclassification of "rural" to "urban" it is not able to keep pace with this urban spread. Therefore there is an "unofficial urbanization" occurring in China as well as an official one. In this chapter we have focused on the spatial aspects of urbanization through these two facets of "official urbanization" and "unofficial urbanization." In the first part of the chapter we look at the "official" patterns of urbanization at the national, regional and city levels. In the second part we look at the "unofficial" urbanization that is illustrated through the growth of "extended metropolitan regions."

Urbanization in China: the official reading

Utilizing the official reading, the particular spatial forms that the Chinese urbanization process exhibits can be analyzed at three levels.

National: the role of urbanization in shaping China's national space

According to the 2000 census China had a population of 456 million people defined as urban giving a level of urbanization of 36.9 percent, which means at this point China was only beginning to enter an accelerating phase of the urban transition.[3] By 2030 this number is estimated to be almost double at 883 million with almost 60 percent of its population urban.[4] Thus in this 30 year period China will have almost doubled its present urban population to urban areas. This estimate is based on the assumption that China will follow a similar trend to that of developed countries of the West and Japan. But there are good reasons for believing that such estimates may severely underestimate the urban population because of the under-bounding of urban activity and trends in demographics of population dynamics particularly internal migration. For example, United Nations' estimates suggest that while the urban levels of China will increase substantially the rural population will only decrease by 251 million leaving 633 million Chinese potentially to be absorbed into urban places.[5] However, these projections of the urban transition are based upon assumptions that urbanization occurs over a relatively long period of time and is sequential. But in fact as Peter Marcotullio and Yok Shu Lee point out with respect to the urban environmental transition the unique feature of our present period is that there is a compression of the time frame in which demographic, economic and social changes occur. This situation is referred to as "a telescoping of the transitional process."[6] The implications of these trends are the focus of our final chapter. Our analysis of the Chinese urbanization process particularly over the last ten years, gives ample evidence of this urban telescoping occurring particularly in the coastal zone. What is more China's urban transition will have to absorb the largest number of people in one country in the history of global urbanization in a very short time frame. This presents huge challenges to infrastructure provision, employment creation, urban infrastructure, social welfare and governance in the context of China's development transition.

The demographic components of the urban transition are well established consisting of (1) natural increase of urban populations from an excess of births over deaths, (2) net migration resulting from an excess of in-migrants over out-migrants in urban areas and (3) the reclassification of rural areas as urban. In the post-reform period the official statistics show these demographic and urban trends for China. As Table 4.1 and Figure 4.1 show, in the 25 year period of the socialist era China's urban population grew from 78 million to 172 million (94 million) but in the 27 year period since 1978 the urban population increased by 402 million, more than three times the previous period. This was despite the fact that the rates of natural population increase fell dramatically during this period indicating that the increase in urban population can be primarily attributed to both rural to urban migration and rural reclassification as urban. This importance of rural–urban migration flow is also indicated by the fact that in this period the proportion of the employed Chinese workforce in the primary sector fell from 70 percent to 50.1 percent while at the same time the contribution of the non-agricultural sectors to the GDP grew to 82.3 percent by 2000.

The interpretation of this table requires closer analysis of these demographic trends as they relate to economic trends. First, despite the fall in birth and fertility rates and natural increase, China continues to add 10 to 11 million people a year to its population. When this fact is linked to the higher birth rates in the countryside where the one child policy is less effective this means that there is a large pool of potential rural migrants available to move into urban occupations. In the period of the mid-1980s this migration accelerated when the demand for

Table 4.1 Demographic and urban trends for China, 1978–2000

Year	Total population (in millions)	Birth rate per 1,000	Growth rate (net natural increase per 1,000)	Urban population (in millions)	Urban %
1953	587.96	37.00	23.00	78.3	13.31
1978	962.59	18.25	12.00	172.5	17.92
1990	1,143.33	21.06	14.39	301.9	26.41
1999	1,259.09	14.64	8.18	388.9	30.89
2000	1,265.00	14.03	7.53	455.9	36.09
2005	1,307.56	12.40	5.89	562.12	43.00

Source: China Statistical Bureau (2006).

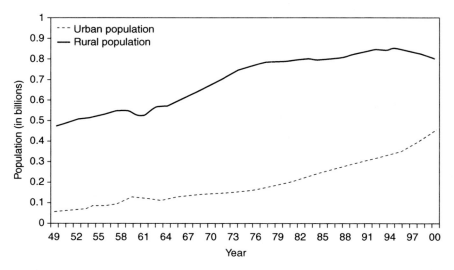

Figure 4.1 Urban and rural population in China, 1949–2000 (sources: China Statistical Bureau (2001); Ma and Cui (1987), p. 388).

labor increased because of the industrial growth particularly in the TVEs of the coastal zone's urban peripheries. This is well illustrated in the following chapters on Guangzhou, Donguan and Kunshan. The employment situation was further exacerbated by the reform of the SOEs from the mid-1990s that caused many workers to lose their jobs or become marginally employed. Thus the sheer volume of China's population provides the demographic imperative to the ongoing surge of urbanization.

Regional urbanization

As is obvious from our earlier discussions the pace and scale of the urban transition in China has been spatially unevenly distributed. Much of the surge of urbanization has been concentrated in the eastern (coastal) region where a large part of the foreign investment, trade expansion, capital formation and most rapid economic growth have occurred in the period since 1978. Figures 4.2 and 4.3 illustrate that the coastal region is the area where the level of urbanization in terms of both urban population and urban built-up area is significantly higher than elsewhere in the country. While the population of the three regions is not very different, the densities of urban population are markedly unequal with the eastern region having almost double the density of the central region and the western region's urban population has a much lower density (Figure 4.2). This is to some extent a reflection of the levels of urbanization but also is a result of the crowded character of the coastal zone. The regional differences in the pattern of urban increase are indicated in Table 4.2, which shows that in the period 1978–98 the increase of the number of cities was fastest in the eastern region.

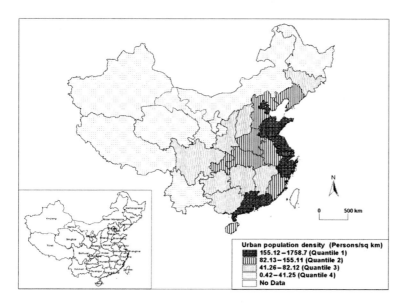

Figure 4.2 Urban population density in China (source: China State Council Popolication Census Office (2002).

Note
Urban population density refers to the ratio of the total population in cities and towns including migrant population in the province to the land area of the province.

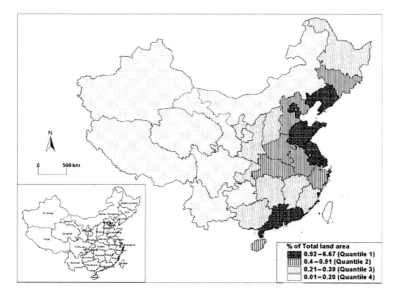

Figure 4.3 Urban built-up area as a percentage of total land area in China by province, 2000 (sources: China Statistical Bureau (2001), p. 345; Lin (2007), p. 18, Figure 1).

Table 4.2 Number of Chinese cities by size and location, 1949–2000

	Number of cities			Annual growth (%)	
	1949	*1978*	*2000*	*1949–78*	*1978–2000*
City size (non-agricultural population in city proper)					
Extra-large (>1 million)	5	13	40	3.35	5.24
Large (0.5–1 million)	7	27	53	4.76	3.11
Medium (0.2–0.5 million)	18	60	218	4.24	6.04
Small (<0.2 million)	102	93	352	−3.18	6.24
Region					
East	69	69	295	0	6.83
Central	50	84	247	1.81	5.02
West	13	40	121	3.95	5.16
Total	132	193	663	1.32	5.77

Sources: China State Statistical Bureau (1999), pp. 6–8; China Statistical Bureau (2002), p. 25.

The emergence of the urban system in China in the post-1978 period

A final approach to the official representation of urban China is to investigate the development of the urban system. Most analyses of the relationship between urbanization and economic growth argue that an important component of this relationship is the development of an urban system that is characterized by the distribution of urban places of different sizes from large to small. In a number of theories emanating from the experience of developed countries it has been argued that there is some ideal distribution of urban places ranging from extra large cities to smaller cities that facilitates distribution and transactional functions in national space.[7] For example, some interpretations of this theory argue that unbalanced urban hierarchies are dysfunctional to economic growth. More recently the work of Scott and others have emphasized the role of the large urban centers as playing a major role in the current phase of globalization.[8]

Statistical data released by the Chinese authorities provides information that enables the analysis of the restructuring of the Chinese urban system in the post-1978 period (see Table 4.2). This data indicates that opening up of the market with the shift from the planned economy has provided the institutional framework for a radically restructured the Chinese settlement system (see Figure 4.4). Between 1978 and 2000, the total number of large and extra-large cities with an urban population of over 500,000 increased from 40 to 93 with a growth rate significantly higher than the previous period (Table 4.2). Although the growth of small cities has also been remarkable, it is large and extra-large cities that have become proportionally more significant ever since the mid-1990s.

In the three years since 2000 these trends in the Chinese urban system appear to have accelerated. Between 2000 and 2003 the number of large and extra- large cities increased from 93 to 448 (an increase of 381.7 percent) while medium and small sized cities fell in number from 570 to 215, which was a loss of 215 percent.[9]

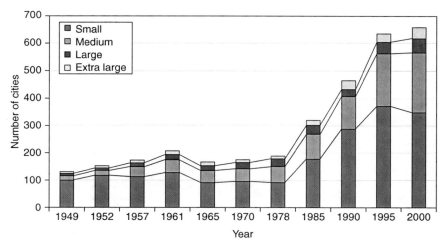

Figure 4.4 The growth of Chinese urban system, 1949–2000 (source: China State Statistical Bureau (1999), p. 8; China Statistical Bureau (2001), p. 339).

While no explanation of this remarkable adjustment is available in the State Statistical Bureau publication, interviews with government officials and academics suggest that these changes are primarily a reflection of the extension of urban political space into rural areas that has been discussed in Chapters 2 and 3. In short China has been involved in remarkable rewriting of the official representation of the urbanization process that is designed to extend political control over "urban space." These trends suggest that it would be a mistake to suggest that the reordering of the urban system is simply a reflection of economic forces and that it also represents the political repositioning of urban space to facilitate economic growth.

The Chinese system of cities that evolved over the past five decades has been shaped by the articulation of the state through the means of investment strategy, administrative changes and reclassification of urban population and urban settlements. Since the 1980s, however, the role played by the central state has experienced significant changes as the national economy started to "grow out of the plan."[10] The power of decision-making has been decentralized as a means to arouse local enthusiasm for development. At the same time, the scope and scale of the state sector under central planning have been gradually reduced to make room for the growth of the private sector and the operation of market forces. The transition of the Chinese political economy from central authoritarianism to local corporatism and from plan to market means that the nature of cities as both administrative and economic entities is undergoing profound transformation.[11] Thus market forces play a greater role in the growth and distribution of cities. Even when the administrative changes are to be made by the state, they are being made in response to the perceived economic benefits that will flow from urban reclassification. To understand better the growth dynamics of the Chinese cities in the new era of market reforms and globalization, it is necessary to analyze the

Table 4.3 Structural and spatial change of Chinese cities, 1984–96 (%)

	Non-agricultural population in city proper		Built-up area in city proper	
	1984	*1996*	*1984*	*1996*
City size (non-agricultural population in city proper)				
Extra-large (>1 million)	39.42	35.69	30.85	27.83
Large (0.5–1 million)	21.00	20.10	21.94	20.27
Medium (0.2–0.5 million)	23.12	23.38	25.12	25.92
Small (<0.2 million)	16.46	20.83	22.09	25.98
Region				
East	49.57	49.70	44.82	46.99
Central	34.76	35.19	39.48	37.91
West	15.67	15.11	15.70	15.10
Total	100.00	100.00	100.00	100.00

Sources: China Statistical Bureau (1985), pp. 35–50; ibid. (1997), pp. 51–90; Lin (2002a), p. 308, Table 3.

"natural" growth of cities without the distortion or "noise" of administrative measures such as the designation of new cities and the elimination of existing ones. Based on detailed statistical data gathered in China's first urban statistical yearbook published in 1985 and the one published recently, Table 4.3 analyzes the expansion of the same 295 cities in the time span of 1984–96.[12]

Two important indicators were used to assess the "natural" expansion of cities: the growth of the non-agricultural population and the built-up area, both in the city proper and in surrounding districts. Among the 295 cities that existed in 1984, more than half of the population and land area remained in large and extra-large cities. Small cities only accounted for 20 to 25 percent despite their larger number. Geographically, cities in the eastern coast accounted for 45–49 percent of the population and land area of the 295 cities. Over the 12 years of 1984–96, these 295 cities experienced a considerable structural change characterized by the proportional increase in the number of small cities and relative decline of large and extra-large cities in terms of both the non-agricultural population and the built-up area in the city proper (Table 4.3). The extent of spatial change in non-agricultural population was limited although the built-up area of the cities in the eastern coast demonstrated significant expansion that appeared to be a logical spatial outcome of infrastructure development that occurred there in order to attract foreign and domestic investment. Altogether, the expansion of the 295 cities existed in 1984, the 12 years of 1984–96 was characterized by a proportional decline of large and extra-large cities, structural increase of small cities and a strengthened dominance of cities in the advanced eastern coast. Since 1996 as our earlier discussions indicated this trend has been reversed with the increase in the number of large and extra-large cities. But at present lack of comparable statistical data prevents analysis at the level of the preceding ten years.

The analysis of Chinese cities thus far has concentrated on the structural and spatial changes of the urban population and the built-up area. But what changes have occurred in the urban economy? What have been the changing roles played by cities as economic centers of investment and production? A series of historically comparable economic data for the same cities recently published by the Chinese urban statistical authorities made it possible for a systematic assessment. Tables 4.4 and 4.5 analyze the economic expansion of 220 cities existing in the period from 1990 to 1998 in three sectors: fixed assets investment, utilized foreign investment and gross domestic product. The picture that emerges clearly underscores the growing importance of larger cities.

The role played by cities of different size and location as the centers of domestic and foreign investment is shown in Table 4.4. Among all cities, large and extra-large cities clearly stand out as the centers of capital investment favored by the post-reform state. Because of their inherent advantages of agglomeration economies, these larger urban settlements received more than 60 percent of all fixed assets capital invested in cities in the 1990s. Moreover, the share of fixed assets capital invested in the extra-large cities grew from 46.5 percent in 1990 to 52.5 percent in 1998 (Table 4.4), suggesting that the extra-large cities have clearly been favored by the Chinese government as the center of fixed assets capital investment. Geographically, over 63 percent of the fixed assets investment in cities was directed to the eastern region, more than the total fixed asset investment of the central and western regions. Such a lion's share was further increased to 65 percent in 1998 (Table 4.4). This is hardly surprising given that all of the special economic zones, open coastal cities and open economic regions were located in the eastern coast. Of all the provinces and special municipalities, Shanghai stood out as the single most important locale receiving the largest increase (6.92 percent) in fixed assets investment during the period of 1990–98. Clearly, Shanghai has recently been selected by the Chinese government as a new growth center along with Guangdong and Fujian for accelerated development. Other locales that displayed a slight increase of fixed assets investment in the urban economy for the same period included provinces in the southeastern coast, the Beijing–Tianjin metropolitan region and the southwestern interior.

In a manner similar to the distribution of fixed assets investment, utilized foreign investment displayed a tendency in favor of large and extra-large cities whose share of the total investment enjoyed a substantial growth at the expense of other smaller cities during the 1990s (Table 4.4). However, the spatial distribution of utilized foreign investment has been somewhat different from that of fixed assets investment. Although an overwhelming proportion of utilized foreign investment (94.5 percent) was located in the cities of the eastern coast, this proportion dropped to 87.4 percent by 1998. This pattern suggests that, unlike the continued concentration of fixed assets investment in the eastern coast, foreign investment has started to disperse from the coastal cities after its initial concentration in the eastern coast. This is evident when the changing distribution of utilized foreign investment in cities was mapped. Jiangsu Province stood out as experiencing the greatest increase of the share of utilized foreign

Table 4.4 Domestic and foreign investment in Chinese cities, 1990–98

	Fixed assets investment				Utilized foreign investment			
	Billion Yuan		Percent		Billion US$		Percent	
	1990	1998	1990	1998	1990	1998	1990	1998
City size (non-agricultural population in city proper)								
Extra-large (>1 million)	86.81	707.23	46.53	52.56	0.84	13.00	35.34	43.56
Large (0.5–1 million)	31.14	184.49	16.69	13.71	0.28	4.87	11.68	16.33
Medium (0.2–0.5 million)	53.61	340.65	28.74	25.32	0.90	8.89	37.88	29.79
Small (<0.2 million)	15.00	113.22	8.04	8.41	0.36	3.08	15.11	10.32
Region								
East	117.58	874.60	63.03	65.00	2.23	26.10	94.54	87.44
Central	47.07	304.17	25.23	22.60	0.10	2.85	4.11	9.55
West	21.90	166.81	11.74	12.40	0.03	0.90	1.35	3.00
Total	186.55	1,345.58	100.00	100.00	2.36	29.85	100.00	100.00

Sources: China Statistical Bureau (2006), pp. 383–8 and 407–12; Lin (2002a), p. 308, Table 4.

Table 4.5 GDP generated by Chinese cities, 1990–98

	GDP		Structure		Per capita GDP	
	Billion Yuan		%		Yuan	
	1990	1998	1990	1998	1990	1998
City size (non-agricultural population in city proper)						
Extra-large (>1 million)	344.14	1,730.14	48.45	48.11	4,403.61	16,922.58
Large (0.5–1 million)	113.28	512.19	15.95	14.24	3,925.57	15,323.32
Medium (0.2–0.5 million)	188.11	1,005.17	26.49	27.95	2,924.13	13,252.92
Small (<0.2 million)	64.70	348.83	9.11	9.70	2,072.29	9,336.64
Region						
East	442.58	2,314.84	62.32	64.37	4,182.58	18,731.93
Central	180.55	848.67	25.42	23.60	2,874.95	10,477.50
West	87.10	432.72	12.26	12.03	2,566.17	9,770.53
Total	710.23	3,596.22	100.00	100.00	3,506.31	14,450.54

Source: China Statistical Bureau (2006), pp. 323–8; Lin (2002a), p. 309, Table 5.

investment followed by provinces along the Yangzi River and in the Shandong Peninsula. By comparison, the dominant position previously held by Guangdong and Fujian provinces experienced a relative decline possibly because of the increase in labor cost and the growing inflow of foreign investment from countries other than Hong Kong to other parts of China.[13]

The functions of cities as centers of production are assessed in Table 4.5. An analysis of the distribution of GDP among cities of different size and location highlights the importance of extra-large cities and cities in the eastern region. Of the total amount of GDP generated by Chinese cities over 62 percent was contributed by large and extra-large cities. A comparison of GDP on a comparable per capita basis among the cities of different size also underscores the importance of large and extra-large cities (Table 4.5). The economic disparity among cities of different regions was even more striking. As listed in Table 4.5, cities in the eastern region produced most of the total GDP generated by the Chinese urban economy (64 percent); more than the combination of those in the central and western regions. As for GDP per capita, cities in the eastern region were also well above their counterparts in other regions (Table 4.5). The tendency of spatial change over time has not been significant except for a slight increase of the share of GDP held by the cities in the eastern region and a widened gap between the cities in the eastern coast and those in the interior in terms of GDP per capita. A closer analysis of the spatial redistribution of GDP among the cities of different provinces unveils another dimension of spatial disparity between north and south China. Figure 4.5 indicates that provinces in the southeastern coast enjoyed a remarkable increase in terms of the share of GDP generated by cities during the years of 1990–98. By comparison, GDP generated by the cities in many northern provinces declined proportionally. This pattern is

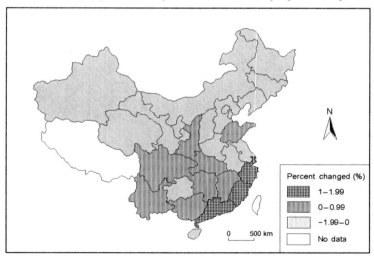

Figure 4.5 Redistribution of GDP among Chinese cities, 1990–98 (sources: China State Statistical Bureau, pp. 323–8; Lin (2002a), p. 311, Figure 5).

consistent with an earlier study of China's regional development since the reforms pointing to the shifting emphasis of the national production space from the north to the south.[14] Such a north–south contrast in the Chinese urban economy has been the complex outcome of the changing regional political economy in which the most vibrant element of growth has been associated with marketization and commercialization located in southern China.

Urbanization in China: the unofficial reading

While the official reading of the urbanization process in China gives us a broad picture it provides only a partial picture that is framed by official government definitions. Chinese urban space is being reconfigured in a manner that is only in part represented by urban statistics. The history of urban growth in the developed countries has been characterized by phases in which the spatial configuration of cities had been influenced by centripetal and centrifugal forces that are a reflection of various political and economic forces. In the early phases of city formation the centripetal forces often drew the population within city walls for reasons of political security.[15] But there were also centripetal forces leading to peri-urban growth that have accelerated in the last two centuries. In the USA this process consisted largely of suburbanization of which the major feature was residential spread of settlement. From the early twentieth century in the USA this process was driven by the private ownership of automobiles which in the post-Second World War period also included the growth of retailing activities and outward movement of industry and services. In the Chinese context these phases of spatial configuration are operating differently because of the two-track land system and limited ownership of private automobiles. In China there is a mixture of urban spaces in the rural areas surrounding the cities that serve as the location for new land development projects including the building of housing estates to accommodate the new urban rich, and industrial zones (*kaifaqu*) to attract foreign investment or relocated industry from the city core. This often occurs along proliferating smaller industries (township and village enterprises) and agricultural activity. As we have indicated in the previous chapters the understanding of the complete dimensions of urbanization is greatly aided by the careful delineation of the major spatial components of these urban spaces. First it is necessary to emphasize that this urban space must be spatially deconstructed. Urban space is best seen as an "assemblage" of interrupted urban spaces that need not to be contiguous to be defined as urban. In this chapter we use the terms "Interlocking Metropolitan Region" (IMR) and "extended metropolitan region" (EMR) to define this expanded urban space. Similarly people residing in the urban assemblages may be earning income from many sources both agricultural and non-agricultural. These urban assemblages are reliant upon transactional environments that are crucial to their activities (see Chapter 8).

Any attempt to configure these urban assemblages involves the construction of some model of this spatial order. The most common approach has been to contrast the city with its rural hinterland.[16] In the Chinese context we have suggested in the preceding chapter that this city dominance was not always true in the pre-socialist period and certainly in an ideological sense it did not occur in the Maoist era. This is well illustrated in the case studies of Kunshan and Dongguan. But in the period since 1992 core cities have begun to assert their control over the urban assemblage and rural spaces that make up an urban region. These developments have been characterized by three features; first, new internal spatial patterns of land use within existing city cores that are a response to industrial decentralization, the growth of the service economy, the increasing role of consumption and the need to create livable environments; second, the physical extension of city political control into the peri-urban regions in the manner we have described in the preceding paragraphs; and third, the rather uneven integration of the urban spaces into a wider assemblage of urban regions (often called city clusters) that have been labeled extended metropolitan regions.

This latter spatial representation of "urban space" is the one that interests us most in this book. There is much controversy over the role and function of these large urban regions in China. They were first recognized by Zhou Yixing[17] who labeled them "Interlocking Metropolitan Regions" that he suggested had some similarities with the concept of "megalopolis" coined by Jean Gottmann to capture the belt of urban activity that stretched from Boston to Washington in the USA.[18] But Zhou also recognized that there were many differences between China and the USA because of the intensity of agricultural activities and the high density of "*in situ*" populations in China. He used a series of criteria to define these interlocking metropolitan regions that included:

> (1) two or more cities with 1 million or more population that acted as growth poles, (2) important ports, (3) convenient lines of communication that act as a development corridor between growth poles and between poles and ports, (4) numerous small and medium sized cities along both sides of the corridor and, (5) intensive interaction between rural and urban areas.[19]

Based on these criteria Zhou delineated four interlocking metropolitan regions and two incipient regions in the coastal zone at the beginning of the 1990s. These were (1) Nanjing–Shanghai–Hangzhou IMR based in the lower Yangzi delta, (2) Hong Kong–Guangzhou in the Pearl River Delta, (3) Beijing–Tianjin in the North China Plain, and (4) Shenyang–Dalian in the central and southern Liaoning Province. The two incipient IMRs were the Shandong peninsula and the Fujian coastal zone from Fuzhou to Xiamen. Data available from the 2000 census suggests that the latter two IMRs now meet the required conditions. In addition the interior IMR of Chengdu–Chonqquing can now be added to this list.

Since 1991 the spatial forms of Chinese urbanization have been the subject of much research and debate among Chinese scholars. Some scholars have pointed out that present spatial patterns of urbanization have well established historical precedents. For example Xu and Yeh point out that the clustering of cities has a long history in China in the Imperial period.[20] In the period since the late 1980s this research has accelerated. Yeung and Zhou's jointly edited papers in Chinese sociology and anthropology were an important benchmark. This was followed by Yao (1992), Yeung and Xu (1992), Tang (1997), Wang (1998), Gu *et al.* (1999), Hu *et al.* (2000), and Sit (2005).[21] Much of this research on EMRs has focused on the four EMRs outlined by Zhou. The lower Yangzi delta has been studied by Marton (1995), Marton and McGee (1998), Yau and Chen (1998), Yu *et al.* (1999), Marton (2000), and Cherod Ltd. (2001), Webster 2002.[22] The Beijing–Tianjin EMR has been the focus of work by Sit (1995), Hook (1998), Laquian (2005) and others.[23] Sit, Yeh, Johnson, Lin and Yeung have all studied the emerging mega-urban region of the Pearl River Delta.[24] Major work on the Fujian IMR has been carried out by Zhu.[25] Finally a most exhaustive study of the Shenyang–Dalian IMR has been carried out by Wang.[26] One of the most comprehensive study of IMRs in China that was published in 1998 presented a strong argument for IMRs functioning as the "pivot, propeller and incubator" for promoting the country's economic and social development. This study revised the earlier criteria of Zhou by suggesting that IMRs should contain a total population of more than 25 million and densities higher than 700 per square kilometer. This is also reflected in recent national policy statements that have emphasized the need to encourage development in major city clusters.[27]

However despite these modifications there is still agreement that the four original IMRs delineated by Zhou still dominate mega-urbanization in contemporary China. Research by Sit (2005) and Wang (2006)[28] shows that in 1999 the four EMRs were approximately the same size (40,000 square kilometers) with populations ranging from 40 million in the Shanghai IMR to 21 million in the Shenyang–Dalian IMR. It is estimated at this time that they generated 45.5 percent of the nation's GDP (a third of the industrial output), were the locations of 76.6 percent of the utilized FDI and were responsible for 75 percent of the nation's exports. The four EMRs were the leading edge of China's modernization and incorporation into the global economy.

Internal differences between the three main zones of core, inner and outer rings indicate that it is the cores of the four EMRs that generally contain the smallest proportion of population in the EMRs. Almost two-thirds of the EMR populations are located in the inner and outer rings that are responsible for the majority of industrial output and exports. The Hong Kong centered EMR varies from this pattern with Hong Kong reflecting the historical trend that developed before it was reincorporated into China politically. Thus the GDP ratio per square kilometer of each zone indicates that the cores are much higher than the surrounding zones reflecting higher income and greater productivity. This pattern is also reflected in utilized foreign direct investment per square kilometer but reversed in the case of exports as a percentage of GDP. Thus this analysis reflects the growing differences between the core and margins that has been suggested in Chapter 3.

This empirical analysis provides the input for models of spatial differentiation of the Chinese extended metropolitan regions that are presented in the next section. Basically these models rely upon the model of EMRs developed by

McGee in 1991 that divided them into three regions: (1) city core; (2) peri-urban; and (3) *desakota*.[29] These correspond to the core, inner and outer rings discussed in the preceding sections. In this earlier work McGee drew attention to the spread of Asian EMRs into surrounding high density rural hinterlands that he argued was very different from the Western experience. McGee's development of the *desakota* model has invoked considerable debate. For many critics the concept of *desakota* placed too much emphasis upon "localized responses" and paid insufficient attention to the role of external forces such as the influence of the urban cores of the EMR and the role of transport and communications in the integration of EMRs.[30] It has been also suggested that the model under-theorizes the mechanisms at work in the rural–urban transformation in China. In particular it is argued that the model should have paid more attention to the role of the state in Chinese society and recognized the "disintegrative" and fragmentation effects of the urbanization process on people and the environment.[31] Perhaps the most constructive critique of the concept of "desakota" has come from the anthropologist Gregory Guldin (1997) who, based upon a careful evaluation of ethnographic studies in China conducted in the early 1990s, introduces the idea of urbanization as continuing along a continuum based upon an increase in "urban lifestyles" that are adopted from the level of the village to the largest municipalities. Thus in the period of the 1980s and early 1990s as industrialization increased in the smaller towns and villages (rural urbanization) the life style dimensions of urbanization began to increase in the countryside. In an economic sense this was indicated by the increase in non-agricultural employment, industrialization and growing agricultural productivity that are all features of the *desakota* enumerated by McGee. Guldin's intervention is valuable because it breaks down the idea of a division between rural and urban that is assumed by the more economic and technocratic critics of the concept of *desakota* which for McGee was a kind of "third space" between "urban" and "rural."[32]

In reflecting upon these critiques it is possible to argue that the critics have seen the "*desakota* model" as something of "strawman" on which to hang their particular predilections. First, we would argue that the original model was essentially an attempt to explain the growth of non-agricultural activities in the peri-urban regions of many of Asia's largest cities. It was also argued that this growth of non-agricultural activity was linked to the city cores of the EMRs and thus "*desakota* zones" should be regarded as part of the extended metropolitan region. Second, the model emphasized the underlying ecology of this process of urbanization into densely crowded rural areas that were often reliant upon irrigation systems that were placed under great stress as urban activities expanded and has therefore provided an important contextual element to the study of environmental problems in China. Third, the model emphasized the role of external factors in the form of improved transaction networks, industrial activity etc., arguing that cheap land and plentiful labor in these peri-urban regions was an important attraction to capital. Within Asian countries, such as Thailand, Indonesia and South Korea the role of the state in promoting export-oriented industrial development was particularly important. Finally the original formulation of this model placed great emphasis on the many problems of environmental pollution, resource degradation, infrastructure requirements, urban management and social disruption that this form of spatial development creates.

On reflection such criticism was hardly surprising. What was essentially a generic model designed to question Eurocentric assumptions concerning the urbanization process in Asia has been subject to critical regional deconstruction through empirical studies including the work of McGee's students that has led to modifications and rethinking of the original idea of *desakota* (see Chapters 5, 6, 8 and 9). It is one of the aims of this book to carry this deconstruction process forward by a closer analysis of the process of Chinese urbanization. In addition to this spatial deconstruction it may also be argued that there is a need for temporal refinement. The original model postulated three phases of *desakota* in Asia that were broadly related to the process of urbanization and economic development that assumes the spatial expansion of *desakota* as the built-up inner margin areas adjacent to the core cities.[33] This is shown in Figures 4.6 and 4.7 that show the development of the main zones of the extended metropolitan regions in Asia. As Figure 4.6 indicates the built-up urban environment has now advanced into former *desakota* regions and the *desakota* regions are now located much further away from the city cores. This has been facilitated by improved an transactional environment and the cheaper land and labor that are available in the outer margins. This is shown in greater detail in Figure 4.7 that draws some inspiration from Webster *et al.* (2003) that shows the types of activities that are spreading into the urban margins. Webster and his associates have argued that there are three stages of peri-urbanization in coastal China that reflect the changes in the period since 1978. Stage 1 peri-urbanization saw a dominance of township and village enterprises, Stage 2 involved the introduction of Economic and Technology Zones and high-tech parks and Stage 3, which is associated with increasing competition from other parts of China, for labor and pressures upon the industries in the coastal zones to produce higher quality goods that involves greater capital intensity, the development of component suppliers in associated spatial clusters and the need for more skilled labor. In addition as the mega-urban region becomes more economically developed it exhibits increasing functional specialization between the core and linked urban places in the margins.[34]

It is interesting to note that in the last five years there has been a growing interest in the concept of *desakota* by GIS specialists and quantitative modelers because of the fact that it represents a particular model of urban development that interlocks bottom-up type development with top-down expansion that occurs in a fragmented and disorganized manner. This attempt to quantify the urban development of *desakota* landscapes has been applied to the Pearl River Delta using multi-temporal aerial images monitoring of rapid urban expansion in the Pearl River Delta.[35] This was followed by work that attempted to build a predictive model of land-use change in different *desakota* areas of China.[36] What is interesting about these works is that they generally find a very good fit between their simulated models and actual existing *desakota* land use, which gives them confidence in the

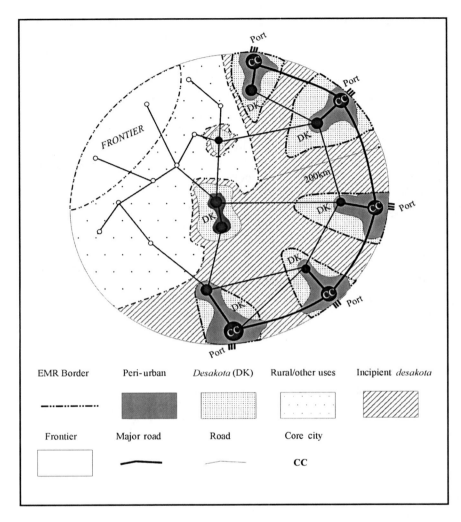

Figure 4.6 Land-use model of urban space at national level.

predictive capacity of such models. This suggests that the *desakota* model as it was first formulated has some conceptual validity as a model for predicting land-use change in these settings of rapid peri-urban urbanization.

Conclusion: core and margins in Chinese urbanization

This empirical and theoretical discourse of the emergence of large urban agglomerations that we have labeled EMRs in the Chinese context returns us to the discussion of Chapter 2 in which we put forward a theoretical formulation of

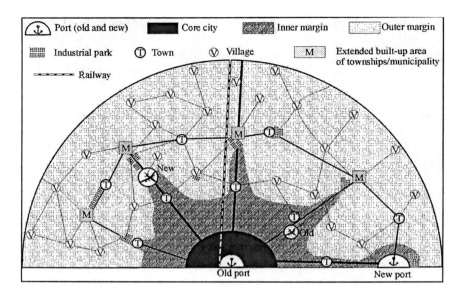

Figure 4.7 Hypothetical model of Chinese mega-urban coastal city.

the political economy of Chinese urbanization. To summarize, there are three main conceptual elements that have to be considered in analyzing this process. The first conceptual element is the recognition that the formulation of the idea of the extended metropolitan regions essentially grew out of a decade of increasing urban growth markedly concentrated in the peripheries of the EMRs, which is well supported by research published in *The Extended Metropolis in Asia: Settlement Transition in Asia* (Ginsburg *et al.* 1991). But in the period since 1990, as our earlier discussion has shown, this pattern of urbanization has begun to change because of a repositioning of the larger urban cores both in terms of economic and political power that is leading to an increasing growth of urban activity in the urban cores and their contiguous built-up areas. The process is causing both detachment and integration of the expanded central core from the hinterland of the EMR. Detachment in the sense that the urban cores of the EMRs are being integrated into wider international and national markets while the outer margins still remain more integrated into the EMR. At the same time the urban margins of the EMRs are becoming more functionally integrated with the core cities as industrial and residential activities proliferate. The outer margins of the EMRs (new areas of *desakota*) characterized by the juxtaposition of agricultural activities and industry now become the main zones of intense negotiation, contestation and reconciliation of the forces coming from all social and political scales (e.g. global, national, local and individual households; urban and rural; local and outsiders; plan and market). There are also important differences in the development of these two areas. In the core areas and the inner margins the built-environment is being transformed to make it more attractive to the forces of globalization. This involves major public and private investment in the enticing infrastructure of globalization; industrial estates, airports, gated communities, road systems and leisure parks. Despite this focus of investment in the core and its periphery the outer margins still remain attractive to both domestic and foreign investment because of cheaper land and labor. In these regions "weak surveillance of economic activity intersects with economic opportunity. At times entrepreneurship goes beyond the limits of legality and the desakota zone which then becomes the site of China's quasi-legal 'hidden economy.' In short ... it is possible to get things done cheaply and relatively expeditiously in these regions."[37]

A second concept may be described as the rural–urban interface that involves, in the context of coastal China, the expansion of urban activities from the core into rural margins characterized by intense agricultural activities and dense populations. One component of this expansion is the demand that core urban areas place upon the resources of their surrounding areas that provide water, food, building materials, land, labor, recreation space and waste disposal sites. As Atkinson points out that this functional analysis of cities and their hinterlands focuses attention on the issue of resource depletion, modification and destruction that it is at the very heart of the debate about urban sustainability that will be the focus of the final chapter.[38]

It is important in the Chinese context (and indeed elsewhere) to emphasize the role that the transactional revolution plays in encouraging the greater spread of urban activity. Thus, as this resource competition becomes more spatially extended, often in areas where there are a multiplicity of administrative entities, this makes policy formulation and implementation difficult, which is further exacerbated in the Chinese context by the influx of urban activities such as industrial estates and the associated movement of migrants to work as factory and agricultural labor. This creates a political environment in which core city governments (often in conjunction with national and provincial government and international funding) can bring about rapid change in expanding core urban areas that is much more difficult within the fragmented governance in the urban margins.

A third concept relates to the issue of the emergence of increasing functional specialization between the larger cities in the urban hierarchy that is related to increasing competition between urban centers within the changing spatial economy of China. There is more research to be done on this emerging facet of Chinese urbanization but much research has been generated that indicates Shanghai and Hong Kong are assuming significant functional domination in the provision of financial services and other cities are attempting to position themselves within the international and national economy as specialized urban centers.[39] There is no doubt that this functional differentiation between cities will grow as the national economy becomes more integrated.

The main thrust of this book is with the parts of the Chinese mega-urban regions that can be defined as urban margins that are constantly changing components of the EMR. The idea of the "restless urban frontier" that is suggested in the image of soft urban edges captures this trope very well. These margins are often the most difficult to investigate because they are outside the "lens of official observation." This feature is seen by the efforts of scholars to capture this ambiguity. For example urban margins that have been variously described as having a "regulation gap" (Ma and Wu, 2005b) and as a "third space" (Lin, 2001b), an "invisible economy" (Wang, 1998) and a "rural agglomeration" (Marton, 2000). This leads to the idea of the urban margins as "hybrid spaces" that we have advanced in Chapter 2. It is in these hybrid urban margins that most urban growth will occur in China in the next 50 years. And it is these margins that the major urban challenges of governance, sustainability and economic development will occur driven by the national, local and international forces.[40] In the next five chapters we present the case studies that focus on urban development in these urban margins.

5   City core and the periphery

The emerging Hong Kong–Guangzhou metropolitan region

Introduction

The preceding chapters have traced the main dimensions of the urban transformation in contemporary China. Our main thesis is that the Chinese urbanization process must be seen as the result of *mélange* of processes that are being driven by globalization, national policy and local bureaucratic entrepreneurial initiatives. We have also emphasized that the urbanization process must be set within the particular regional context in which it is occurring. In the midst of these dramatic changes it is possible to identify three main directions. First, city leaders are repositioning their cities so that they capture an increased proportion of global, national and regional transactions. Most obviously this is done by building new "gateway functions" such as international airports, freeway systems and container ports. Part of this package are attempts to market the city as livable, sustainable and efficient, which are often parts of newly developing city strategic plans. But this process is intensely competitive, none more so than in the province of Guangdong where Hong Kong had assumed a leading role in global interactions in the post-war period while it remained a British colony. But in the post-1978 period as Guangdong was opened-up to global investment as a result of Deng's open door policy, that has enabled Guangdong to become the leading industrial province in China (in terms of exports). Many new cities have sprung up in Guangdong including the special cities of Shenzhen and Zhuhai and many of the county urban cores such as Dongguan, Shunde, Zhongshan and Nanhai. This has presented a major challenge to the city core of Guangzhou as the provincial capital and forced city administrators to attempt to find new roles for the city in the urban system of the province.

This repositioning has been accompanied by a restructuring of economic activity at the provincial level that has seen a sharp decline in agricultural employment and a large increase in industrialization based in the smaller towns up to the mid-1990s. Since that date industrial activities also increased in the new towns such as Shenzhen and Zhuhai as well as administrative centers of the counties that have been reclassified as municipalities. Increasingly industry in the urban centers is becoming more capital intensive while labor intensive industry set up in the earlier period characterizes the smaller towns of the urban margins. Within this emerging urban system Guangzhou is also experiencing structural transformation with the increase of services that has particular implications for the spatial structure of the city and its margins.

These processes of repositioning and restructuring combined with administrative policies have also produced changes in the spatial patterns of the cities of the region that include: (1) the expansion of core cities into adjacent areas through the annexation of counties; (2) the creation of new zones for service and retailing and residential land uses; and (3) the establishment of new high-technology zones on the periphery of the city. This case study of Guangzhou shows that all these developments are occurring in the broader context of the reshaping of urban space.

In order to explore these developments the chapter is divided into three parts. The first part describes the pattern and processes of spatial restructuring in the Guangzhou and Hong Kong extended metropolitan region (Figure 5.1). The second part examines the processes of repositioning and economic restructuring of the city core of Guangzhou, which is illustrative of what has been taking place in many Chinese metropolises since the mid-1990s. The final part explores the changes in the spatial structure of the city as a reflection of these processes.

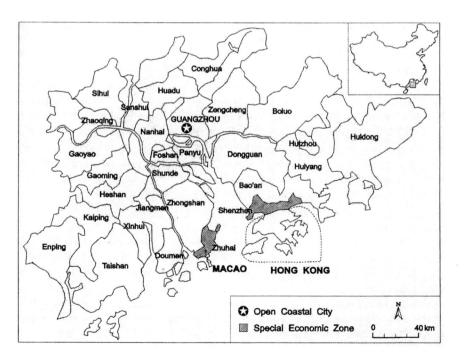

Figure 5.1 The Hong Kong–Pearl River Delta region, China.

Regional economic and spatial transformation in the 1980s

Since the 1980s, the regional economy in southern China extending from Hong Kong to Guangdong Province has experienced profound economic and spatial transformation as a result of increased globalization and marketization. Despite the existence of traditional cultural links, intensified interaction between Hong Kong and Guangdong Province has essentially been a recent phenomenon that has taken place since the late 1970s as a response to the restructuring of the political economies at both the national and global level. As the world capitalist economy moved from the stage of Fordist mass production to the new era of post-Fordist flexible specialization, from Keynesian welfare-statism to global capitalism, and from managerialism to entrepreneurialism, the Chinese economy has gone through an unprecedented process of transition from central planning to market coordination and from state monopoly to decentralization.[1] Almost in parallel to the ascendance of the Reagan and Thatcher "new right" administrations, which popularized the ideas of deregulation, privatization and industrial rationalization, the pragmatic leadership of Deng Xiaoping, who took power after the demise of the radical Maoist regime, adopted a new approach that favored efficiency over equity, individual creativity over collectivization and outward looking over self-isolation. While the emergence of the new regime of flexible accumulation in North America and Western Europe has been primarily a response to deepened international division of labor and intensified global competition, the formation of liberal economic policies in China has stemmed from a keen recognition that endless revolutionary upheavals in the past several decades had brought little improvement to the lives of the Chinese people and that drastic policy changes must be made to lead the nation out of the deadlock of isolation and stagnancy.[2]

One of the most important actions taken by the new Chinese leaders has been the introduction of an Open Door Policy as a means to attract foreign investment, bring advanced technology and know-how into the country, and promote export production. Under the Open Door Policy, foreign investors are given preferential treatments including tax concessions, duty-free imports of machinery and equipment, and other benefits to facilitate their investment and production in China. As a major objective of the Open Door Policy was to attract foreign capital, it is not surprising that the geographical focus of this new practice has been on the coastal zone, which is more easily accessible than the interior to potential investors overseas.

The Open Door Policy has been implemented through a process of spatial reorganization, which leads China to enter the world step by step. It began with the establishment of four Special Economic Zones in the southern provinces of Guangdong and Fujian where overseas connections are extensive and the tradition of international trade is strong.[3] This was followed by the opening up of 14 port cities along the eastern coast in 1984 and the designation of three major river deltas as Open Economic Regions in 1985.[4] Finally, the policy was further extended to cover all coastal provinces in 1988. Increasingly, China's coastal zone has been seen as a "development catalyst" or a stepping stone for the country to move up to the stage of Pacific regional cooperation and newly international division of labor.[5]

Although Chinese coastal provinces are now all open to receiving foreign capital, the most dynamic region capturing much international attention thus far has been the province of Guangdong, which is located in the southern frontier of the mainland facing Hong Kong across the border. When measured by its size of population or land area, Guangdong is not a prominent province in China. With a population of 85 million and a territory of 17.97 million hectares, Guangdong is ranked second in population and fifteenth in land area among China's provinces.[6] The province is, however, distinguished by its geographic proximity to Hong Kong, which used to be a British colony but was returned to Chinese rule in July 1997. Despite their political and economic differences, Hong Kong and Guangdong share a common Cantonese culture based on which extensive social ties had been developed over the past several decades. Even in the Maoist era when Guangdong's connections with Hong Kong were limited, the two territories maintained minimum economic exchanges because the city state of Hong Kong had to rely on Guangdong for the supply of fresh water and farm products. However, social and economic linkages between Hong Kong and Guangdong were not extensive at the time. They did not benefit the development of Guangdong either because the province's frontier location to Hong Kong was perceived to be highly vulnerable to the penetration of capitalism and to possible military invasion by overseas enemies including Taiwan and the United States. For this and other reasons, Guangdong had never become a prime location to receive sizable state capital investment for most of the years since 1949.[7]

The implementation of the Open Door Policy since 1979 has not only renewed traditional social and economic linkages between Hong Kong and Guangdong but also greatly facilitated the intertwining of the two neighboring territories. The opening up of Guangdong coincided with a time when Hong Kong was seeking ways to cope with the growing competition from countries of the capitalist world and other newly industrializing economies. As the cost of labor and land continued to rise, it became profitable to relocate the labor-intensive manufacturing factories of Hong Kong to Guangdong. In this way Hong Kong's industry could meet the challenges of new international division of labor and global competition.[8] With its geographic proximity to and special cultural and linguistic connections with Hong Kong plus a newly introduced Open Door Policy, Guangdong Province naturally became the first choice for those Hong Kong manufacturers who had been desperately looking for low-price production outlets to relocate manufacturing facilities in the face of increasing competition from newer low-cost locations in other parts of Asia.

The combined effect of the forces of globalization and national policy changes has intensified economic interaction between Hong Kong and Guangdong and the emergence of an integrated economic region in southern China. It has been estimated that of the total direct foreign investment received by Guangdong, 70 percent came from Hong Kong. As many as three million workers in Guangdong have been hired to work for Hong Kong manufacturing firms, more than the total manufacture labor force of Hong Kong itself.[9] From the national point of view, available data clearly identify Hong Kong as the single largest source of foreign direct investment flow into China. During 1992–99, for instance, China received a total of US$282.57 billion foreign direct investment from all over the world. Of this amount, US$140.69 billion or 49.7 percent came from Hong Kong alone. The inflow of foreign capital in China has been highly concentrated in Guangdong Province. In the two decades of 1979–99, China received an estimated US$459.56 billion utilized foreign capital investment, of which US$110.67 billion or 24 percent of the national total ended in Guangdong Province. Of the total US$305.92 billion foreign direct investment that China received during this period of time, as much as US$86.58 billion or 28 percent was found in Guangdong Province alone.[10] Hong Kong and Guangdong, as the major origin and destination of the foreign capital investment flow into China, have played a leading role in the re-articulation of China with the global economy.

The integration of Hong Kong and Guangdong has resulted in a process of economic restructuring in both places. As many industrial facilities have been relocated from Hong Kong to Guangdong, the number of employed in the manufacturing sector in Hong Kong dropped from 755,000 in 1971 to 574,000 in 1996 and its share of the total employment declined from 48 percent to only 19 percent. Meanwhile, the number of employed in the service sector rose from 640,000 to 2.18 million and its share of the economy increased from 41 percent to 72 percent for the same period of 1971–96.[11] While Hong Kong was undergoing a process of deindustrialization and tertiarization, Guangdong started to experience accelerated industrialization and urbanization. The emphasis of the regional economy shifted from the primary sector to the secondary and tertiary sectors, with the proportion of employment in the primary sector dropping from 71 percent to 42 percent and the percentage of people engaged in the secondary sector increasing from 17 percent to 31 percent during the years of 1980–99. The composition of GDP also demonstrated a similar pattern of restructuring.[12]

The process of regional integration has been most remarkable in the area extending from Hong Kong to the Pearl River Delta (PRD), which is both the core of Guangdong Province and the immediate hinterland of the capitalist enclave. Since the implementation of liberal economic policies, the PRD has played an exceptionally significant role in both exports and the attraction of foreign investment. Geographically, the spatial pattern of export-led industrialization in the delta region has been characterized by a relative decline of Guangzhou city as a dominant metropolitan centre, the accelerated growth of the counties and cities located in the areas outside and between metropolitan centers and the persistent stagnancy of places in the periphery of the region.[13] While the dominance of Guangzhou city in the region has weakened, the triangular area between Guangzhou, Hong Kong and Macao has quickly emerged as a developing zone where industrial and agricultural production has advanced quite dramatically. The concentration of economic activities in the triangular zone bordered by Hong Kong–Guangzhou–Macao has been the result of inter-action of various internal and external forces.

First, this zone is where land and labor can be obtained easily and cheaply when compared with the large city. This situation has been particularly attractive to foreign industrial entrepreneurs who are looking for locational alternatives to reduce production costs. It also represents an important outlet for the relocation of older manufacturing facilities from the large cities where congestion and environmental pollution have become a major concern of the government and the general public. Second, since the 1980s the zone has experienced a massive development and dramatic improvement of the transportation infrastructure. Improvement of the regional transportation infrastructure has no doubt increased the accessibility of the zone and helped attract production facilities. Finally, many townships and villages in this zone have been the ancestral home of the Chinese people in Hong Kong and overseas. Extensive pre-existing personal connections between this area and overseas investors have been found con-ducive to foreign investment and export processing activities.[14] The existence of these place-specific kinship ties helped explain why many manufacturing activi-ties financed by Hong Kong and overseas investors had taken place here in this zone rather than the large city of Guangzhou despite its advantages such as agglomeration economies.

A remarkable spatial configuration of economic growth and structural change has been the reinforced concentration of population in the Guangzhou–Hong Kong–Macao triangle zone. Under the population control policy particularly, the policy that allows for one child per couple, there was no significant change in the growth and spatial distribution of the local population in the delta region. However, population mobility has significantly increased as a result of both the process of economic restructuring and the recent relaxation of state control over population movement. As the regional economy experienced a significant restructuring characterized by a relative decline in traditional farming and the rapid surge of the rural industry, the potential for the people to move has been increased significantly. On the one hand, the demise of traditional food-grain production released a sizable number of rural laborers from the field. On the other hand, the flourishing of numerous rural industries and the revitalized com-mercial activities in small towns created phenomenal employment opportunities for the rural exodus. The combined effect of these push-and-pull forces has been a movement of people from farming to non-farming activities, and from rural to urban settlements. Such a movement has been facilitated since the mid-1980s by the state's deregulation of rural–urban migration.[15]

One of the most important indicators of rural–urban migration in the Chinese statistics is what is termed as "temporary population" (*zanzhu renkou*), which refers to migrants who have lived in a locale for longer than one year without holding a permanent household registration of that locale.[16] Data show that between the two national census years of 1982 and 1990, "temporary population," essentially migrants moving to and within the PRD, increased by 42 percent, or an average of 350,000 persons per year. This growth rate was much higher than the provincial average of 29 percent per year. The total number of the "temporary population" rose from 184,000 in 1982 to 2.98 million in 1990. Almost 80 percent of the temporary population found in Guangdong Province in 1990 ended up in the PRD.[17] It is obvious that the PRD has become the chief destination for migrants moving to and within the province.

When analyzed at the intra-regional level, the growth and distribution of migration exhibits a spatial pattern similar to the one associated with industrial and agricultural production. Table 5.1 analyzes the changing distribution of the temporary population in the region between 1982 and 1990. Not surprisingly, the most dramatic growth of migration occurred in the two Special Economic Zones of Shenzhen and Zhuhai, both of which recorded an extraordinary annual growth rate of over 75 percent. Their share of the regional total of temporary population rose significantly from a mere 2.4 percent to 21 percent during the eight years between 1982 and 1990 (Table 5.1). The largest city Guangzhou and other existing designated cities, such as Jiangmen, Zhaoqing and Huizhou, did not receive many in-migrants during this period. The growth rates of migration to these cities were all lower than the regional average. Consequently, their

Table 5.1 Changing distribution of temporary population in the Pearl River Delta, 1982–90

	1982		1990		Annual
	Number	*Percent of total*	*Number*	*Percent of total*	*growth (%)*
Guangzhou	70,541	*38.38*	451,761	*15.14*	*26.13*
SEZs	4,438	*2.41*	640,593	*21.46*	*86.18*
Shenzhen	2,925	1.59	506,185	16.96	90.45
Zhuhai	1,513	0.82	134,408	4.50	75.22
Existing cities	23,312	*12.69*	217,996	*7.30*	*32.24*
Foshan	4,929	2.68	81,280	2.72	41.96
Jiangmen	3,325	1.81	22,827	0.76	27.23
Zhaoqing	8,724	4.75	43,837	1.47	22.36
Huizhou	6,334	3.45	70,052	2.35	35.04
Selected counties and cities	27,106	*14.75*	1,335,329	*44.74*	*62.77*
Zhongshan	6,368	3.47	108,884	3.65	42.60
Dongguan	5,228	2.84	453,005	15.18	74.67
Shunde	5,294	2.88	76,312	2.56	39.59
Nanhai	4,956	2.70	123,167	4.12	49.42
Panyu	2,904	1.58	44,795	1.50	40.78
Baoan	2,356	1.28	529,166	17.73	96.76
Other counties	58,381	*31.77*	339,109	*11.36*	*24.59*
Total	183,778	100.00	2,984,788	100.00	41.69

Source: Guangdong Province Population Census Office (1991), pp. 40–4; Lin (2001a), p. 396, Table 4.

Note
SEZ stands for Special Economic Zone.

share of the total temporary population of the region has dropped significantly (Table 5.1). The only exception is Foshan city, which had moderate growth and a slight proportional increase in temporary population. This increase is partly because of its intense economic linkage with counties in the central delta, and partly because it contains the small town of Shiwan, which is relatively accessible to in-migrants.

The most remarkable increase in temporary population occurred in the newly developing counties within the Guangzhou–Hong Kong–Macao triangle. As revealed in Table 5.1, these counties, especially Baoan and Dongguan, have experienced not only a much faster growth rate of in-migration than other parts of the region, but also a dramatic increase in their share of the regional total of temporary population. As a group, they tripled their share of the regional total in eight years, accounting for a disproportionate 45 percent of all temporary populations in 1990. While the Special Economic Zones (SEZs) and the newly developing counties were receiving an increasing and disproportionate number of in-migrants, cities and counties on the periphery were left far behind. These peripheral cities and counties accounted for 72.97 percent of the delta's land area and 47.88 percent of its total population, but received only 31 percent of the total in-migrants in 1982. That disproportionately low percentage dropped even further to 11 percent in 1990 (Table 5.1).

That the extended metropolitan region has accepted a large number of in-migrants as a result of economic restructuring may not be unique to the PRD. While in North America and Western Europe in the 1960s the growth of urban peripheries was primarily the result of intra-urban residential relocation facilitated by freeway development, in the PRD it has been primarily because of employment creation. What, then, are the distinct features of population redistribution in this Chinese region? Who are the migrants? Do they originate from the central cities? Why do they move into the peri-urban regions outside and between metropolitan centers? According to a 1 percent sample survey of migrants conducted by the provincial census authorities in 1988, increased migration since the reforms has been predominately intra-provincial. Migrants who originated from areas outside of the province accounted for only 11 percent.[18] The majority of migrants (57 percent) are female. In terms of their origins, most migrants (72 percent) come from villages in the countryside. Over 70 percent ended up in towns (Table 5.2). As for the motive of migration, seeking employment, including job transfer, job assignment and to enter business or do factory work, was reported by most migrants (70 percent) as the main reason to change their residence.[19] When the results of this survey are pieced together, it becomes clear that recent migration in the PRD since the reforms has involved primarily an internal movement of surplus rural laborers from the countryside to towns in the quickly developing corridor between metropolitan centers for the purpose of seeking a factory job or for other more profitable non-agricultural pursuits. This pattern stands in sharp contrast with the earlier American experience of suburbanization that primarily involved the relocation of urban residents from the central cities to the suburb for a greater

Table 5.2 Population migration to and within Guangdong Province, 1982–87

	Number (thousands)	*Percent*
Total	2,535.6	100.00
Male	1,094.1	43.15
Female	1,441.4	56.85
Destinations		
Cities	698.5	27.55
Towns	1,776.0	70.04
Villages	61.1	2.41
Origin		
Cities	198.4	7.82
Towns	519.5	20.49
Villages	1,817.7	71.69

Sources: China State Statistical Bureau (1988), pp. 677, 706; Lin (2001a), p. 397, Table 5.

open space. It is also different from the current Western urban process, which involves mainly consolidation rather than physical and population expansion.

The distinct pattern of internal migration to the towns in the metropolitan areas of the PRD has been a complex outcome of a number of factors including the changing state policies from above, spontaneous rural industrialization from below and inflow of foreign investment from outside. Prior to the reforms, rural to urban migration was constrained by the socialist state for the strategic consideration of minimizing the cost that might involve in the provision of urban services. Since the reforms, however, the state has adopted a more flexible yet differentiated approach to migration to cities and towns. While rural to large cities migration remained limited by the state, peasants have since 1984 been allowed to move into towns nearby provided that they looked after their own needs for food-grain, housing and other urban services. The state's partial relaxation over the control of rural–urban migration took place at a time when rural industries particularly township and village industries (*xiangzhen qiye*) flourished in the countryside.[20] Geographically, these township and village industries have been better developed in the areas between and surrounding major metropolitan centers, which function as not only a source of technological transfer but also a market for the industries. The interaction of new state policies from above and rural industrialization from below has been reinforced by the establishment of export processing facilities from Hong Kong and overseas. As discussed in the foregoing section, many manufacturing facilities set up by Hong Kong investors have been located in the corridor between Hong Kong, Guangzhou and Macao partly because of the availability of cheap land and labor and partly because of the existence of kinship ties on which business relationships were built. Along with the township and village industries, the export processing ventures located in the metropolitan corridor have created considerable employment opportunities to accommodate the rural migrants who have been allowed by the state to move into towns. The living costs for

Table 5.3 Changing non-agricultural population for the Pearl River Delta, 1980–90

	1980	1990	Increase 1980–90	Share of total increase (%)
Largest city of Guangzhou	2,264,470	2,577,883	+313,413	9.77
Designated cities	580,172	1,603,086	+1,022,914	31.89
Designated towns	1,422,157	3,292,584	+1,871,427	58.34
Total	4,266,799	7,474,553	+3,207,754	100.00

Sources: Guangdong Statistical Bureau (1986), pp. 2–41; ibid. (1990), pp. 108–30; ibid. (1991), pp. 111–12; ibid. (1992), pp. 83–206; Lin (2001a), p. 398, Table 6.

Note
Data for designated cities do not include designated towns contained in their suburbs. They have been separately counted as designated towns.

migrants, which are lower in small towns than in large cities, have also been considered an important factor explaining the revealed pattern of rural – urban migration.[21]

The process of economic restructuring and population redistribution has found its way to reorganize the settlement system of the region. Tables 5.3 and 5.4 analyze the changing settlement system of the PRD, using non-agricultural population as the basis for assessing urban population size.[22] Given the above-revealed fact that most migrants have chosen small towns as their destinations, it is not surprising that these towns have become the most dynamic element in the settlement system, accepting the largest share of the increased non-agricultural population (Table 5.3) and experiencing the fastest growth rate (Table 5.4). By comparison, the largest city of Guangzhou showed little expansion. Its share of the regional total dropped from 53 percent in 1980 to only 34 percent in 1990 (Table 5.4). This pattern is consistent with the reduction of the city's dominance in the regional economy as discussed earlier. What is worthy of attention is the fact that the growth of cities other than Guangzhou has not been substantial. Most cities were in the small-city group, and the large-city category remained empty after ten years of rapid economic growth and development (see Table 5.4). The result of this analysis seems to suggest that cities, especially large cities, did not set the pace for change in the delta's urbanization in the early period of rural industrialization in the 1980s. This has posed great challenges to the leaders of many large cities especially the city of Guangzhou and forced them to adopt new strategies of urban repositioning and restructuring.

Repositioning and restructuring of the city core

While the period up to the mid-1990s, as the preceding discussion has indicated, was a phase in which small and newly established towns dominated the industrialization process, since the 1990s the larger towns have begun to

Table 5.4 Distribution of non-agricultural population among cities and towns in the Pearl River Delta, 1980–90

Cities and towns: growth by size	1980			1990			Annual (%)
	No.	Number of people	% of total	No.	Number of people	% of total	
Extra-large (> = 1 million)	1	2,264,470	53.07	1	2,577,883	34.49	1.30
Large (500,000–1 million)	0	0	0	0		0	
Medium (200,000–500,000)	0	0	0	2	604,780	8.09	
Small (100,000–200,000)	6	580,172	13.60	7	998,306	13.36	5.58
Towns (< = 100,000)	235	1,422,157	33.33	435	3,293,584	44.06	8.76
Total	242	4,266,799	100.00	445	7,474,553	100.00	5.77

Sources: Guangdong Statistical Bureau (1986), pp. 2–41; ibid. (1990), pp. 108–30; ibid. (1991), pp. 111–12; ibid. (1992), pp. 83–206; Lin (2001a), p. 399, Table 7.

Note

Data for cities do not include those towns contained in their suburbs as they have been separately counted in the category of towns. The three new designated cities in 1990 were Zhongshan, Dongguan and Qingyuan.

assume a more important role as they have attempted to reposition themselves so as to receive maximum benefits from China's increasing globalization and economic growth. The recent development of Guangzhou appears to be illustrative of such attempts. Since the 1990s, Guangzhou has experienced a process of urban economic restructuring similar to that occurring in other large Chinese cities. That process is characterized by a dramatic expansion of the tertiary sector in the urban economy, accompanied by a proportional decline of the primary and secondary sectors in output and employment. In other words, large Chinese cities are repositioning themselves in response to the growth of manufacturing activities in the small and medium-sized cities and towns.

Situated at the confluence of the three major tributaries (west, east and north branches) of the Pearl River (*Zhujiang*), Guangzhou (Canton) has long been the southern gateway to China, the capital city of Guangdong Province and an economic center of the PRD region. The city enjoys geographic proximity to Hong Kong and shares a common Cantonese culture with the former British colonial enclave ever since it was formed in 1842. For decades, Guangzhou has been China's designated city to host its national exports commodity fair.[23] Its external orientation makes the city an interesting case illustrative of how the urban economy and space have been repositioned, restructured and reshaped in response to the growing influence of globalization and increased competition from other cities in the region. The reorientation of the urban economy in

Guangzhou has to be understood in relation to the established tradition of the city in the region and the country.

Historically, urban services and commercial functions have been the areas in which Guangzhou has the comparative advantages and strength. Compared with other Chinese cities, Guangzhou has never been strong in the manufacturing of heavy machinery or capital goods production partly because of the lack of industrial energy and raw materials in the region and partly because of the shortage of an industrial labor force. However, Guangzhou is endowed with a favorable location for international ocean transportation and a strong tradition in international trade. Geographically, Guangzhou enjoys an accessibility much more favorable than any other coastal cities including Shanghai and Tianjin as far as ocean transportation and trade links with the European continent are concerned. For this and other reasons, Guangzhou was the first port city reached by the European (Portuguese) in 1516 and by the Americans in 1784. When the entire China coast was closed in 1757 for defense reasons, Guangzhou was the only port city that remained open for trading with the outside world.[24] When the Treaty of Nanjing was signed to end the Opium War in 1842, Guangzhou was among the first five "Treaty Ports," along with Shanghai, Ningbo, Xiamen and Fuzhou, opened to trade in addition to the concession of Hong Kong as a British colony. With this historical background and geographic foundation, it was not surprising to see the economy of the city highly reliant upon commerce, trade, businesses and services when the Communists took over Guangzhou on 14 October 1949. The tertiary sector provided jobs for 44 percent of the labor force whereas the primary sector accommodated 36 percent and the secondary sector only 20 percent.[25] Guangzhou was essentially a mercantile city at the outset of the socialist revolution.

The mercantile nature of the city of Guangzhou had naturally become the subject of constant assault and transformation in the era of socialism under Mao. For ideological and strategic reasons, the dominance of trading and service activities in the urban economy was unacceptable to the new regime. Ideologically, trading and service activities were considered to be "nonproductive" and exploitative in the nature that should be restrained. Strategically, industrial production, especially the production of basic industry or capital goods such as iron and steel, was identified as the key to building a great socialist enterprise, strengthening national military might and "catching up the US and overtaking the UK." Great efforts had therefore been taken by the municipal government to transform Guangzhou from a "city of consumption" into a "city of production."

The death of Mao in 1976 and the subsequent demise of the radical leadership set Guangzhou on a new path of economic restructuring and urban development. Although there was no drastic privatization in the form of "big bang therapy" as experienced in the former Soviet Union and Eastern European countries, decentralization of the power of decision-making from the central government to Guangdong Province in 1979 was significant enough to allow the municipal government of Guangzhou to proactively develop a market economy and interact with forces of globalization on the basis of its inherent comparative advantages. Ideologically, the overarching concern of the post-Mao regime was no longer to comply with the scripture and restrain "non-productive" consumption activities. Instead, it is the generation of income and employment to satisfy the actual needs of the general population and raise the standard of living to a "moderately well-off" level (*xiao kang shui ping*). Strategically, to have a coastal and gateway location is no longer seen as vulnerable to possible naval attacks. On the contrary, a coastal city like Guangzhou has now been considered to be the spearhead for the socialist nation to reintegrate itself with the global capitalist economy through the attraction of foreign investment and promotion of exports.[26] Subsequent to the establishment of four SEZs in southern China and the allowance of Guangdong and Fujian provinces to practice "special policies" (*teshu zhengce*) in 1979, Guangzhou, capital city of Guangdong Province, was designated as one of the 14 "open coastal cities" in 1984. With this new atmosphere favoring marketization and globalization, the "seeds" of mercantilism deeply sown in Guangzhou prior to the Communist revolution but forcefully suppressed by Mao's regime for nearly three decades, could now germinate, bloom and bear impressive fruits.

At the outset in 1980, the urban economy of Guangzhou was overshadowed by the legacy of the earlier practice of transforming the city from consumption into production. The secondary sector took the lion's share of employment providing jobs to 46 percent of the urban labor force. Since then, the share held by the secondary sector in the total employment of the city has steadily declined from 46 to 34 percent whereas the balance has been taken up by the tertiary sector whose share enjoyed a dramatic growth from 35 to 57 percent during 1980 to 2000. Not only has the tertiary sector resumed its dominant position in the urban economy as it used to be prior to the Communist revolution, it has led the other two sectors by a margin even greater than it was in 1949. If the occupational structure of the urban labor force is taken as an important indicator of sectoral transition, it is quite obvious that the urban economy of Guangzhou has undergone a significant process of tertiarization. The arbitrary distortion of the Maoist regime to the natural structure of Guangzhou's urban economy has eventually given way to the operation of forces of marketization and globalization.

The restructuring of the urban economy toward a service orientation has owed a great deal to the articulation of the central and local states for political and social considerations. Although the share of the tertiary sector in the urban labor force has grown steadily since the 1978 economic reforms, it was not until the mid-1990s that the tertiary sector surpassed the other two economic sectors and became the most important source of employment for the city. Such a shift of emphasis was associated with the growth of per capita income during this period and the increase in market demand for services. Statistical data released by the Guangzhou Statistical Bureau show that the average annual salary for a worker in the city rose from 714 yuan in 1978 to 3,504 yuan in 1990 and then 19,091 in the year 2000.[27] In a similar manner, per capita annual disposable income for urban residents grew considerably from 442 yuan in 1978 to 2,749 yuan in 1990 and 13,967 by the turn of the century. Increase in per capita income is logically one of the important market forces facilitating the growth of services because, to follow Engel's law, consumers normally spend proportionally less of any increase in their income on basic material needs and proportionally more on immaterial services. In other words, a rising per capita income will logically increase the market demand for services and China is no exception.[28] However, the upsurge of the tertiary sector as the leading economic sector since the mid-1990s cannot be fully explained without analyzing changes in state policies at the time.

The early 1990s was a time when China started to deepen reforms of the national economy particularly the money-losing state-owned enterprises (SOEs). With a keen understanding that reforms or privatization of the SOEs might result in massive layoffs and rising unemployment that could threaten social stability, the post-reform regime had to find an outlet alternative to SOEs so that the industrial exodus could be accommodated. On 16 June 1992, the Central Committee of the Chinese Communist Party and the State Council jointly made "The Resolution to Speed Up the Development of The Tertiary Industry" and disseminated it to the entire nation. Among other things, the resolution spelt out the definition of the tertiary industry, highlighted the "strategic importance" of the tertiary industry as "the main outlet to relieve the growing employment pressure faced by the nation," and listed a series of approaches that should be adopted for faster development of the tertiary industry. The growth of the tertiary industry has since then become not simply a market-driven economic affair but one on the political agenda with important implications for urban manageability and social stability.

The growth of a service economy in Guangzhou has also been an integral part of the strategy adopted by the municipal government. If municipal fixed asset capital investment and city planning were previously used to transform the city of Guangzhou from consumption into production in Mao's era, then they are now to be used as the instruments to promote the tertiary industry. This is evident when the changing composition of Guangzhou's fixed asset capital investment is analyzed. The proportion of fixed asset capital investment allocated to the tertiary sector, after a slight drop from 67 percent in 1985 to 65 percent in 1990, increased dramatically to 76 percent in 1995 and has kept its dominance ever since.[29] By the year 2000, the tertiary industry had taken 85 percent of the total fixed asset capital investment in the city. Of this investment, the bulk was found in real estate development (39 percent), social services (19 percent) and wholesale, retail and catering activities.[30] In a similar manner, the tertiary industry occupied a prime position in city planning and land-use arrangement in the most recent comprehensive plan for the terms of 1991–2000 formulated in 1994.

Since the late 1990s, the municipal government has taken important steps to drastically reorganize the existing urban space and upgrade the existing urban built-environment. A strategy of urban development was formulated aiming at "a minor change in one year, medium-scaled change in three years, and major change in five years" (*yinian yixiao bian, sannian yizhong bian, wunian yida bian*). Under this new strategy, a large number of urban development projects were initiated, including the building of a new international airport with the largest capacity of handling passenger and freight transport in southern China and comparable to the one in Hong Kong, a new metro railway system, the International Convention and Exhibition Center, the Olympics Sports Center, the 63-story-high Tower of CITIC as the signature building of the new central business district and a planned sea port in the Nansha Economic and Techno-logical Development Zone (see Plates 5.1, 5.2, 5.3 and 5.4). These development projects required not only a huge amount of capital input but also a large area of land. To meet the demands of these development projects for land, the municipal government took drastic action and incorporated two of its sub-urban counties into the urban district. Panyu in the south and Huadu in the north of Guangzhou city were both taken over by Guangzhou in June 2000. As a result, the urban space has been dramatically expanded and restructured so that Guangzhou could compete with its rivals and reassert its central function in the region and the country.

Plate 5.1 The newly developed international airport in Huadu, Guangzhou.

Plate 5.2 Tower of China International Trust and Investment Corporation (CITIC).

Plate 5.3 The new subway system in Guangzhou.

Plate 5.4 The Nansha economic and technological development zone.

The changing urban economy and space of Guangzhou

The practice of a new place-making strategy has found its way to restructure and reshape the urban economy and space. Table 5.5 analyzes the changing position of Guangzhou city (urban district) in the PRD regional economy after 1992 when the importance of the tertiary sector was officially recognized and promotion of service activities was initiated. It has been extensively documented that recent economic development in the PRD since the reforms has been characterized by rapid rural industrialization, dramatic upsurge of many sub-urban economies and a relative decline of the leading position held by Guangzhou in the region.[31] This observed pattern is confirmed by the data on population and GDP listed in Table 5.5. As many sub-urban economies grew vigorously and upgraded themselves in the region, there has been a proportional decline in terms of both population and GDP contributed by Guangzhou city. While the share of Guangzhou in the total population of the region dropped only by a small margin (from 18 to 17.9 percent), the proportional decline of the GDP generated by Guangzhou city has been significant, a drop from 34 percent to 23 percent in less than ten years (Table 5.5). This decline has been due to in part a rapid industrialization of the delta region and in part a shift of plants out of the city center to the urban outskirts.

There are some important exceptions, however. When the contribution of Guangzhou city to the total retail sales of the region is scrutinized, a growing

Table 5.5 Guangzhou *shiqu* in the Pearl River Delta region, 1992–2000

			1992	*1995*	*2000*
Population	Delta	million	20.08	21.38	23.07
	Guangzhou	million	3.67	3.85	4.14
	Guangzhou as % of delta	%	18.28	18.01	17.95
GDP	Delta	billion yuan	115.93	389.97	737.86
	Guangzhou	billion yuan	39.60	89.62	171.51
	Guangzhou as % of delta	%	34.16	22.98	23.24
Retail Sales	Delta	billion yuan	67.08	154.47	278.14
	Guangzhou	billion yuan	16.72	43.44	93.05
	Guangzhou as % of delta	%	24.93	28.12	33.45
Utilized Foreign	Delta	billion USD	3.22	8.58	12.54
Investment	Guangzhou	billion USD	0.47	1.36	2.47
	Guangzhou as % of delta	%	14.60	15.85	19.70

Sources: Guangdong Statistical Bureau (2001), p. 626; Guangzhou Statistical Bureau (1999), pp. 208, 230, 567 and 613; ibid. (2001), pp. 29, 38, 39, 54, 401 and 470; Lin (2004a), p. 34, Table 6.

trend becomes evident. Over the eight years from 1992 to 2000, Guangzhou's share of the total retail sales of the delta region increased from 25 to 33 percent. In Chinese statistics, the output of retail sales has been the main indicator of the magnitude of trading or commercial exchange in a city or town. The share of a city in the total retail sales of a region represents to a great extent the role played by the city in trading or commercial exchange of the region. The increased contribution of Guangzhou city to the total regional retail sales suggested that the city has played an increasingly important role as the regional center of trading and commercial exchange. Apparently, Guangzhou's upgraded position in regional trade has been one of the direct consequences of the dramatic expansion of the tertiary sector.

Another interesting exception lies in the role played by Guangzhou city as a major recipient of foreign investment. As shown in Table 5.5, utilized foreign investment in Guangzhou city has been growing steadily in both absolute amount and its proportion of the delta region. Guangzhou's share of the total utilized foreign capital invested in the delta region expanded from 15 percent in 1992 to nearly 20 percent in the year 2000. This trend has been particularly evident toward the end of the 1990s when China's accession into the WTO eventually occurred. The increase in Guangzhou's share of the total utilized foreign investment in the delta region in recent years suggested that the city has reclaimed its position as the regional center of transnational capital and multinational corporations subsequent to both China's accession into the WTO and improvements of services in the city that have made it more attractive to foreign investment. Looking at all the data listed in Table 5.5, Guangzhou city has recently resumed its function as a regional service center for both domestic traders and foreign investors despite its relative decline in terms of its role as a center of industrial production.[32]

Economic restructuring has also found its way to reshape urban land use and transform the urban landscape. The earlier practice of industrial-biased urban development under socialism in the Mao era had left Guangzhou city with a land-use structure preoccupied by industrial production. Even in the early 1990s after a decade of market reforms, the land occupied by industrial production still represented the most important type of urban land use accounting for 27 percent of all urban construction land (Table 5.6). This pattern of urban land use dominated by industrial production has since 1992 experienced profound restructuring as a result of the phenomenal development of services within the city proper. As the city resumed its traditional strength in merchant trading, commerce and other services, existing industrial premises have been converted into commercial purposes that are simply more profitable than industrial production, and new land has been developed to accommodate the explosive market demand for services. The result has been a significant restructuring of urban land use characterized by a proportional decline of industrial land use and expansion of the land used for urban services and residential purposes. Whereas industrial land dropped its share of the total urban construction land from 27 to 21 percent, urban services expanded from 27 to 33 percent of the urban construction land during 1992–2000 (Table 5.6). By the year 2000, urban services had exceeded industrial land use and become the most important category among all types of urban construction land. It should be noted that all types of urban construction land including industrial land continued to grow in absolute amount in this period of time. The total urban construction land actually expanded from 18,820 hectares in 1992 to 43,070 hectares in 2000. The shift of emphasis in urban land use from industry to services revealed in Table 5.6 suggested that the land used for services has expanded in a pace much faster than its industrial counterpart. As

Table 5.6 Structure of urban construction land in Guangzhou, 1992–2000 (%)

Year	Residential	Industrial	Transport/ storage	Urban facilities	Others	Total
1992	26.94	27.05	17.11	26.94	1.96	100.00
1993	28.08	26.53	15.82	27.79	1.78	100.00
1994	29.60	25.62	15.41	27.61	1.76	100.00
1995	32.34	24.86	14.13	27.09	1.58	100.00
1996	32.37	24.74	14.02	26.98	1.89	100.00
1997	32.36	24.73	14.02	27.00	1.89	100.00
1998	32.28	23.81	13.55	28.49	1.87	100.00
1999	31.59	23.05	14.87	28.69	1.80	100.00
2000	30.59	20.67	13.86	32.63	2.25	100.00

Sources: China's Ministry of Construction (1993 to 2001) – (1993), p. 99; (1994), p. 106; (1995), p. 116; (1996), p. 118; (1997), p. 182; (1998), p. 176; (1999), p. 190; (2000), p. 187; (2001), p.179; Lin (2004a), p. 37, Table 8.

Note
Urban services include land used for public utilities, roads, squares, parks, open spaces and other urban facilities.

Plate 5.5 The renewed commercial center on Beijing Road.

Plate 5.6 The Tianhe shopping Mall: the first shopping mall open in China.

the land in the old city proper has been converted into commercial purposes, industrial facilities have been relocated to the sub-urban areas particularly in the newly annexed sub-urban districts of Huadu and Panyu.

More striking has been the dramatic expansion of the urban space. Using Landsat images taken in the years of 1986, 1991 and 1996, China's central authorities found out Guangzhou had expanded its urban land (*chengshi yongdi*) by 109 percent during the ten years of 1986–96, making it the third largest rate of expansion among 27 super large cities in the country, next to Dalian (213 percent) and Shijiazhuang (110 percent).[33] A similar but more updated study by Ho and Lin reveals that Guangzhou had doubled its non-agricultural land from 35,000 hectares to 70,000 hectares between 1988 and 2000.[34] With a negligible amount of unused land in the city, the increase in non-agricultural land was largely at the expense of agricultural land located primarily in its newly annexed sub-urban counties of Panyu and Huadu. Indeed, the Guangzhou city region lost nearly 47,000 hectares of agricultural land, and much of that was cultivated land. Of the increase in land occupied for non-agricultural uses, the expansion of urban built-up area accounted for 55 percent and industrial and development zones 25 percent.

The internal structure of the city has also shown profound changes. A classic socialist city is usually characterized by an absence of a central business district (CBD) and the occupation of a public square with monuments in the city center. This was the case in the city of Guangzhou when the Haizhu Square with a monument of the People's Liberation Army used to be the center of the city for public gatherings, social functions and political events. Marketization and globalization have not only revitalized the two traditional commercial centers (one on Beijing Road and the other on Upper/Lower Ninth Road) as CBDs but also led to the emergence of two new commercial centers in the newly developed areas on the outskirts of the old urban district (one in the Tianhe District and the other on the Ring Road). A much more colorful, diversified and business oriented new urban space is quickly taking shape to characterize Guangzhou as a post-socialist and globalizing city (see Plates 5.5 and 5.6).[35]

Conclusion

This chapter has shown how the broad processes of globalization, national policy and "entrepreneurial bureaucratism" have drawn the re-emergence of Guangzhou as the service center of the region and the province. This was a slow process and only accelerated after 1998 when Guangzhou began to lose its competitive position in the Chinese urban system. The case study suggests that the urban system of China is beginning to develop functional specialization that reflects changes in the spatial and structural economy. This process is leading to the creation of "new urban spaces" in China with skyscrapers, office buildings, hotels etc., often scattered throughout the cities. The process also appears to be accelerating the growth of large city cores and their immediate built-up areas as illustrated in the case of Guangzhou's annexation of Panyu and Huadu and the creation of high-tech zones in the sub-urban county of Zengcheng. This has enabled the Guangzhou administration to move ahead with the construction of a new international airport in Huadu and a planned container port in the south of Panyu. Thus the process of "urban expansion" enables the city administration to position its city and province in response to intensified domestic and global competition for mobile capital.

It should not be taken that the urban explosion that is occurring in China's cities today is without its problems. The human consequences of this "infrastructure-led development" are not all beneficial. People are being forcibly evacuated from their land and their homes and forms of urban poverty are emerging particularly among the migrant communities. There are also many problems in the "encapsulated villages" that have been submerged on this wave of urbanization. Although the upgrading and expansion of the urban spaces have brought benefits to the urbanites who have long suffered from the urban bottleneck left over from the early socialist negligence of urban services, it remains questionable that such immediate benefits will be able to cover the social and environmental costs that will have to be covered by this and future generations.

6 Urbanization of the Pearl River Delta

The case of Dongguan

Introduction

This chapter attempts to investigate the changing pattern and processes of urbanization in one of the most rapidly growing peri-urban regions in southern China experiencing export-led industrialization and widespread urbanization. Most of the existing documentations of Chinese urbanization adopt a top-down approach and focus on some officially designated cities especially large cities. This study adopts a different yet complimentary bottom-up approach to analyzing the dramatic transformation of urban activities and settlements outside large cities with a magnitude no less spectacular than that within the large cities. The objective is to identify the new urban forms evolving in southern China in the recent decade, analyze the processes that have given rise to these urban forms and evaluate the thesis of Chinese urbanization in the light of the rapidly changing real world situation. The hypothesis made and tested in this study is that, despite the growing convergence in *urban forms* under the Chinese and American contexts, Chinese urbanization as locally constituted *processes* remains significantly distinct from what has been observed in the West. Moreover, urbanization in contemporary China differs significantly from what was described in the past so that the conventional emphasis on uniqueness is no longer adequate to enlighten the complex and hybrid nature of Chinese urbanism in a globalizing context. A new and innovative approach with local sensitivity and historical contingency is in order for a better understanding of urbanization within the different regional contexts of the globalizing world.

Dramatic economic, spatial and social changes recently taking place in the peri-urban region of Dongguan in Guangdong Province provide a significant case for scrutinizing the complex patterns and processes of urbanization unfolding in the context of a rapidly urbanizing and globalizing socialist economy. Dongguan is a relatively advanced city region that is not entirely typical to the general situation of China. For a number of reasons, however, Dongguan stands as a rare and valuable laboratory for the study of changes in Chinese urbanization under globalization. First, with a location falling in the middle of the two metropolises of Hong Kong and Guangzhou (see Figure 5.1 in Chapter 5), Dongguan can illustrate well the changes undergoing in the peri-urban zone of a Chinese extended metropolitan region. Such a middle location means that the city region can enjoy simultaneously an easy access to both the Hong Kong metropolis (to the south) as a gateway to the world and Guangzhou (to the north) as the largest political and economic center in the region. It also enables Dongguan to embark on a path of export-led industrialization by merging the capital and industrial facilities relocated from Hong Kong with the influx of interior cheap labor transferred primarily from the transportation hub in Guangzhou.

Second, Dongguan is a peri-urban region where the influence of global market forces has been felt earlier and arguably stronger than elsewhere in the country. With a land area of 2,465 square kilometers and a local population of 1.56 million in 2002, Dongguan is a medium-sized municipality converted from originally a county-level economy. It is distinguished, however, by the leading role it has played in the attraction of foreign investment and promotion of exports in the national economy. Table 6.1 lists Dongguan's disproportionate contribution to the province and the nation in terms of exports and the attraction of foreign investment. With a total population (including migrant workers) of less than 8 percent and land of less than 2 percent of the provincial total, Dongguan contributed to the province 20 percent of exports and attracted over 12 percent of utilized foreign investment. Among China's 660 cities, Dongguan occupied the third most important position (next only to Shenzhen and Shanghai) in exports and was ninth in the attraction of foreign direct investment in 2002. A detailed study of urban transformation in an externally oriented regional economy such as Dongguan can help evaluate the prevailing notion that the forces of globalization facilitate the diffusion of Western urbanism into regions worldwide including the socialist economies under reform.

Third, Dongguan is characterized by an extraordinarily large volume of migrant workers that outnumbers the local population by a huge margin. The fifth national population census revealed that in 2000 Dongguan had a temporary population of nearly five million, which was more than three times that of

Table 6.1 Basic economic indicators for Dongguan, 2002

	Dongguan	*Dongguan as % of Guangdong*	*Dongguan as % of China*
Total population* (million)	5.89	7.56	0.46
Area (thousand km²)	2.465	1.39	0.02
GDP (billion yuan)	67.3	5.76	0.66
Export (billion $)	23.7	20.03	7.29
Utilized foreign investment (billion $)	2.1	12.94	3.91

Source: Dongguan Statistical Bureau (2003), p. 391.

Note
* Total population include 1.56 million local residents and 4.33 million migrant workers. The fifth national population census in 2000 revealed that Dongguan had a total population of 6.44 million of which 1.4 million held local household registration and the remaining 5.04 million were temporary population. This total population was 7.56 percent of the total population in Guangdong (85.22 million) in 2000.

the local residents. Over half (53 percent) of the migrant population were female and the majority (83 percent) came from other provinces.[1] A detailed study of the growth and distribution of migrant workers in Dongguan can help reveal how population mobility responds to both the relaxation of state control and the intrusion of global market forces.

Finally, Dongguan is administratively a regional economy consisting of a city center of 14 square kilometers and another 31 towns under its jurisdiction. Prior to economic reforms, Dongguan had long been a rural county with agriculture being the mainstay of the local economy. The initial success of Dongguan in the attraction of foreign investment and promotion of exports since 1979 has eventually led to its administrative upgrading from an ordinary county to a county-level municipality in 1985 and then further to a prefectural municipality in 1988. Despite these administrative changes, the local economies at the township and village levels have played a role no less important than that of the municipality. Administratively and politically, Dongguan is an interesting case, big and diversified enough to warrant an analysis of how changes in urbanization involved the reshuffling of power relations among various administrative and geographical scales under globalization.

The globalizing regional context

Among the many local Chinese economies at the county level, Dongguan is one of the first that has actively articulated itself with the forces of global capitalism coming into the socialist territory through Hong Kong, which had been a British colony until 1997. Such an active articulation with global forces started in 1979 when profound structural changes took place at the global, national and regional scales. As the world economy moved away from Fordist mass production toward post-Fordist flexible specialization, from welfare to workfare and from managerialism to entrepreneurialism, the Chinese political economy underwent a major transition of leadership and policies. Almost parallel to the ascendance of the Reagan and Thatcher "new right" regimes in favor of deregulation, privatization and industrial rationalization, the pragmatic leadership under the late Deng Xiaoping replaced the radical regime under Mao and instituted a gradual shift of emphasis from central planning to market coordination and from "self-reliance" (*zili gengsheng*) to "reforms and opening up" (*gaige kaifang*). One of the important initiatives of "reforms and opening up" was to allow Guangdong and Fujian provinces in southern China to practice "special policies" (*teshu zhengce*) and move "one step ahead of the country" in attracting foreign investment and promoting exports. This initiative coincided with a time when Hong Kong was desperately looking for ways to reduce the cost of production for its industry so as to meet the new challenges of international division of labor and intensified global competition. China's opening up has offered Hong Kong an enormous and cheap production outlet nearby for industrial outsourcing. The result has been an intensified economic and social interaction between Hong Kong as both a main source of capital and window to the capitalist world and mainland China, particularly Guangdong Province, as a new base of manufacturing for Hong Kong and the global economy. These changes at the global, national and regional scales have effectively exposed Dongguan, originally an agrarian local economy under socialism, to the new forces of global capitalism and urbanism.

The influence of the forces of global capitalism has been particularly strong in Dongguan for several reasons. Geographically, Dongguan is situated in the frontier of the socialist territory immediately next to the Shenzhen Special Economic Zone and with close proximity to the capitalist enclave of Hong Kong. Such a frontier location brought no benefits to Dongguan for most of the three decades under Mao as it was considered vulnerable to the contamination of capitalism. In the new era of reform and opening up, geographic proximity to Hong Kong has become an advantageous condition for Dongguan to play with global capitalism ahead of other places in the region. Apart from being a pioneer initiating export-led industrialization, Dongguan was one of the first where local people were able to receive radios and TV programs broadcast from Hong Kong when people elsewhere were still limited to only a few channels of political propaganda broadcast by the Central Television Station in Beijing. Although Dongguan is next to the Shenzhen Special Economic Zone (SEZ) in terms of geographic closeness to Hong Kong, its pre-existing personal ties with Hong Kong and overseas Chinese are more extensive than the Shenzhen SEZ simply because of its earlier and better record of development. A two-year comprehensive survey conducted in 1997–99 revealed that Dongguan residents had 653,729 compatriots (*gang'ao tongbao*) in Hong Kong and Macau and another 217,853 relatives (*huaqiao*) who lived overseas.[2] These pre-existing personal ties suggest that the penetration of the forces of global capitalism into the socialist territory here could be more efficient and effective than elsewhere.[3]

Finally, the entrepreneurial attitude of the local cadres in Dongguan and the flexible approach they have adopted also help facilitate the intrusion of global forces into the local economy and society. Economic cooperation between Chinese and foreign firms usually takes a number of forms including equity joint ventures (*hezi jingying*), cooperative ventures (*hezuo jingying*), wholly foreign-owned ventures (*duzi jingying*) and others such as export processing (*lailiao jiagong*) and compensation trade (*buchang maoyi*). Dongguan was the one that pioneers the model of "three supplies with one compensation" (*sanlai yibu*) for export processing. This model involves the Hong Kong contractor supplying raw materials, equipments and models for what is to be processed while the Dongguan contractee is responsible for the provision of labor, land, buildings, electricity and other local utilities necessary for production. A "processing fee" (*jiagongfei*) is then paid by the Hong Kong contractor to Dongguan as a compensation for the cost of labor, land and other utilities involved in the production. Arrangements are also made on a compensational basis, in which the Dongguan side does the processing or assembling jobs for a specialized period of time, for example five years, and at the end of this period assumes ownership of the machinery or equipment provided by the Hong Kong firm as compensation.

These flexible arrangements, combined with geographic closeness to and strong social ties with Hong Kong, have greatly facilitated Dongguan's articulation with global forces and its growth of export-led industrialization.

The intrusion of global market forces into Dongguan has had its own configuration, however. Its initial growth occurred in the mid-1980s when the liberal leadership of Hu Yaobang and Zhao Ziyang relaxed central control over local economic development. After a brief episode of stagnation in the late 1980s subsequent to the 1989 Tiananmen incident, there was a renewed rally of investment after 1993 as a direct consequence of the late Deng Xiaoping's visit to Shenzhen in the spring of 1992 when foreign investors were reassured of Deng's determination to reforms and opening up. In other words, the intrusion of the forces of economic globalization into Dongguan has been very sensitive to changes in the political environment of the nation. Prior to 1990, foreign investment in Dongguan took primarily the form of compensational processing (*sanlai yibu*), which accounted for over 50 percent of all utilized investment. It was only after 1990, 11 years after the opening up, that foreign investment with more formal arrangements such as equity joint venture, cooperative venture and wholly foreign-owned venture has taken over and become the dominant mode. This pattern suggests that the inflow of foreign investment into Dongguan has been a gradual and transitional process starting with some informal, locally based and tacit arrangements that are then followed by more formal and legalized forms that are in line with international conventions. Apparently, foreign ventures, including those from Hong Kong, have been cautious in entering the socialist territory where the institutional environment remains incomparable with that of the capitalist world. There were two periods of time, one in the mid-1980s and the other the mid-1990s, when foreign loans took a significant portion of the utilized foreign investment. The increase of foreign loans in the mid-1980s corresponded with the massive development of the local transportation and telecommunication infrastructure. The increased use of foreign loans in the mid-1990s was a result of the new development of a number of industrial complexes to attract high-tech industry. After 1999, foreign loans have been reduced substantially both in amount and proportion of the utilized foreign investment. It appears that the Chinese governments have learnt important lessons from the 1997–98 Asian financial turmoil.

The shifting emphasis of the modes of foreign investment is closely related to changes in the origins and nature of investment. For most of the years until the mid-1990s, an overwhelming majority of foreign investment was initially obtained from Hong Kong where Dongguan enjoyed favorable geographic closeness and extensive social ties. This was also a period of time when most of the foreign investment came in the form of "three supplies and one compensation" (*sanlai yibu*). It was estimated by local officials that about half of the contracts they had signed during the 1980s were with their country-fellows in Hong Kong, many of whom were former Dongguan residents who fled their native villages to Hong Kong during the disastrous years of the Cultural Revolution.[4] Since the mid-1990s, however, significant changes have taken place in the origins of foreign investment. Although Hong Kong remains the single most important source of capital overseas, its share has reduced from 84 percent in 1996 to less than 50 percent in 2002, and the balance has been picked up by countries and regions elsewhere such as Taiwan, Japan, Singapore, the US and South Korea.

Unlike the earlier investment from Hong Kong, which involved primarily some compensational export processing activities that are labor intensive, small scale and low-tech in the nature, investment from non-Hong Kong sources have a broader industrial spectrum extending from the making of fashion shoes and apparels to the manufacturing of electronic and telecommunication products such as cellular phones, computers and various peripheral devices. Official statistics reported that a total of 2,800 enterprises were engaged in the IT industry by 2000 and Dongguan is now one of the largest IT industrial bases of the world. It produces over 40 percent of the world's computer cases and computer magnetic heads, 30 percent of computer disk drivers, 20 percent of scanners and mini-motors, 16 percent of keyboards and 15 percent of computer motherboards.[5] Whereas the externally financed export processing industry was dominated by the labor intensive sectors of textile, apparel and toys relocated from Hong Kong in the 1980s, foreign investment in Dongguan now has a new industrial spectrum that includes electronics (33 percent), machinery and metal processing (14 percent), textiles and garments (11 percent), rubber and plastic products (11 percent), shoemaking (6 percent) and paper and paper products (5 percent).[6] Clearly, the penetration of the forces of economic globalization into Dongguan has since the 1990s expanded both in breadth and depth as China furthers its opening up and, as the global economy deepens, its international division of labor.

Export-led industrialization and rural urbanization

The impacts of global forces on the transformation of Dongguan's economy and society have been profound and pervasive, some of which can be identified statistically and others cannot. The most noticeable effect of economic globalization has been a distinct process of export-led industrialization fueled primarily by the capital, technology and employment brought into Dongguan by the industrial firms relocated from Hong Kong, Taiwan and other countries overseas. Available statistics suggested that by the end 2002 a total of 10,035 compensational export processing firms were put in place and another 5,428 joint ventures, cooperative ventures and wholly foreign-owned ventures were established. These export-oriented industrial establishments have brought into Dongguan a total utilized foreign capital of US$17.3 billion and imported modern machinery that worth US$12.51 billion.[7] Over 1.43 million workers were employed directly by the compensational processing firms and another 1.08 million by foreign ventures in 2002. This means that the total number of workers (2.5 million) directly employed by export processing firms and foreign ventures exceeded the total local population (1.56 million). The result is an influx of a huge number of migrant workers, three times the local population, to fill the gap, and this influx of outside population has profoundly reconstituted the local economy, society and space. In addition, the taxes and processing fees paid by foreign ventures and export processing firms have become one of the most important sources of local revenue. On top of the various taxes collected from foreign ventures, local governments of various levels collected a total of US$1.74 billion processing fees from compensational processing firms in 2002. While the collection and distribution of taxes are subject to central taxation regulations, the processing fees are usually remitted to local governments at the village and township levels for their own consumption. With the inflow of an extraordinary amount of processing fees, coupled with the decentralization of the power of decision-making, the towns and villages in Dongguan are financially and politically in a stronger position to promote industrialization and urbanization in its own way. Official statistics indicated that government fiscal income rose from only 5 percent of GDP in 1990 to 23 percent in 2002 and the total fixed asset capital investment increased from 12 percent of GDP to 29 percent for the same period.[8] Much of the fixed asset capital investment was directed toward industrial and urban development as well as the improvement of the local transportation infrastructure. The result has been an industrialization and urbanization of an enormous scale.

The scale and speed of export-led industrialization and urbanization taking place in Dongguan over the past two decades have been astonishing. Table 6.2 lists some of the key demographic and economic indicators to illustrate the transformation of the local economy and space. At the eve of economic reforms in 1978, Dongguan was an agrarian economy with 73 percent of the population recognized as agricultural and 72 percent of the labor force working in the primary economic sector. Rural per capita income was less than 150 yuan a year and there was hardly any sign of modern urbanism except a county-seat and a number of commune centers scattered in the countryside. This situation has changed dramatically in the two decades that followed as the local economy was firmly dragged onto the global theatre of flexible capital accumulation. While the local population grew slightly from 1.1 to 1.5 million in 22 years due to the population control policy, non-agricultural population as a proxy of urban population grew from only 17 percent of the total population to 36 percent (Table 6.2). More significant is the influx of migrant population from 660,000 in 1990 to over four million in 2002. When the migrant population were taken into account, population density increased by four times in 12 years, rising from 800 to 2,400 persons per square kilometers. Equally significant is the transition of the economy from one dominated by the primary sector into one led by manufacturing and services. In the 12 years of 1978–2002, employment in the primary sector dropped substantially from 72 percent to 15 percent while the secondary and tertiary sectors expanded their share from only 28 percent to a dominant position of 85 percent. While the growth of the secondary sector is primarily a result of export-led industrialization, the accelerated growth of jobs in the tertiary sector since 1990 has been a direct consequence of the inflow of

Table 6.2 Dongguan's demographic, economic and social change, 1978–2002

	1978	1980	1990	1995	2000	2002
Population (million)	1.11	1.12	1.32	1.44	1.53	1.56
Non-agricultural (%)	16.62	17.60	23.41	24.63	25.96	36.03
Migrant population (million)			0.66	1.42	2.55	4.34
Population density (person/sq km)			801	1,160	1,652	2,393
Employment (%)	100.0	100.0	100.0	100.0	100.0	100.0
Primary	71.6	64.1	36.2	23.3	19.4	14.6
Secondary	16.8	24.6	40.6	46.9	48.2	48.8
Tertiary	11.6	11.3	23.2	29.7	32.4	36.6
Cultivated land (thousand ha)	78.92	78.49	58.84	47.24	44.22	33.38
Urban built-up area (thousand ha)		2.387		8.248	14.768	18.846
GDP (billion yuan)	0.611	0.704	6.46	20.56	49.27	67.29
Per capita GDP (yuan/person) (including migrants)			3,263	7,189	12,076	11,405
Highway density (km/100 sq km)		49.70	53.75	94.40	102.15	107.14
Mobile phone users (million)					1.24	4.12
Urban resident disposable income (yuan/person)			2,508	9,588	14,142	16,949
Rural per capita income (yuan/person)	149	266	1,359	3,988	6,731	7,907

Sources: Dongguan Statistical Bureau (2003), pp. 59–62; Lin (2006), p. 41, Table 1.

migrant population most of whom are factory workers creating high market demands for services. The industrial sector has also gone through a process of restructuring as a consequence of the inflow of foreign investment and growth of exports. Figure 6.1 analyzes the restructuring of the industrial sector according to different ownerships. At the eve of reforms and opening up, the industrial economy was dominated by state and collectively owned enterprises. This situation has changed since the mid-1980s when Hong Kong and Taiwanese firms started to come in. This was then followed by the growth of foreign ventures beginning in the early 1990s. By 2002, state and collectively owned industrial enterprises had given way to those from Hong Kong, Taiwan and other foreign sources (Figure 6.1).

The process of demographic and economic restructuring has found its manifestations over space. As foreign ventures and export processing firms built their factories and transportation facilities often on ground that was previously farmland, a huge amount of farmland was taken over and converted into industrial, transport and commercial developments. Cultivated land shrank dramatically from 79 to 33.38 thousand hectares during 1980–2002 while the urban built-up area expanded from 2.3 to nearly 19 thousand hectares (Table 6.2). For an efficient transportation of goods in and out of Dongguan, the local highway network has been substantially extended and upgraded so that highway length extended by more than twice from 1,259 to 2,641 kilometers during 1978–2002. By 2000, Dongguan had been ranked first among all Chinese prefectural municipalities in terms of its highway density (102 kilometers per 100 square kilometers). Dongguan was also among the first where mobile phones enjoyed great popularity with over four million users in 2002, which exceeded its total local population by a large margin. Finally, labor productivity as measured by per capita GDP showed a steady growth and per capita income soared for both urban and rural residents (Table 6.2). Taken

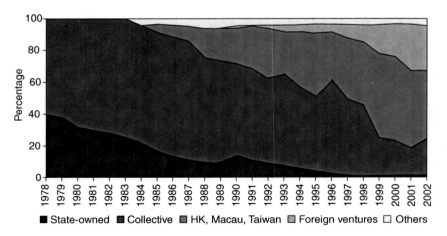

Figure 6.1 Dongguan's industrial restructuring (% of output), 1978–2002 (source: Dongguan Statistical Bureau (2003), p. 147).

together, the process of demographic, economic and spatial changes identified here, characterized by growing urbanization, increased population density and heterogeneity, the growth of industry and services, and the conversion of farmland for industrial, transport and urban developments, suggests that some of the salient features of modern urbanism as observed historically in the West and recently in other socialist transitional economies have been emerging in Dongguan. This process is unprecedented in Dongguan and it has firmly set the local economy apart from the earlier practice of self-isolation, collectivization and controlled urbanization in Mao's era of utopian socialism.

If important features of modern urbanism are emerging in Dongguan, does this then suggest that Dongguan is showing evidence of converging with the Western norm of urbanization? A closer analysis reveals that there exists distinct local processes of urbanization and that it is still too soon to reach the conclusion of convergence. First, the process of suburbanization that has taken place in North America since the 1960s involves primarily an outward movement of urban residents from the city center to the suburb in search of a better living environment with greater open space and a wider range of facilities for shopping, recreation and entertainment. In his seminal work of the emergence of megalopolis on the northeastern seaboard of the United States, Jean Gottmann highlighted the importance of such factors as rising income, improved transportation and the growth of tertiary economic activities, which gave rise to the new urbanized region.[9] Recent documentation of "Edge City" has identified such "characteristic monument" as "the atria reaching for the sun and shielding trees perpetually in leaf at the cores of corporate headquarters, fitness centers, and shopping plazas" and such "landmark structure" as "the celebrated single-family detached dwelling, the sub-urban home with grass all around that made America the best-housed civilization the world has ever known."[10] In other words, what has happened in the case of the "Edge City" of the US is closely associated with the transition from an industrial to post-industrial society, extensive land development for residential use and the growth of recreation and leisure. By comparison, what has been taking place in Dongguan involves essentially an industrialization of the rural economy and urbanization of the countryside. Although there have been real estate developments in selected towns (e.g. Zhangmutou) to attract Hong Kong residents, the main driving force for urban development in China has been export-led industrialization.

Tables 6.3 and 6.4 illustrate the dominant position held by industry in foreign capital investment and the employment structure for both the local and outside labor force. An overwhelming majority of utilized foreign investment, ranging from 87 to 99 percent, has been placed in the industrial sector. Industry has taken the lead in the employment composition of the local labor force, accounting for over one-third of the total. For migrant workers, the dominant position held by the industrial sector is even more striking–over 80 percent of all. The dominant role played by industrialization in Dongguan's space economy could also be seen from its land-use pattern. Table 6.5 analyzes Dongguan's land use pattern and compares it with the general situation in the province and the nation. Industrial

Table 6.3 Utilized foreign investment in Dongguan by sectors, 1990–2002

	1990		1995		2000		2002	
	million US$	%	million US$	%	million US$	%	million US$	%
Agriculture	2.60	2.56	5.44	0.79	–	–	0.30	0.01
Industry	88.59	87.13	629.12	91.93	1,611.15	97.82	2,137.21	99.48
Wholesale, retail, catering	10.41	10.24	4.56	0.67	2.25	0.14	3.66	0.17
Real estate	–	–	37.51	5.48	11.53	0.70	2.44	0.11
Others	0.07	0.07	7.75	1.13	22.19	1.35	4.87	0.23
Total	101.67	100.00	684.38	100.00	1,647.12	100.00	2,148.48	100.00

Source: Dongguan Statistical Bureau (2003), p. 282.

Table 6.4 Employment structure for Dongguan, 1990–2002

	1990		1995		2000		2002	
	No.	%	No.	%	No.	%	No.	%
Local labour force	750,809	100.00	869,154	100.00	977,798	100.00	1,040,953	100.00
Primary	271,513	36.16	202,914	23.35	189,926	19.42	151,802	14.58
Secondary	305,190	40.65	407,923	46.93	471,365	48.21	508,070	48.81
Industry	266,867	35.54	373,459	42.97	434,696	44.46	464,725	44.64
Construction	38,323	5.10	34,464	3.97	36,669	3.75	43,345	4.16
Tertiary	174,106	23.19	258,317	29.72	316,507	32.37	381,081	36.61
Migrant workers			1,265,368	100.00	2,448,415	100.00	4,260,142	100.00
Industry			1,084,860	85.73	2,043,270	83.45	3,573,355	83.88
Agriculture			54,714	4.32	88,195	3.60	127,584	2.99
Commerce			52,965	4.19	187,015	7.64	300,642	7.06
Services			72,829	5.76	129,935	5.31	258,561	6.07

Sources: Dongguan Statistical Bureau (2003), pp. 86–8; Lin (2006), p. 43, Table 2.

Table 6.5 Land-use pattern in Dongguan, 2000

	Dongguan			Guangdong		
	Area (ha)	% total	% sub-total	Area (ha)	% total	% sub-total
Total area	247,170.3	100.0		17,964,326.5	100.0	
Agricultural land	126,546.0	51.2	100.0	14,239,486.2	79.3	100.0
Cultivated land	34,700.0	14.0	27.4	3,127,832.9	17.4	22.0
Orchards and plantations	42,919.1	17.4	33.9	835,555.1	4.7	5.9
Forest	48,837.9	19.8	38.6	10,248,692.9	57.1	72.0
Pasture	88.9	0.0	0.1	27,405.3	0.2	0.2
Industrial and urban land	54,352.1	22.0	100.0	1,239,305.2	6.9	100.0
City	2,204.4	0.9	4.1	118,610.9	0.7	9.6
Town	4,056.6	1.6	7.5	127,095.3	0.7	10.3
Rural settlements	19,418.6	7.9	35.7	647,045.0	3.6	52.2
Industrial	27,517.0	11.1	50.6	270,459.0	1.5	21.8
Others	1,155.3	0.5	2.1	76,094.9	0.4	6.1
Transportation	7,353.0	3.0		155,127.2	0.9	
Water area	45,657.2	18.5		1,373,409.3	7.6	
Unused land	13,262.1	5.4		956,998.6	5.3	

Source: Internal documents; Lin (2006), p. 44, Table 3.

land use accounts for 11 percent of the total land area, which exceeds the averages of the province (1.5 percent) and the nation (0.3 percent) by a large margin. Among the 97 cities and counties in the province, Dongguan has the second highest proportion of land used for industry, next only to Nanhai. The dominance of industry in capital, labor and land suggests that whatever is observed in Dongguan must be closely associated with the growth of externally fueled and export-oriented industrialization. The local trajectory of global metropolitanism is based upon a transition from an agrarian to industrial economy that is distinct from the Western norm of suburbanization in a post-industrial society.

Second, the export-led industrialization process in Dongguan has taken a widespread spatial pattern and has been located primarily at the village level. Figure 6.2 analyzes the changing composition of industrial production according to the ownership of five different administrative levels. At the eve of the opening up, industries owned and run by the municipal and township governments took the lion's share (86 percent) of the total industrial production. In the following 14 years, industries located and operated at the village level continued to expand so that their share of the total industrial production increased from only 14 percent in 1978 to 46 percent. By 2002, village industries had become the leading component. This pattern suggests that what has been taking place in Dongguan involves more an industrialization of the countryside at the village level than anything based on the urban centers. The fact that industrial development is widely scattered among many villages without any concentration in the urban center has been described by the local people as "a spread of numerous stars in the sky without a large shining moon in the center" (*mantian xingdou queshao yilun mingyue*). This process of rural industrialization in Dongguan as an urban

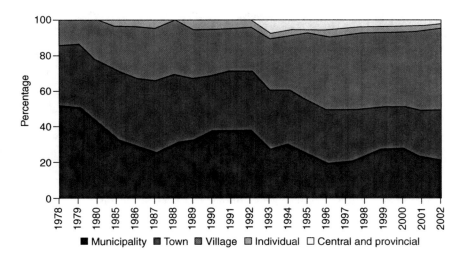

Figure 6.2 Dongguan's industrial output by administrative levels, 1978–2002 (sources: Dongguan Statistical Bureau (2003), p. 153; Smart and Lin (2007), p.292, Figure 3).

margin of the Hong Kong–Guangzhou extended metropolitan region stands in sharp contrast with what has been observed in the West where metropolitan development is driven primarily by the force of urban sprawl. If what has happened in the West could be understood as a top-down and city-driven process of urbanization, then what Dongguan has shown is one characterized by a bottom-up process of industrialization and urbanization of the countryside.

The distinct spatial pattern of widespread industrialization observed in Dongguan requires explanation. For the investors from Hong Kong, Taiwan and other countries overseas, subcontracting with and industrial outsourcing to Dongguan are motivated primarily by the desire to reduce production costs. While the control functions and the core of production functions are retained in the home countries, only those technologically unsophisticated tasks are horizontally separated and outsourced into China. Most of the export-processing industries established in Dongguan involve simple and repetitive production that requires a great deal of time and labor but little knowledge and skills. This type of production does not necessarily have to be located in the urban center where a better economic infrastructure and educated labor force are available for exploitation at a higher price. On the contrary, many townships and villages are no less attractive to foreign investors than the urban center because of their pre-existing personal connections for a secured return of investment, improved transportation and telecommunication infrastructure, an abundant supply of cheap surplus rural laborers and land, and a less-regulated environment. Furthermore, the local scalar distribution of the power over the use of land and labor also contributed to the predominance of the village level in the location of industries. Prior to 1985, Dongguan had long been a county where land was owned by the rural collective, except that in the county-seat and designated towns. By law, the collectively owned land is owned and operated by a villagers' committee, village economic entity and/or township economic entities.[11] In other words, the village, as the basic unit of the rural collective on which landownership is ultimately rested, has the basic and direct authority to determine how the rural land is to be used. A development project may be initiated by foreign investors and local governments at a higher level, but it ultimately has to be accepted and located in the town or village. For the foreign investors coming to Dongguan, dealing directly with the local cadres at the township or village level could save unnecessary transaction costs. The hiring of labor faces a similar situation. After Dongguan was upgraded administratively to a county-level municipality in 1985 and then a prefectural municipality in 1988, its landownership based on the rural collective has remained unchanged, and this has been one of the important factors underlining the dominance of the village and town levels in the location and spatial distribution of industries.

Third, in close relation to the distinct processes identified above, there is intensive interception of industrial and urban activities into the agricultural economies or the pursuits of the rural households. Because industrialization and urbanization are taking place in the grassroots level, many of the agricultural population are diversifying their occupations and shifting away from farming into more profitable non-agricultural activities. Such a diversification is made possible by a spontaneous and flexible division of labor for the maximization of profits. For a typical farm household, farm cultivation is either subcontracted to migrant workers or looked after by the housewife or elderly, whose task is to ensure fulfillment of the farming quota set by the state. The husband, son and daughter may engage in more lucrative non-agricultural activities such as manufacturing, trade, transportation, services or construction. A similar division of labor also takes place on a seasonal basis. Often peasants will concentrate on agricultural production during the planting and harvest seasons when the demand for labor on the farm is high. They will then shift to non-agricultural pursuits for the rest of the year, thus raising income and maximizing profits. The result of this flexible division of labor on both family and seasonal basis has been a remarkable mix or interception of agricultural and non-agricultural, urban and rural activities, which makes it increasingly difficult to delineate agricultural and non-agricultural population or urban and rural settlements.

Many of the local population wearing an "agricultural" or "rural" hat are actually involved in a variety of non-agricultural or urban activities. Figure 6.3 shows the changing occupational structure of Dongguan's rural labor force. When economic reforms were initiated in 1978, an overwhelmingly large majority of the rural labor force was affiliated with agricultural pursuits. Since then, agricultural pursuits as a share of the total occupations of the rural labor force have declined steadily and substantially from 84 percent to only 20 percent. By 2002, the majority of the rural labor force had shifted occupations into non-agricultural sectors such as industry, commerce, transport and telecommunication, and construction. This rural labor force is considered "rural" because it is found in rural

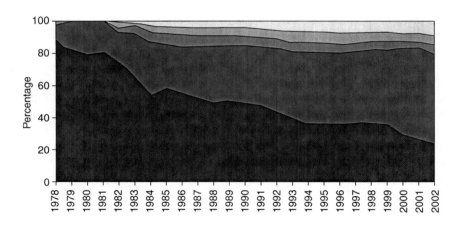

■ Agriculture ■ Industry ▨ Construction ▨ Transport and Telecom. ☐ Commerce

Figure 6.3 Occupational structure of Dongguan's rural labor force, 1978–2002 (sources: Dongguan Statistical Bureau (2003), p. 112; Smart and Lin (2007), p.292, Figure 4).

settlements. In other words, those who live in rural settlements are now pursuing a wide range of activities associated more with an urban society. Increased occupational diversity and the growth of urbanism in the rural areas can also be detected from an analysis of income and expenditure of rural households listed in Table 6.6. While basic income per household increased steadily from 30,842 to 34,998 yuan in the recent seven years for which data are available, agriculture as a share of rural household income (excluding wages and salaries) dropped dramatically from 71 to 12 percent and the balance was picked up by non-agricultural sources. The income sources that enjoyed the largest increase are industry, transport, catering and services. As a result, rural household income has become much more diversified than before. The expenditure of rural households also displays some interesting changes. Expenditure in housing as a share of the total declined from nearly 40 percent to 26 percent while spending in transport and telecom, leisure, clothing and health care enjoyed an expansion (Table 6.6).

The fact that the rural labor force and agricultural population are pursuing industrial and urban activities without leaving the rural areas is in part a consequence of the widespread rural industrialization identified earlier (see Figure 6.3). It is also a direct outcome of the partial relaxation of state control over rural to urban migration. For most of the years under Mao, rural to urban migration was tightly controlled by the state because of the fear that the influx of rural migrants into cities might create a huge burden on the state for the provision of urban facilities and services. Since the reforms and opening up, the new liberal regime has recognized the increased demands for urbanism as a consequence of accelerated economic growth and made important attempts to relax, partially at least, its control over rural–urban migration. While migration into cities, especially large cities, remains restricted, the state relaxed its control over rural to towns migration in 1984.[12] Peasants are now allowed to move to the towns nearby to work and to settle permanently there. Rural individuals who wish to open stores or undertake construction, transportation or other service jobs in towns and who intend to stay for a prolonged period of time can apply for a "lodging card" (*zanzhu zheng*) and be registered as "lodging population" (*zanzhu renkou*). They are treated like other town residents except that they are not entitled to state-subsidized grains and cooking oils. The implementation of this policy has given rise to a new type of population known as "population engaged in both industrial and agricultural work" (*yigong yinong renkou*). These peasant workers may work and live in towns and return to the fields during the harvest and planting seasons as described above. The intense interception of industrial and urban activities into the agricultural economy and rural society in the Chinese case may bear resemblance to what has been observed in East and Southeast Asia. However, the processes involved are locally specific and contingent on the institutional changes in a transitional socialist political economy.

Finally, local governments have played a role instrumental to the transformation of the space economy in Dongguan. The importance of municipal governments in urban growth is not unique to China. It has been well documented that in response to intensified global competition, many municipal

Table 6.6 Income and expenditure of rural households in Dongguan, 1996–2002

	1996		2000		2001		2002	
	Average household income	%	Average household income	%	Average household income	%	Average household income	%
Total income (yuan)	40,065	100.0	47,115	100.0	48,509	100.0	47,242	100.0
Basic income	30,842	77.0	34,887	74.0	34,752	71.6	34,998	74.1
Wages/salaries	7,590	18.9	21,866	46.4	24,264	50.0	26,452	56.0
Household income	23,252	58.0	13,021	27.6	10,488	21.6	8,546	18.1
Agriculture	16,412	70.6	6,297	48.4	3,682	35.1	994	11.6
Side-line business	1,874	8.1		0.0		0.0		0.0
Industry	253	1.1	2,028	15.6	2,563	24.4	2,800	32.8
Construction	2,153	9.3	582	4.5	509	4.9	291	3.4
Transport	213	0.9	630	4.8	802	7.6	1,107	13.0
Commerce	269	1.2	1,629	12.5	917	8.7	788	9.2
Catering	957	4.1	1,610	12.4	1,435	13.7	1,637	19.2
Services	1,120	4.8	245	1.9	581	5.5	929	10.9
Expenditure	35,031	100.0	28,614	100.0	34,416	100.0	32,089	100.0
Food	14,010	40.0	12,853	44.9	12,907	37.5	13,925	43.4
Cloth	320	0.9	1,192	4.2	874	2.5	1,252	3.9
Housing	13,790	39.4	6,595	23.0	11,918	34.6	8,240	25.7
Homeware	2,587	7.4	889	3.1	725	2.1	938	2.9
Health care	575	1.6	966	3.4	763	2.2	1,149	3.6
Transport and telecom	658	1.9	2,644	9.2	2,563	7.4	2,800	8.7
Leisure	882	2.5	2,711	9.5	2,722	7.9	3,016	9.4
Others	2,209	6.3	764	2.7	1,944	5.6	769	2.4

Sources: Dongguan Statistical Bureau (1998), pp. 383–4; ibid. (2000), pp. 370–1; ibid. (2001), pp. 347–8; ibid. (2003), pp. 319–20; Lin (2006), p. 47, Table 4.

governments in North America have increasingly shifted emphasis from welfare provision to workfare creation, from government to governance and from managerialism to entrepreneurialism.[13] Local governments have played a key role in the formation of public–private partnerships or pro-growth coalition either to drive the urban "growth machine" or to consolidate the "urban regime."[14] However, municipal governments in the West remain political organizations and are seldom involved directly in capital investment and business affairs. By contrast, local governments in the Chinese socialist economy undergoing transition have usually functioned as not only chief decision-maker but also the largest investor directly responsible for investment, development and operation of key industrial, transport and urban projects. Prior to the 1978 economic reforms, local economic development had to rely on state budgetary allocation and the role that could be played by local governments was rather limited. The institutional changes made since 1978 have decentralized the power of economic decision-making and greatly expanded the room for local governments to occupy. The local governments in Dongguan have probably made the best use of the room opened because of the decentralization.

Apart from making flexible arrangements with foreign investors for export processing, the municipal government in Dongguan has invested heavily in the local transportation and telecommunication infrastructure. It was reported that a total of 105.76 billion yuan was invested in fixed assets and economic infrastructure during 1978–2002.[15] Unlike the previous situation under Mao when state budgetary allocation dominated capital formation, the bulk of capital has been mobilized by local governments of the municipal, township and even village levels, from different channels including bank loans, foreign investors and self-fund-raising. Figure 6.4 illustrates capital formation in Dongguan since 1990. State budgetary allocation only accounted for a very small proportion of

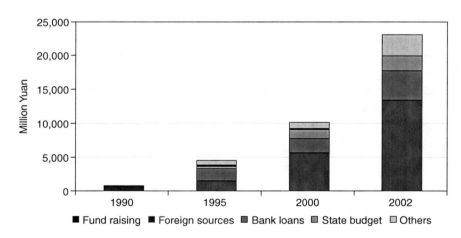

Figure 6.4 Capital formation in Dongguan, 1995–2000 (sources: Dongguan Statistical Bureau (2001), p. 568; ibid. (2003), p. 205; Lin (2006), p. 39, Figure 3).

the capital mobilized and invested, and local governments were responsible for the capital mobilized from foreign and local sources. This pattern sets itself apart from the past under Mao. It is also different from what has been observed from urban development in the West.

One of the results of heavy investment in fixed assets and economic infrastructure has been a significant improvement of the local highway network doubling its length from 1,259 to 2,641 kilometers for the same period. By 2000, Dongguan had more highways per square kilometers than all other prefectural municipalities in the country. Dongguan was also the very first prefectural municipality in China that installed a digital telephone system in 1987 to connect its towns and villages with 250 cities domestically and 150 countries and regions internationally. The role played by local governments has also been instrumental to the spatial restructuring of production activities. Until recently, the location of foreign investment and export processing activities had been located primarily along the Guangzhou–Shenzhen highway running through the eastern part of Dongguan. This tolled highway was built by the Hong Kong developer Gordon Wu in the 1980s and its tolled fees were high in the local standard. To reduce the cost of transportation so as to keep and attract foreign investment, the municipal government mobilized 1.74 billion yuan and started to build an alternative highway connecting Dongguan with Shenzhen and Hong Kong. The project broke the ground in March 1997 and was put in use in September 2000. It became China's first highway that was planned, invested and constructed completely by a prefectural municipality without any input from the central or provincial government. Because the locally built Dongguan–Shenzhen highway has offered a cheaper alternative than Gordon Wu's Guangzhou–Shenzhen highway, new foreign investment and export processing activities are now moving into the western wing of Dongguan, giving rise to a more diversified and balanced spatial pattern of foreign investment, exports and production. Clearly, local governments have taken a proactive approach to strengthen constantly the competitiveness of the local economy and to meet the new challenges of its rivals domestically and internationally. Despite the overwhelming influence of global forces, local governments in Dongguan have managed to find their own ways to shape the construction of infrastructure and the reconstruction of space.

The role played by the municipal government of Dongguan can also be illustrated by a constantly repositioning and rescaling strategy adopted in response to growing domestic and international competition. Since the mid-1990s, Dongguan has faced growing competition from newly developed economies in the lower Yangzi River delta such as Suzhou and Kunshan both of which have managed to attract an increasing amount of foreign investment from Taiwan, Singapore and other advanced countries, and promote exports. Prior to 2003, Dongguan had occupied the third position among all Chinese municipalities in terms of its volume of exports, next only to Shenzhen and Shanghai. This changed in 2003 when Suzhou, originally next to Dongguan, took over Dongguan's position and became the third most important center of exports among all Chinese cities.[16] This shifting of position greatly alarmed local officials in Dongguan and forced the local government to re-evaluate its comparative advantages. A critical comparison between Dongguan and its formidable rival Suzhou has led local officials to recognize the fact that Suzhou has had a more urbanized and attractive built-environment whereas Dongguan has suffered from a pattern of scattered and dispersed industrialization focusing on the village level without a concentrated and urbanized environment to attract headquarters of multinational corporations.

A new *rescaling* strategy has subsequently been adopted to "group industries into parks, merge individual housing estates into urban districts, and link scattered towns to form urbanized regions" (*gongye jinyuan, minzhai jinqu, chengzhen jinquan*). The idea essentially is to create an urbanized environment with a higher degree of concentration of the population and economic activities. To this end, the municipal government substantially increased its investment in capital construction from 6.1 to 9.7 billion yuan and expanded the urban built-up area from 14,768 to 24,552 hectares during 2000–03. A large number of new urban projects has been added to the built-environment, including a new city hall and city center, an international convention center and a modern sports stadium (see Plates 6.1, 6.2, 6.3 and 6.4). On top of these projects is the Songshan Lake Industrial Park of Science and Technology established and financed by the municipal government. Located in the center of the municipality with a clean and green environment, the park covers a large land area of 7,200 hectares. It broke the ground in 2002 and involved a capital investment of 1.5 billion yuan plus a contracted foreign investment of US$2.3 billion. Any

Plate 6.1 Dongguan's new city hall and city center (source: Lin (2006), p. 49, Figure 8).

Plate 6.2 Dongguan sports stadium (source: Lin (2006), p. 49, Figure 8).

Plate 6.3 Zhen'an high-tech industrial park (source: Lin (2006), p. 49, Figure 8).

Plate 6.4 Songshan Lake industrial park under construction (source: Lin (2006), p. 49, Figure 8).

enterprise entering this zone can enjoy free administrative fees and a simplified approval procedure that can be completed within five working days. It was hoped that the creation of an urbanized environment would be conducive to industrial clusters and agglomeration that would in turn help overcome the perceived disadvantages associated with scattered industrialization focusing on the village level. It was reported that by the end of 2003 a total of 150 enterprises had expressed an interest in entering the Songshan Park. It remains to be seen how effective this new approach of concentrated industrialization and increased urbanism will be in strengthening the competitiveness of Dongguan in the attraction of foreign investment and promotion of exports. It is obvious, however, that peri-urbanism has been actively pursued by the municipal government as a strategy of place-promotion or what Jessop called "glurbanization" to induce and "fix" mobile capital in the era of intensified global competition.[17]

Conclusion

This chapter moves beyond the conventional approach whereby urbanization is evaluated on the basis of changes in cities particularly large cities and examines widespread urbanization on the grassroots level in a peri-urban region experiencing marketization and globalization. A detailed study of rural urbanization in Dongguan, a rapidly globalizing and urbanizing peri-urban region lying in the middle of the Hong Kong–Guangzhou corridor, has generated interesting results to interrogate the convergence thesis. The intrusion of the forces of economic globalization has facilitated an export-led industrialization of the local economy and contributed to the increase in population density and mobility, personal income, economic diversification and social as well as spatial heterogeneity. On the surface, some of the salient features of modern urbanism seem to be emerging in the Chinese peri-urban region in the era of market reforms and globalization. A closer scrutiny has, however, revealed some fundamental processes distinct from the Western norm. Manufacturing rather than services has been the most important driving force behind the growth of urbanism in this previously agrarian society. Villages and towns have been the major loci where external (global) technology and culture landed and sprouted leading to the growth and diffusion of urbanism from below. There is an intensive interception of industrial and urban activities into the agricultural economy and rural households. Local governments at the municipal, township and village levels have functioned as both decision-makers and investors directly involved in urban development. These processes have blended the persistent legacy of earlier state socialism and agrarian economy with the new elements of market reforms, export industrialization and global capitalism. As a result, the earlier space of an agrarian society has been transformed and reconstituted into multiple spaces of representation (space of local–global negotiation, space of rural–urban interaction, and space of local–outsider contesting etc.) in which new urbanism finds its room.[18]

Obviously, the patterns and processes of change in urbanization identified in Dongguan are place specific and therefore cannot be used to make theoretical (over)generalizations applicable to the entire country. Nevertheless, this case study does bring out several significant theoretical issues for re-evaluation and further investigation. First, studies of Chinese urbanization in a comparative perspective have traditionally focused on the degree of resemblance or difference in the characteristics of urbanization between the Chinese case and the Western norm. Relatively little attention has ever been paid to the distinction between form and processes. This has not been a critical problem in the cases of imperial and socialist China when economic and social interchanges with the outside world were limited. With the recent widespread penetration of global forces into China bringing about new features of urbanization without overriding the persistent influence of the socialist legacy and local tradition, there is clearly a need to make a distinction between the globalizing urban forms and the locally evolving processes in the study of Chinese urbanization in a comparative perspective. This distinction may also provide a key to resolve the controversial thesis of convergence and solve the riddle of converging urban forms with diverging processes.

Second, the Chinese experience analyzed in both national and local perspectives has clearly shown the hybrid, path-dependent and locally sensitive nature of growth and spatiality of rural urbanization. Despite the seemingly irresistible and irreversible tendency of globalization, Chinese rural urbanization on the grassroots level has not been devoid of the effect of past state ideologies, practices, institution and locally specific cultural conditions. Geographically, the emergence of new urban spaces has not totally replaced the "old" under state socialism. Instead, it is the coexistence and overlapping of the new and the old that have made new Chinese rural urbanization so complex, heterogeneous and intensively mixed that its exact nature can be elusive, obscure and easily confused.

Finally, the importance of the peri-urban region in Chinese urbanization processes warrants serious theoretical consideration. The emergence of "Edge City" and the growth of suburbanization in North America has been extensively documented. On the Chinese side, existing studies of the growth of "the New Chinese City" have been based primarily on the growth and transformation of officially recognized cities and towns. With its marginal status both administratively and geographically, the growth of the peri-urban region and the role it has played in Chinese urbanism have rarely been addressed. The case of Dongguan has shown a distinct process in which the growth and diffusion of urbanism takes place in the grassroots level and in a widespread manner. It remains to be seen whether or not the process of urbanism from below in Dongguan can also be found in varying degrees elsewhere in the country. It appears certain, however, that there is urgent need to move beyond the traditionally city-centered approach and take the seemingly marginal peri-urban region more seriously than it has been treated. If the processes of urbanism are no less significant than the urban forms, then it will not be possible to understand fully Chinese urbanism without careful studies of what has been taking place in many of the rapidly growing quasi-legal peri-urban regions where things can get done relatively easily, cheaply and expeditiously.

7 Manipulating the margins
The case of Shanghai

Introduction

Since the 1990s, extended metropolitan regions in coastal China have developed rapidly and have become major centers of "place marketing" in China. These fast growing urban regions are now the focus of China's attempts to develop a globally competitive economy that will enable China to achieve the status of a developed country by 2050. Grounding the analysis in theoretical frameworks introduced in Chapters 1 and 2 this case study investigates the urban transformation that is occurring in Shanghai's urban margins, which in this case are the sub-urban rural counties under the jurisdiction of the city.

Shanghai, the core city of the extended metropolitan region (EMR) of the lower Yangzi River delta, is a municipality of provincial status that incorporates several different levels of administration: the city, the special economic zone of Pudong New Area, urban districts and sub-urban rural counties. It has experienced the most rapid economic growth of all of the Chinese coastal cities in the last ten years as well as the most furious pace of change in the transformation of the built-environment. Images of the financial district of Pudong with its towering Manhattan-type skyline conjure up the image of global cities such as New York. This image contrasts with the Bund across the Huangpu River in which the nineteenth century architecture of banks and offices reinforce the reality of the early incorporation of Shanghai into the world system from the mid-nineteenth century. But surrounding this urban core are the margins of the municipality that are rapidly changing from rural to urban landscapes and that are the focus of this chapter.

While rural–urban boundaries tend to be blurred in EMRs,[1] state administration and spatial policies remain important for the production of urban space. Local administrations are the basic units from which statistical materials are gathered, to which state developmental resources are allocated and different policies are adopted for economic development and the accumulation of capital. This engenders a unifying territorial consciousness for the people who live there. With the decentralization of decision-making power, the structural importance of local governments is growing, forcing higher levels of the state to use their political power by reorganizing and restructuring territorial conditions under which "spatial fixes"[2] occur. The transition of urban margins reflects a unique arena in which these "spatial tactics" and "spatial targets" can be applied. "Spatial tactics" refers to the various instruments that the state utilizes in the production of space while "spatial targets" suggests the divergent territorial scales on which these instruments are deployed.[3] The urban margins are thus shaped by each of these "actors" through a series of comprehensive metropolitan plans, municipal policies and regulations, focused to a large extent on land-use zoning plans.

In the Shanghai context, urban transformation of the margins is closely associated with the integration of the EMR in the lower Yangzi River delta and industrial restructuring of the old urban core. This case study focuses on this important aspect of the production of urban space that brings about a rapid shift in the agricultural base of the margins by implanting a mix of industrial estates and residential sprawl among the ongoing rural activities. This is an overall state urban project, but manifests itself in different levels of social, economic and political practices, particularly in the expansion of urban political control and activities into the immediate margins of the old urban core. This case study emphasizes one aspect of the spatial expansion of urban activity into Shanghai city margins that have some different features from others in the book.

This chapter is structured into six main parts. Following the introduction, Shanghai's urban margins are defined and their development during the centrally planned period is briefly reviewed. The third section discusses how the state policies and other forms of intervention have been implemented in the margins in Shanghai since 1978. The fourth section looks at the impacts of changing fiscal policy and land-use arrangements and the utilization of foreign capital on the development of the urban margin. The fifth section focuses on the population movement and patterns of urban development in the urban margins. This is followed by some concluding comments in section six.

The urban margins of Shanghai

For the purpose of this analysis we make a division of Shanghai municipality into three zones. As Figure 7.1 shows, the outer margins consist of Chongming county and the districts of Qingpu, Songjiang, Jinshan, Fengxian and Nanhui.[4] The inner margins include the four sub-urban urban districts of Pudong New Area, Minhang, Jiading and Baoshan. The inner-city is the old city proper of Shanghai including nine inner-city districts. The terms urban margins, margins, margin areas and margin regions are used interchangeably throughout this chapter.

Historically, Shanghai had been a compact city, derived from an indigenous "walled city" and the development of foreign settlements before 1943. Both the built-up area and the margins of the city have been expanded dramatically since the establishment of the People's Republic of China in 1949. Ten rural counties from the neighboring provinces of Jiangsu and Zhejiang were placed under

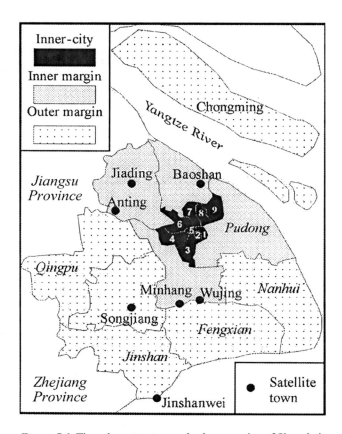

Figure 7.1 The urban structure and urban margins of Shanghai.

Notes
Shanghai's inner-city district: 1 – Huangpu; 2 – Luwan; 3 – Xuhui; 4 – Changning; 5 – Jing'an; 6 – Putuo; 7 – Zhabei; 8 – Hongkou; and 9 – Yangpu.

Shanghai's jurisdiction in 1959 and 1960, enlarging the municipality from 590 square kilometers to 6,340 square kilometers. It was expected that such an expansion of the sub-urban rural counties would ensure a secure supply of agricultural products to the inner urban districts. During most of the time between 1960 and 1978, the municipality of Shanghai was organized into ten urban districts and ten sub-urban rural counties. The rural counties housed most of the agricultural population and supplied agricultural products to the urban districts, aiming to develop self-sufficiency in agricultural products and minimize unnecessary inter-urban transportation. In contrast, the urban districts consisted almost entirely of the "urban" population who held urban household registration and engaged in "urban" activities.

The areas of both urban districts and rural counties were organized into centrally planned units during the centrally planned period. In the rural counties, the agricultural population was organized into the basic units, which were known as the communes, whereas in the urban area, *danwei* were formed in almost all urban sectors in order to carry out the production plans and facilitate control of the urban population and the growth of the state economy. Residential apartments, workshops, schools, shops and other services were mixed together and enclosed by walls.

The functional differentiation between the two kinds of planned units established a "hard edge" that indicated the end of "urban" and the beginning of "rural" in Chinese cities during the period of central planning. This resulted in a system of classification whereby the Chinese population could be categorized not only by their household registration status[5] (*hukou* see Chapter 3) but also in terms of their urban or rural location. People with non-agricultural household registration living in the margins were often seen as "rural folk" compared to those who resided in the "urban" areas. Such divisions were produced through the "formal urbanization" of central plans and statistics, and became symbolically constructed and accepted in the minds and social practices of individuals who lived within urban and rural space.

During the Maoist period, the central allocation of funds from Beijing was largely invested in urban development, accounting for over 83 percent of the city's total investment during the period between 1950 and 1957, reaching 97 percent in 1958, and remaining over 90 percent until 1961. Then, for most years until 1978, it accounted for more than 85 percent of the city's total capital formation.[6] The investment was mainly allocated through central government ministries and the central economic plans. Production and consumption quotas were applied to each district, industrial sector, enterprise and household with priority given to the development of manufacturing activities, in particular, heavy industries involved in the production of iron, steel and machinery – and confined to the urban districts. The margin areas were regarded as a source for food for the core city and largely ignored in financial allocation.

The only exception took place in a few inner margin regions. After the end of the 1950s, due to the high density of population and industry in the inner-city and its adjacent districts, some investment in industrial and housing projects went to some of Shanghai's urban margins. This was focused on the development of industrial estates and new worker villages in the inner margins. These inner margins were ultimately incorporated into the jurisdiction of the urban districts. This was the major process of expansion of officially defined urban area into Shanghai's inner margin areas. Such urban growth primarily occurred through an incremental expansion of areas controlled by the urban district, with the total area of Shanghai's urban districts increasing from 82 square kilometers in 1949 to 149 square kilometers in 1960. However, between 1964 and 1980, the area officially defined as urban districts was unchanged. The officially defined urban area was expanded after 1980 when the adjustment of inner urban district boundaries resumed. For example, the total area of the ten inner urban districts was expanded from 261.4 square kilometers in 1985 to 289 square kilometers in 2000.

Thus during the Maoist period, these political divisions between rural counties and urban districts were important but did not totally constrain state-led "urban" expansion. Urban development beyond the fringe areas into the margin areas was mainly driven by the satellite town programs. Five industrial satellite towns of Minhang, Wujing, Anting, Songjiang and Jiading based on the British town-planning model were planned and built from 1959 (see Figure 7.1). The population proposed for each satellite town varied between 25,000 and 50,000. The establishment of the Shanghai Petrochemical Complex in Jinshanwei and the Shanghai Baoshan Iron and Steel Complex in Baoshan added another two industrial satellites to the city at the end of the 1970s. The development of these satellite towns has been well documented, and contributed to the decentralization of industries to a certain extent, but did not attract a large population from the urban districts.[7]

There was also an "invisible" urbanization process in Shanghai's urban margins. From 1960 to 1984, Shanghai's rural margins were organized into 230 communes, which were the basic units formed to carry out agricultural production plans, to bond rural labor to their localities and help alleviate overpopulation in urban districts.[8] These communes were encouraged to develop the so-called "five small plants,"[9] which were oriented to the production of agricultural machinery and other inputs such as cement etc., that were needed in the communes. As a result, the population engaged in non-agricultural activities but living in rural communes increased considerably. For example, employment in township manufacturing activities increased from 3.5 to 18 percent of the total labor force in Changzhen Commune in Shanghai, during the period between 1961 and 1978.[10] However, because these people remained under agricultural household registration, this growth of non-agricultural activities was rarely reflected in the published statistics. The urbanization involved was "unofficial" and not included in official statistics.

But these developments did not change the rural–urban dualism and overall differentiation between urban margin and inner-city persisted. Shanghai's outer margins were primarily "rural." For example, in 1978, over five million people lived in the rural counties of Shanghai and accounted for half of the city's total population. Over three-quarters of rural laborers were engaged in agricultural activities. They produced a major proportion of the grain, vegetables, edible oil, milk and freshwater fish for the urban districts in their support of the self-sufficiency of the city. The population density in the margins averaged 879 persons per square kilometer compared to 37,000 persons per square kilometer in urban district areas at that time.

Since 1978, many changes have occurred, resulting in the communes being dissolved and the central control being reduced. The agricultural population could now look for employment in manufacturing and commercial activities within, or beyond, the regions in which they lived. This has resulted in a decline in agricultural land use and a reduction in the number of workers in the agricultural sector.

Urban planning and management of Shanghai's margins since 1978

Shanghai's margin regions have been gradually incorporated into the municipal government's overall plan and more importantly into its official "urban" development strategies. This is partially due to the fact that one important consequence of the incremental boundary expansion that categorized urban development in Shanghai from the 1950s through to the late 1970s was a failure to plan for future infrastructural needs. In an effort to provide more effective management of the urban growth of Shanghai, a comprehensive metropolitan plan was created at the beginning of the 1980s and was centrally approved in 1986. A "multi-centered structure" model was introduced to regenerate the inner-city, in which the People's Square was designated as the center of the city while several ancillary urban centers (*chengshi fu zhongxing*) were proposed on both the northern and the southern banks of the Suzhou River. In addition, nine sub-urban centers (*chengshi ci zhongxing*) were planned: six in Puxi (the west side of Huangpu River) and three in Pudong (the east side of Huangpu River).

A series of sub-urban centers in the margins were designed, based on the theory of rank–size distribution. They constituted of three levels of urban settlement: satellite towns, rural administrative towns and rural market towns. Under the plan the urban infrastructure of the seven industrial satellite towns that were established in the 1960s and 1970s would be improved. The plan also envisaged that the population in each of these towns would increase to 100,000–300,000 by 2000. These towns would serve as comprehensive urban centers in the margins and be linked to the central city through an expressway network. The population of the satellite towns collectively would rise from 0.64 million in 1982 to 1.3 million in 2000. On average, three to four rural administrative towns were proposed in each county, each with 2,000–5,000 inhabitants. These were expected to extend the provision urban services to people living in rural market towns and villages.

To ensure the developments progressed according to the plan, a new urban planning regime was established based on the Planning Ordinance in 1984 and later the Planning Act of 1989.[11] Under the new arrangement, all developmental projects had to be registered with the local urban planning authority. These required detailed regulatory plans to be provided for urban developments and planning permits to be issued for all new developments and changes of land use. In principle, development approvals could only be granted when both the assessment criteria and detailed plan were in accordance.

The authority for urban planning in the city was also decentralized from the municipality to urban districts and sub-urban rural counties. In the early 1990s, the planning departments of Shanghai's district and county government were established and authorized to prepare detailed plans for their territories, excluding the regions labeled as "important areas" by the municipal planning authority, such as the "historical conservation" area of the Bund and the new central business district (CBD) in Lujiazui in Pudong. In the rural counties, almost all residential, infrastructural, commercial and industrial projects could be developed without the consent of the municipal planning authority, with the exception of those that might impair conservation areas. Permits issued by planning authorities from the district and county government accounted for over 90 percent of Shanghai's total development approvals between 1996 and 1999.[12]

The rapid industrialization and the changes in land use and occupations of agricultural laborers have resulted in significant changes to the administrative management of the margins. By 2005, all rural counties but Chongming Island in Shanghai had been granted urban district status, increasing the area of urban districts to 4,865 square kilometers. This involved a change in the political status of the sub-urban rural counties from the county level to the prefecture level and entitled them to more funding allocation for urban infrastructure. However, the development characteristics of these newly designated urban districts were quite different from that of the inner urban districts as they remained rural in character. The average size of the inner urban districts was only 32.1 square kilometers with a population density of 33,605 persons per square kilometer, while the average size of these newly designated urban districts in inner and outer margins was 557 square kilometers, in which the population density was of 2,310 persons per square kilometer.

The comprehensive metropolitan plan was soon revised after the opening of Pudong New Area in 1990, targeting Shanghai as the "dragon head" of the Yangzi valley and delta. The latest attempts of the new plan are designed to integrate the urban margins into the development of the municipality as a whole, while at the same time developing the regional and international role of the municipality. Land use is to be optimized by relocating manufacturing activities to the urban margins and bringing a prosperous tertiary sector as well as production services into the inner-city. These planning policies, along with other intertwined factors of decentralization of fiscal arrangements, development of the land market and global and regional integration, have all had a profound impact on urban transition in the margins.

Changing development practices of the urban margins

What forces are driving such a transformation? This section will discuss how the following factors have contributed to Shanghai's urban transformation: the policies of fiscal decentralization, the development of the Pudong New Zone, the growth of new industrial estates designed to attract foreign investment, improvements in transportation infrastructure, industrial relocation from the core city, the outwards spread of population and the rapid commodification of the land market that encouraged the growth of new housing developments and estates in the city's margins.

Decentralization of fiscal arrangement

The central allocation process has been reformed and decentralized as discussed in Chapter 2. In the new reform structure, the central government granted

Shanghai a preferential fiscal contract system of "self-responsibility" in 1988. Accordingly, Shanghai only needed to remit an annual fixed sum of 10.5 billion yuan to Beijing during the period between 1988 and 1990. In 1991 and 1992, it was required to remit this base amount and half of all revenues collected in excess of 16.5 billion yuan.[13] This greatly increased Shanghai's financial capacity to improve its urban infrastructure.

Following the central government's decision, the Shanghai municipal government has gradually decentralized its power to the local levels, moving its unified leadership over the city down to the district and county governments under a so-called "Two Level Governments and Two Level Management" program since 1992.[14] Local governments at district/county level are allowed to retain revenues based on a similar formula to that between the central and Shanghai municipal government. Since the introduction of the tax sharing system in 1994, an average of 90 percent of local development expenditure is sourced from local revenue. In order to generate more revenue, efforts of local governments have focused on developing tax incentives and competing for new investments from the market. The importance of a partnership between local authorities and other Chinese agencies and private/foreign investors has increased, determining the level, pace and location of developments within the city.

Global and regional integration

The developmental enthusiasm of local governments in Shanghai has been greatly stimulated by increased access to sources of capital, which is illustrated by the establishment of foreign direct investment (FDI)-oriented development zones. The first three small economic and technological development zones (ETDZs) in Minhang, Hongqiao and Caohejing areas were established by the central government in the mid-1980s (see Plate 7.1). Since then, many FDI-oriented development zones have been designated by different levels of governments with different names and industrial specializations in the margin areas of Shanghai. The most impressive ones with national and international significance are those located in Pudong. The opening of Pudong New Area, an area of 522 square kilometers on the eastern bank of Huangpu River in 1990, was a catalyst for the FDI-oriented preferential policies in Shanghai municipality. It also shifted the development focus from the old city on the western bank of the Huangpu River to a greenfield site on the eastern bank of the river. The area had a population of 1.3 million, but most was farmland with only 38 square kilometers of built-up area in 1990, within which four large FDI "themed zones"[15] with a total area of 83 square kilometers were planned. These are the Waigaoqiao Free Trade Zone, the Jinqiao Export-Processing Zone, the Lujiazui Financial and Trade Zone and the Zhangjiang High-Tech Park (see Plates 7.2 and 7.3).

Following Pudong's themed zones idea of using tax incentives, streamlining the administrative system and providing a well-equipped infrastructure, the municipal government designated the Songjiang Industrial Park 30 kilometers

Plate 7.1 Hongqiao economic and technological development zone: FDI-related commercial and office centers in Shanghai's urban fringe.

Plate 7.2 Entry gate of the Waigaoqiao free trade zone in Pudong.

from downtown on the southwest part of Shanghai in 1994, with a planned area of 20 square kilometers (Plate 7.4). This has been followed by the establishment of industrial parks of Jiading, Jinshan, Fengpu, Xinghuo, Xinzhuang and Chongming, Baoshan and Qingpu successively. Each has a similar scale and role in attracting foreign capital and rearranging the city's industrial spatial

Plate 7.3 Lujiazui financial and trade zone, Pudong, Shanghai.

Plate 7.4 Songjiang industry park, Shanghai.

system. By 2001, the total area of centrally designated ETDZs and themed zones in Pudong and municipally designated industrial parks had reached 250 square kilometers, almost equal to the size of the inner-city. Geographically, the industrial parks designated by the municipal government are mainly located in the outer margin areas while those by the central government tend to be focused in the inner margins. The average distance of the industrial parks to downtown is 35 kilometers, whilst the centrally designated ETDZs and Pudong's themed zones are only 12 kilometers from downtown. This suggests a desire of the central government to reinforce the dominance of the city core consisting of the old city and the new zones across the river.

The establishment of development zones has been decentralized and widely spread. They have become an effective tool for the local government to concentrate on using scarce resources to create urban land for lease, which is an important way for generating local revenue. Furthermore, industrial pollution treatment facilities set up in these zones can lessen the degree of any negative environmental effects caused by manufacturers within the zones. Many lower level governments of urban districts, rural counties and towns set up local industrial parks within their jurisdiction to compete with those designated by municipal and central governments.[16] By 2001, there were 36 development zones established by district and county government and 196 established by township government, in addition to the numerous areas designated by many other institutions and private firms.[17] For example, the Textile Ministry of China and Qingpu district jointly developed the 2 square kilometer International Textile Industrial Park in Qingpu, which has become one of the largest textile industrial parks in Shanghai.

Many of these development zones, especially those of state and municipal rank, have attracted substantial foreign investment. The past two decades have witnessed a huge amount of FDI flowing into Shanghai, which has attracted nearly one-tenth of China's total FDI annually since the mid-1990s albeit with fluctuation in some years. By the end of 2005, the city's cumulative FDI totaled US$98.8 billion in over 36,000 projects of which over half of the FDI are concentrated on manufacturing activities.[18] Pudong has performed exceptionally well. For example, in 2004, Shanghai successfully attracted 4,321 foreign invested projects totaling US$11.69 billion. A total of 39 percent of the projects (55.5 percent of investment) went to Pudong whilst 37.7 percent of the projects (27.6 percent of investment) were distributed amongst the other marginal areas.[19]

These projects have been important driving forces for Shanghai's urban development in terms of being important capital sources that can be used for urban infrastructure. Before 1980, almost all investment in fixed assets of Shanghai originated from the central government and collective enterprises. The importance of foreign capital increased from zero in the early 1980s to a third of the total investment in fixed assets in Shanghai in the early 1990s.[20]

The desire for foreign capital is driving Shanghai's urban development. For example, heavy investment has been used to improve the urban infrastructure of the city, to facilitate foreign operators. From 1991 to 1995 (the Eighth Five Year Plan), a total of RMB82.5 billion was spent on urban infrastructure, of which 29 percent went to transportation and communication improvement. Thus the urban infrastructure has been allocated both to the inner-city and Shanghai's margins. For example, modern transport linkages between Pudong and Puxi have been built, including the development of two major bridges, a tunnel, an inner ring road, 65 kilometers of elevated freeways and the Metro line 1. An investment of RMB227.4 billion was further invested in the Ninth Five Year Plan (1996–2000), extending the infrastructure to the whole metropolitan area. This included a number of regionally significant projects. For example, the Maglev line connection between the Pudong International Airport and the Lujaizui Finance and Trade Zone, the extension of Mass Transit Mode to Zhangjiang High-Tech Park in Pudong and Minhang district. This investment increased to RMB325.7 billion from 2001 to 2005 (the Tenth Five Year Plan), of which 46 percent was spent on transportation and communication. The expressway network in Shanghai has been rapidly developed, increasing from 98 kilometers in 2000 to 560 kilometers in 2005. The linkages between the central city and the margins and between Shanghai and Nanjing and between Shanghai and Hangzhou have been greatly improved. Overall, the capacity for Shanghai to be globally competitive and act as the economic node of the lower Yangzi valley has been improved.

Development of land market

The introduction of the land market is a major feature of China's urban reform but the market reform of urban land use in China's cities did not officially start until the amendment of the constitution in 1988 that has been discussed in Chapter 2. The ability for urban governments to transfer land-use rights to developers or individual users by tender, auction or contract while the ownership of urban land remains with the state has been a major source of capital generation. In Shanghai, it was first attempted in Hongqiao ETDZ, where the right to use the first piece of urban land in the city was put up for tender in 1988. Since then, the transfer of land-use rights has become the main impetus for urban development in Shanghai, both through the conversion of rural to urban land and through the raising of revenue to update urban infrastructure and support development projects. Accordingly, 95 percent of the income from land leases remains with the municipality, which remits only 5 percent to the central government. In 1992 alone, Shanghai collected US$35 billion from land transfer,[21] which has been an important factor in restructuring the social and spatial patterns of Shanghai.[22]

The transfer of land-use rights is an administrative means to convert rural land into urban land in particular in the development zones. The administrative commissions of development zones usually employ a form of quasi-expropriation that involves the payment of a certain percentage of the price of the land as an acquisition fee to obtain the land-use rights of the rural land from the rural households. The rest of the payment would be made after the land was developed and sold to urban land users. For example, the Administrative Commission of Pudong New Area obtained the land-use right for 107 square kilometers of land in 1993 by paying 30 percent of the negotiated price of the land to the rural households while the rest would be paid after the land use was changed. They then transferred the land-use rights to land developers and land users in the market. The recipients could use the rights to obtain credit from financial markets. Beginning with the development and transfer of a small area, the administrative commissions could collect money for new land acquisition and infrastructure provision.

Meanwhile, existing land occupants that could not afford the high cost of land, or those who wanted to make a profit from sale of their land in the inner-city have moved out of the city centre. As a result, economic activities, labor and population within the metropolitan area are being rapidly redistributed.

Industrial relocation

An increase in land-use fees in the inner-city has forced the relocation of manufacturing activities to the urban margin areas. In 1990, 58 percent of Shanghai's industrial output was produced in the inner-city. To implement the new comprehensive metropolitan plan, a planning policy was proposed in the mid-1990s that permitted only one-third of the manufacturing enterprises that were compatible with functions of the inner-city to stay in the inner-city while one-third would be closed down due to poor performance and another one-third would be moved out of the inner-city to make room for tertiary sector activities. The majority of the relocated manufacturing enterprises were located in the margins.

The textile industry is a good illustration of such massive industrial restructuring. Historically, the textile industry was the largest industrial sector in Shanghai in terms of both output and employment. In 1952, it produced about half of the industrial output of the city.[23] In 1990, there were 495 textile factories directly under the administration of the Shanghai Textile Industrial Bureau, employing half a million workers and producing half of the city's total textile output. Over 90 percent of these factories were located in the inner-city, especially in the Yangpu and Putuo districts, occupying 8 square kilometers of land.

With the introduction of land market, factories began to be charged for the land they occupy. In addition, the key raw material, cotton, that used to be supplied through the central plans, now need to be purchased from the market.[24] All of these developments placed increased financial pressure on the textile enterprises forcing them to close down, or relocate to the margins of Shanghai. Many of these relocated factories chose to join with foreign firms to establish joint ventures. An example was the Seventeenth Shanghai Textile Factory in the Yangpu district, which joined with Hong Kong and Taiwanese investors to establish two joint projects. Both the projects were relocated in the margins in 1996; one in the Minhang district and the other in the Qingpu district. In 2000, the number of factories that were controlled by the Shanghai Textile Holding Corporation (renamed Shanghai Textile Bureau) decreased to 386, a third of which are now joint venture firms. Employment in the textile industry dramatically declined to 165,000. In addition, the land occupied by the textile industry in the inner-city was reduced to 3 square kilometers.

Table 7.1 Changing spatial shares of industrial output by value in Shanghai, 1985, 1990, 1995, 2000, 2005 (RMB billion)

Years	Total output	Inner-city		The margin area	
		Output	% of total	Output	% of total
1985	83.0	59.4	71.6	23.6	28.4
1990	105.9	61.5	58.1	44.4	41.9
1995	466.3	162.8	34.9	303.5	65.0
2000	660.4	145.0	22.0	514.2	77.9
2005	1,576.7	179.8	11.4	13,396.9	88.6

Source: Shanghai Statistical Bureau (1986, 1991, 1996, 2001, 2006).

Notes
Shanghai experienced many times of administration adjustment. The area of inner urban districts was 261.4 square kilometers in 1985, then extended to 280 square kilometers in 1990 and 289 square kilometers in 2000.

Table 7.1 shows a rapid growth of the urban margins' share of total industrial output and a decline in the share of the inner-city. Shanghai's margin regions increased their share in industrial output value from 28.5 percent in 1985 to nearly 89 percent in 2005 (see Table 7.1). The urban margins have now become the industrial base of Shanghai (see Plate 7.5).

Plate 7.5 Teli Leather Products factory in Fengxian District, Shanghai.

The relocation of manufacturing enterprises has reduced industrial pollution in the inner-city area. However, the urban margins are now suffering. In fact, manufacturing is still the major source of Shanghai's pollution, accounting for 93.3 percent of gaseous emissions in 2004.[25] The treatment rate of domestic sewage in the urban margins is particularly low with huge volumes of waste water discharged directly into urban water bodies. For example, it was reported that in 2000 over three million cubic meters of sewage in Shanghai were directly discharged into the East China Sea each day. The black water belt can be seen and smelled over a dozen kilometers away from the sewage outlets.[26] Some outlets are even close to water intake points, such as the Dianshan Lake, located at the upper reaches of the Huangpu River. In the meantime, the urban margins have gradually lost their agricultural role of providing food and other agricultural products. Furthermore, the environmental and resource situation regarding wildlife habitats and breeding areas, water supply sources, purification and pollutant assimilation and climate regulation has seriously deteriorated.

Population movements

As a consequence of the relocation of manufacturing activities from the inner-city to the urban margin areas, the growth of commercial and office development in Shanghai's core and the commodification of the housing market, Shanghai's population distribution pattern has changed radically over the last 25 years. The inner-city of Shanghai has experienced rapid redevelopment.[27] Office space of the city increased from 5.99 million square meters in 1990 to 43.34 million square meters in 2005 while commercial space increased by over 28 million square meters in the same period. In the same period over 55 million square meters of building floors among which three-quarters was housing were demolished during the period between 1995 and 2005. This involved 843,000 households and resulted in a large scale population displacement.[28] Most of these out-migrants were relocated in the newly developed areas in the inner margins because they could not afford the price for new apartments in their original sites, or because the old residential areas in which they were located were redeveloped for non-residential purposes.

The population in Shanghai's margins has increased rapidly in the last two decades. The number of long-term residents living in the urban margins doubled from 5.77 million in 1990 to 11.24 million in 2005 while the population in the inner-city increased only slightly from 6.37 million to 6.54 million.[29] Population growth has been focused on the inner margin, increasing by 87.4 percent during the five years between 2000 and 2005. The past ten years saw over 1.3 million more people in Pudong, almost doubling the population density from 2,854 persons per square kilometer in 1995 to 5,341 persons per square kilometer in 2005. A total of 1.16 million people was added to the Minhang district while the population in the Baoshan and Jiading districts increased by 0.61 million and 0.3 million respectively during the same period. The population in the outer margins has also grown, increasing by 35 percent during the first five years of the new century after experiencing a 3.3 percent decline in the second half of the 1990s (see Table 7.2).

These changing patterns in the distribution of long-term population have also been duplicated by the growth of floating population.[30] The 2000 census data show that almost 60 percent of the city's total migrants were concentrated in the inner margins while only 8 percent of them chose to live in the outer margin areas. The district of Minhang had more migrants than its local population (see Figure 7.2).

The floating population's social and economic status largely determines the location of their residence. In fact, they have limited options and choices as to where to live in Shanghai. Furthermore, they have been treated as second class citizens who are usually underpaid with most having to return to their home villages after a period in the city. They have limited access to the local school, government jobs and government housing due to their "temporary" migration status. Most of them live in farmer rental houses or temporary quarters that were formerly workshops or storage facilities. Overcrowding and lack of facilities is a common feature of the housing of this group of migrants.[31]

The growing number of foreign firms in the city has increasingly attracted temporary or long-term international migrants, in particular the overseas Chinese. There were over 90,000 foreigners living in Shanghai in 2005. In contrast to the floating population, they usually hold high-rank management positions in foreign firms. The growth of these so-called "golden-collar" elites in combination with the distribution of commercial housing has increased the diversification of social spaces in Shanghai. The development of Shanghai's commercial housing was classified into those for foreigners (including overseas Chinese) and for the local Chinese people.[32] Between 1988 and 1998, 8.7 million square meters of the first category housing were built.[33] Houses with backyards and "gated communities" are being built for foreigners and high income Chinese people.[34] For example, among the 1,200 households in Binjiangyuan (a small residential area in Pudong), 40 percent consist of foreigners.[35] Gubei New Resident Area, which is next to the Hongqiao ETDZ, has earned the nickname of "Taiwan Village" in Shanghai.[36]

Table 7.2 Population movements in Shanghai 1995, 2000, 2005 (in 1,000 persons/square kilometer)

	1995		2000		2005	
	Pop.	*Pop. density*	*Pop.*	*Pop. density*	*Pop.*	*Pop. density*
Shanghai total	13,013.70	2,033	13,216.30	2,084	17,784.0	2,805
Inner-city	5,346.60	19,095	6,282.40	21,705	6,544.2	22,644
Inner margin	3,200.90	1,809	3,601.30	2,037	6,747.7	3,817
Outer margin	3,447.10	779	3,332.60	752	4,492.3	1,014

Source: Shanghai Statistical Bureau (1996, 2001, 2006).

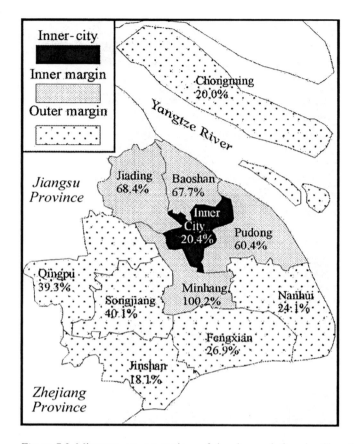

Figure 7.2 Migrants as proportion of local population in Shanghai (2000) (source: Shanghai Census 2000).

Notes
Migrants include both those from other provinces and other districts of Shanghai.

Meanwhile, the numbers of people engaged in agriculture in Shanghai's outer margins has changed dramatically. For example, in 1978, the agricultural population in Shanghai was 4.53 million, accounting for 41 percent of the city's total population. Almost all of these people were located in the margin regions. The proportion of the agricultural population decreased to a third of the city's total population in 2000. It further decreased to 15.5 percent of the total population in 2005 with the increase of both the city's total population and the proportion of laborers engaged in non-agricultural jobs.[37] Rural labor engaged in agriculture dropped from 77.8 percent in 1978 to 28.7 percent in 2005 while those engaged in manufacturing activities increased from less than 20 percent of total rural labor to over half during that period (see Plate 7.5). The proportion of rural labor engaged in other non-agricultural sectors of commercial activities, transportation, communications and construction also increased, accounting for 15 percent of the total labor force in 2005.

The changing urban landscapes of Shanghai municipality

These processes of change since 1978 have produced a rapidly changing urban landscape in the Shanghai Municipality. While the "old city" is now undergoing "urban renewal" and "gentrification," the distinctive feature of the inner margins is the emergence of diverse and large numbers of residential blocks and the specialized centers based on centrally designated development zones. For example, the Hongqiao area, which is located 6.5 kilometers from the city centre was rural in character in the early 1980s, but has been transformed into a major FDI-oriented office centre with a large amount of apartment space. It was initially proposed as a "foreign consulate area" in 1984 and was designated as an ETDZ by the central government in 1986. The planned use of the land in the area was substantially amended in order to accommodate the interests of foreign investors, which resulted in the production of urban space as a high-rise office center, attracting foreign trade-related management along with large retail stores that had previously been confined to downtown. Infrastructure improvement and the concentration of manufacturing activities have also resulted in the Caohejing and Minhang ETDZs.

The most impressive example of the development of these specialized centers has been the themed zones in Pudong. The high-rise district of the Lujiazui Finance and Trade Zone has formed a new part of the central business district of Shanghai.[38] This zone is becoming the regional headquarters of multi-national corporations, international organizations, agencies of other centers of the Yangzi delta EMR, international fairs, exhibitions and conferences, as well as other producer services. Over 400 high-rises with five-and-a-half million square meters of floor space were built. A total of 63 percent of the buildings are for business and commercial use while 37 percent are for residential purposes. The high-rise buildings have been laid out to around 400,000 square meters near the central park. A public poll shows that the Oriental Pearl Tower, Jinmao Plaza, the Shanghai Convention Centre and the Pudong International Airport were listed as Shanghai's "icons"; three of them are in Lujiazui.[39] Similarly, the Waigaoqiao Free Trade Zone, about 20 kilometers from the city centre, was developed for harbor use, warehouse use and free trade while Jinqiao and Zhangjiang themed zones focused on the development of manufacturing activities, research and development institutes. Related to this functional differentiation was the development of transport links. These included global connections, such as the Pudong International Airport and the Waigaoqiao Deep-water Berths; city-wide connections such as the four bridges that cross the Huangpu River, a ring road and subways for integrating with Puxi; regional connections such as the three axes for commuting between themed zones and a Maglev line between Pudong Airport and Lujiazui; and inner zone connections. The integration of these transport connections with the expressway network and the Yangzi River has extended the functions of these themed zones to serve the delta and valley of the Yangzi River.

Development zones designated by the municipal and lower levels of government have become the growth engines in the outer margins. Industrial parks planned by the municipal government have been well equipped with urban infrastructure and become the focus of manufacturing activities that produced RMB245 billion or 18.3 percent of total industrial output of the margins in 2005.[40] A number of district and town designated development zones scattered throughout the urban margins were suddenly "transferred" from the rice fields to the "urban area" overnight. Some of these zones have been successfully developed with paved roads, buildings and other facilities attracting foreign or domestic manufacturing projects while some have had little development. With the duplication of development zones, each had to compete with others for FDI and relocated manufacturing activities. As a result, it has become increasingly difficult for the outer margins to follow development objectives set in the comprehensive metropolitan plan.

Urban development in Shanghai's outer margins is widely dispersed. There were 156 towns in Shanghai's margins in 2000. The distribution of towns in the margins varied from only 1.8 towns per 100 square kilometers in Qingpu to five towns per 100 square kilometers in Baoshan. On average, each town covered 31.4 square kilometers and had 43,300 people. The population size of the towns varied. Only three of them had a population over 100,000 and another six towns having a population between 40,000 and 100,000. These nine largest towns together held 935,000 people, accounting for only 21 percent of the population in the urban margins. In other words, 79 percent of the total margin town population was located in much smaller towns, each with a population of less than 40,000 people. Thus the municipal government's 1986 Metropolitan Comprehensive Plan, which proposed that urban expansion be centered on the satellite towns, has only been partially accomplished. For example, the plan estimated that Songjiang Town would eventually house 300,000 people, but only had 100,000 people by 2000.

The rapid urban transformation in Shanghai has not occurred without problems. The development centered on the ETDZs, themed zones and other incentive zones has consumed huge amounts of agricultural land. In Pudong, for example, it caused over 10,000 rural laborers to lose their land. Some of them, instead of being absorbed into the industrialized process, are forced to become "floaters" and leave Pudong due to a lack of relevant job skills. It was reported that the rate of rural labor transfer to manufacturing activities in the Pudong actually decreased from 2.2 percent per year (between 1984 and 1990) to 1.1 percent per year (between 1990 and 1997).[41] In addition, the urban development in zonal areas has focused on the need for foreign investment and a facilitated industrial restructuring strategy. However, construction and maintenance of public facilities such as health, education, sport and culture in the margins have not evoked much consideration. For example, Pudong may have the city's, even the nation's best physical infrastructure, but its ratio of doctors per 10,000 people is very low; only 20 in the year 2000. It is not only far less than that of the inner-city in which the number was 47, but is also less than the average of the city as a whole where the number was 38.[42]

The scattered nature of productive sites in general makes environmental management more difficult, particularly since transport activity and the costs of providing services to an increasingly spread out and poly-nucleated urban form has grown. The number of private cars and passenger vehicles in the city has increased from 190,000 in 1996 to 1,070,000 in 2003. The number of motor-cycles has increased from 93,000 to 985,000 during the same period.[43] This large increase in vehicles places great pressures on the existing transport systems and creates many challenges to develop an efficient transportation system.

Conclusion

The transformation in Shanghai's margins has been manifested at different levels of social, economic and political practices in which the overarching met-ropolitan level plans designed to create a more efficient and sustainable metro-politan region have been in constant interaction with local initiatives that have led to the modification of the plan and the emergence of new urban forms in the margins of the metropolis. This transformation has eroded the sharp rural–urban dichotomy that existed during the central planning period. A clear spatial division – the city center as a manufacturing center and urban margin as the city's food basket – has been replaced by increasing rural–urban integration and intra/inter-city and international links for commodities, services and population movement. The margin areas have been rapidly industrialized as a result of Shanghai's industrial restructuring policy, which aims for a new service role to be played by the inner-city in the regional, national and global systems. The increase of manufacturing activities concentrated in the development zones has absorbed a large proportion of the workforce released from agricultural activities in the margins, which have become more integrated with the inner-city, the EMR and the global economy. Such trends have been recognized and reflected by the administrative upgrading of all of sub-urban rural counties (except Chongming Island) to urban district status.

The overall development of Shanghai has been very scattered and diversified. The inner margin has been rapidly urbanized, characterized by a mixture of the new residential blocks – which host the population moving from the inner-city, the floating population from other provinces and international migrants – and a number of emerging specialized centers, while rural activities have rapidly diminished. The growth of the outer margins is mainly driven by the newly established development zones, resulting in the dispersal of urban development in Shanghai. Such phenomena can be explained by the increasing role of the local governments. Along with the increasing autonomy of the local government and administration commissions of development zones in revenue, preparation and implementation of urban plans, the urban margins have become detached from and more integrated with the inner-city, the EMR and the global economy. The increasing role of the local governments in the development of Shanghai's margins has been the major influence.

Meanwhile, the development outcomes of local projects have reshaped the municipal government's plans. It was expected that manufacturing activities and population movements would be mainly concentrated in a few planned sites – designated towns as intended under the municipal urban plans. However, the establishment of various types of development zones by the local governments has meant that urban growth in Shanghai's margins is dominated by these development zones and existing towns. Therefore, the urban margin transformation in Shanghai has resulted in an uncontrolled spread of urbanization in the outer margins that has in the short term defeated the intentions of the municipal plan to create a more rational and efficient landscape.[44] These development trends in the outer margins of Shanghai exhibit features similar to those of other case studies of outer margins in this book, and thus reinforce arguments about the important role of local "bureaucrat entrepreneurs" in urban development. They have also shown that even in a situation of a powerful government administration of a provincial status municipality, an elaborate planning system and clearly formulated development goals, local urban authorities still play an important role in the shaping of Chinese metropolitan regions. To return to our division between spatial targets and tactics discussed in the introduction this case study illustrates how "spatial tactics" at the local level have modified the "spatial targets' of the Shanghai municipality.

8 Rural agglomeration and urbanization in the lower Yangzi delta

The *urban echo* in Kunshan

Introduction

This chapter engages the notion of the production of urban space in China as a state project through an examination of spatial economic transformation in the lower Yangzi delta. The morphology of urban forms in this region arise from shifting local institutional structures and how these are embedded in the reconfiguration and consolidation of political and administrative jurisdiction and space. Areas within extended metropolitan regions in coastal China are repositioning themselves in the wider space economy by adopting functional specialization. This chapter invokes an analytical framework that unpacks local institutional and administrative frameworks to illustrate how these phenomena have impacted the emergence of a new urban form in the region of the lower Yangzi delta. Information for this analysis was collected over a period of more than two decades of fieldwork in the region, including extended discussions with key informants involved with the reform of administrative divisions and in the local Land Resource Management Bureau.[1]

Spatial economic transformation in the lower Yangzi delta in the post-reform period to 1998 has been characterized as a process of rural agglomeration through the "expanding power and influence of local governments, to promote growth, and the rising appreciation of, and localized attempts to respond to external economies and the dynamics of conventional agglomeration."[2] While the role of foreign direct investment was very important in the early post-1978 reforms in places like Guangdong, locally driven domestic capital formation was the main source of investment for this rural agglomeration in the lower Yangzi delta. This involved investment in transportation, and other core infrastructure often in special development zones and industrial parks. While the proportion of the population engaged in agriculture decreased with the rapid growth of industry in the countryside, this did not result in a commensurate increase in the proportion of the local population living in urban areas – at least up until about the mid-1990s. While the restructuring of agricultural production did result in increased productivity, the regional economy also became more diversified and commercialized and household incomes increased.[3]

The processes and mechanisms of this transformation were facilitated by institutional and administrative structures the details of which constituted the fundamental elements of a "transactional environment" that was closely associated with "local growth machine politics."[4] Thus, the urban pattern of these coastal regions exhibited three main patterns. The first was a pattern of regional and urban development that was closely associated with intensely localized exigencies and opportunities. A second feature was the movement of goods, people, manufacturing inputs and other transactional activities, and overlapping interrelationships and interdependencies, administrative imperatives and complex patterns of jurisdiction and power that facilitated a highly dispersed and mixed pattern of economic activity and urbanization. Third, external economies, the dynamics of agglomeration and the role of large cities and other exogenous forces, while important, operated in conjunction with local forces that made the role of large cities less important.[5] This was markedly the case in the period between 1985 and 1998 in the lower Yangzi delta – a region dominated by patterns of rural agglomeration. As will be demonstrated through a case study of Kunshan, a county-level municipality in Jiangsu Province between Shanghai and Suzhou, the notion of rural agglomeration also captures the paradox of economic development as it was associated with the power and influence of local actors to promote growth, and the growing awareness of and desire to respond to external economies and the need to stimulate and manage conventional agglomeration, but at a very local level.

From 1995 onwards the coastal zones of China have accelerated economically, with average annual growth in GDP exceeding 7 to 8 percent and a flood of overseas and domestic investment. In the lower Yangzi delta these developments have generally taken spatial form in the creation of special economic zones (and occasionally export processing zones) combined with incentives and improved infrastructure intended to attract foreign investment. In places like Kunshan since 1998 this has resulted in an increase in the number of people living in expanded built-up areas and designated special zones in and around key central towns. It is possible to suggest that the pattern of urbanization in coastal China is beginning to exhibit tendencies for urban concentration in which economies of scale and agglomeration are playing a more important role in urban formation. However, the processes and mechanisms driving this urban formation, and the transactional environment within which these occur, are also fundamentally different from large cities. The result is a "new model of urbanization" that will be explored in the latter part of this chapter.[6]

This chapter explores these issues through an investigation of developments in Kunshan, located in southern Jiangsu Province adjacent to the Shanghai municipal region in the lower Yangzi delta. In 1978 Kunshan was a peripheral county known for its rather backwards largely agricultural character. In those days Shanghai and the prefectural capital of Suzhou were distant entities with no significant positive economic or indeed other links to Kunshan. In a dramatic change of fortune, by 2005 Kunshan was attracting more than 2 percent of China's total annual foreign direct investment, surpassing Shunde in Guangdong, to become China's richest county-level municipality, and producing 15 million laptops accounting for about a third of total world output.[7]

The following section introduces the spatial and economic circumstances of the lower Yangzi delta and Kunshan. This provides a foundation for examining the growth of urbanization and economic activity in Kunshan from 1978 to 1998. Major changes to the patterns of spatial change that occurred between 1998 and 2005 are then discussed with a view to highlighting recent outcomes of urban development in the lower Yangzi delta. Finally, the chapter concludes with a discussion of the implications of the Kunshan case study for the future patterns of urban formation in east coastal China.

The lower Yangzi delta and Kunshan: the fringe to the fore

For the purpose of this chapter the lower Yangzi delta is defined as including the eight prefectural divisions of Suzhou, Wuxi, Changzhou, Zhenjiang, Nanjing, Yangzhou, Taizhou and Nantong adjacent to the Yangzi River in southern Jiangsu Province and the Shanghai municipal region. Figure 8.1 illustrates the location of the nine major cities and 42 county-level administrations that comprise the lower Yangzi delta in 1998.

It is the southern Jiangsu region of the lower Yangzi delta (often referred to as Sunan) wherein the initial spatial economic transformation from the early 1980s to 1998 was most dramatically demonstrated. The clearest indication of this transformation can be seen when passing through the delta's countryside. Infused into the agricultural landscapes, among the dense clusters of rural settlements and crop production, were tens of thousands of industrial enterprises. "Rural" is defined here initially as areas that were administratively classified below the county level including towns (*zhen*), townships (*xiang*) and villages (*cun*). County-level administrative seats, usually large towns (*xianshu zhen*) or small cities (*xian cheng*) were excluded for the purposes of this analysis. Meanwhile, for the period to 1998, the term "rural industry" refers to industrial enterprises owned and operated at or below the level of towns, townships and villages.

Table 8.1 positions the 54,645 square kilometers of the lower Yangzi delta in a national context in the late 1990s as the most important economic region in China. Nearly 52 million people – 4.19 percent of the national total – lived here in 1997, on only 0.57 percent of China's territory, making the delta one of the most densely populated contiguous concentrations of people in Asia. It generated 11.11 percent of China's gross domestic product in 1997, and 4.66 percent of total agricultural output. However, the delta's most significant contributions to the national economy at that time were in terms of industrial production. Nearly 14 percent of China's industrial output was concentrated here in 1997. The relative importance to China of industrial output in the lower Yangzi delta was almost four times its population and 29 times its area. Even more noteworthy was that nearly 50 percent of industrial output in the delta in 1997 was generated by rural enterprises, accounting for well over one-fifth of the nation's total rural industrial output. The 1980–97 average annual growth rates in agri-

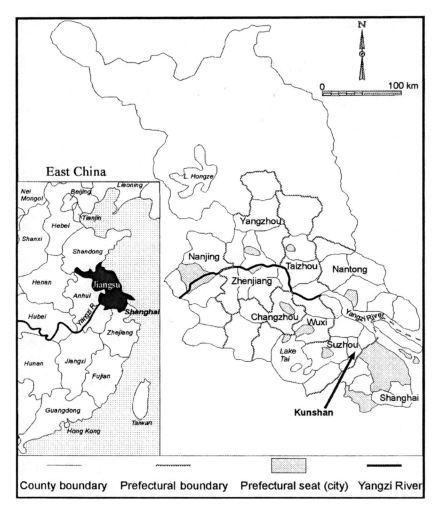

Figure 8.1 East China, the lower Yangzi delta and Kunshan, 1998 (source: Adapted from Marton (2000), p. 4).

cultural output (7.6 percent), industrial output (20.6 percent) and rural industrial output (29.3 percent) shown at the bottom of Table 8.1 were also substantial. These latter figures refer to all of Jiangsu Province excluding Shanghai, and should be considered the minimum average values for the region of the lower Yangzi delta within southern Jiangsu. The average annual growth rates in Shanghai over the same period were 3.7 percent for agriculture and 10.4 percent for industry, while for China the growth rates in agriculture and industry were 6.9 percent and 15.8 percent, respectively over the same period.[8]

Table 8.1 The lower Yangzi delta in China, 1997

Area (km²)	54,645
Share of national area (%)	0.57
Population (millions)	51.75
Share of national population (%)	4.19
Average population density (people/km²)	947
Gross domestic product (GDP) (billion RMBᵃ)	83,1.05
Share of national GDP (%)	11.11
Gross value of agricultural output (GVAO) (billion RMBᵃ)	114.65
Share of national GVAO (%)	4.66
Gross value of industrial output (GVIO) (billion RMBᵃ)	1,563.86
Share of national GVIO (%)	13.75
Rural GVIO (billion RMBᵃ)	815.49
Share of national GVIO (%)	22.61
1981–97 Average annual growth in GVAOᵇ (%)	7.6
1981–97 Average annual growth in GVIOᵇ (%)	20.6
1981–97 Average annual growth in rural GVIOᵇ (%)	29.3

Sources: adapted from Marton (2000), p. 7.

Notes
a US$ 1 = RMB8.3 (midpoint in 1997).
b figures here are for Jiangsu Province.

These impressive values for output and growth of rural industry in the lower Yangzi delta provide a context and baseline for understanding more recent spatial economic restructuring and urban transformation in this region.

Changing patterns and processes of urbanization and economic activity: a case study of Kunshan

The institutional dimensions of this restructuring will be explored in a detailed case study of Kunshan, a county-level municipality (sometimes city) (*xianji shi*) located in southern Jiangsu Province adjacent to the Shanghai municipal region (see Figure 8.1). The first part of this case study reviews the period of restructuring in Kunshan from 1978 up to 1998.[9] The second part undertakes a preliminary analysis of key changes in Kunshan since 1998 up to the end of 2005.

Rural agglomeration triumphant 1978–98

The centre of Kunshan is located 55 kilometers from downtown Shanghai and 36 kilometers from the city of Suzhou. In the early 1990s Kunshan comprised 20 towns and 466 villages. Kunshan covers an area of 865 square kilometers, 52.4 percent of which was arable land in 1998, with another 22.3 percent containing lakes, rivers and canals.[10] At the end of 1998 the officially registered local population was 587,509.[11] The average annual growth rate of industrial output in Kunshan between 1979 and 1996 was 32.7 percent.[12]

More detailed data for the growth of restructuring in Kunshan for the period 1988 to 1998 are presented in Part A of Table 8.2. Total GDP rose from RMB1.63 billion in 1988 to RMB15.05 billion in 1998. The share of GDP from industry showed a modest increase from 45.4 percent to 53 percent, while growth in the share of GDP from construction, transportation and commerce increased from 28.9 percent to 39.3 percent in Kunshan over the same period. Meanwhile, the proportion of GDP from agriculture declined significantly from 25.7 percent in 1988 to just 7.7 percent in 1998, although productivity on a per unit area basis and total yield continued to increase.

Comparable data presented in Part B of Table 8.2 show much less intensive, though still significant, restructuring for China as a whole over the same period. Perhaps the most noteworthy phenomenon was that nearly one-fifth of the nation's total GDP was still attributed to the agricultural sector as late as 1998. This was well over twice the proportion in Kunshan, which sits in the heart of one of the nation's most productive agricultural regions. Moreover, while the importance of agricultural production has not diminished in terms of the output of staple grains, new roles in industrial production and other non-agricultural activities have emerged that create locally specific opportunities for accumulation making rural areas the focus for socio-economic transformation. The unit area yield of stable grains in Kunshan, for example, was 7,000 kilograms per hectare in 1996, 56 percent more than the national average at the time. Per capita GDP in Kunshan in 1998 was RMB25,625, the fourth highest in Jiangsu Province behind three other

Table 8.2 GDP and sectoral distribution: Kunshan and China, 1988–98 (selected years, billion RMB (current values for the year shown))

Year	Total (%)	Agriculture (%)	Industry (%)	Other[a] (%)
Part A: Kunshan				
1988	1.63 (100)	0.42 (25.7)	0.74 (45.4)	0.47 (28.9)
1991	2.44 (100)	0.46 (18.9)	1.36 (55.7)	0.62 (25.4)
1993	6.04 (100)	0.58 (9.6)	3.13 (51.8)	2.33 (38.6)
1996	11.43 (100)	1.15 (10.0)	6.10 (53.4)	4.18 (36.6)
1998	15.05 (100)	1.16 (7.7)	7.98 (53.0)	5.91 (39.3)
Part B: China				
1988	1,492.83 (100)	383.10 (25.7)	577.72 (38.7)	532.01 (35.6)
1991	2,161.78 (100)	528.86 (24.5)	808.71 (37.4)	824.21 (38.1)
1993	3,463.44 (100)	688.21 (19.9)	1,414.38 (40.8)	1,360.85 (39.3)
1996	6,788.46 (100)	1,384.42 (20.4)	2,908.26 (42.8)	2,495.78 (36.8)
1998	7,955.30 (100)	1,429.90 (18.0)	3,354.10 (42.2)	3,171.30 (39.8)

Sources: Adapted from Marton (2000), p. 88.

Note
a includes construction, transportation and commerce.

areas in Suzhou and Wuxi, and six to ten times larger than the 17 least developed counties in the province.[13] The gross value of agricultural and industrial output per-capita in Kunshan in 1998 was RMB 55,969, fifth highest in Jiangsu and six to ten times that of the fifteen least developed countries in the province.[14]

However, the rapid growth of industrial activity in Kunshan during this period neither required, nor resulted, in a commensurate shift in residential urbanization. That is not to say that there was little or no mobility of local labor and population. In fact, significant proportions of the officially designated peasant population either resided in or commuted on a daily basis to work in or near the town centers resulting in an *in situ* shift of rural labor into non-agricultural activities. According to the official statistical classification, 20.2 percent of the population in Kunshan in 1992 was considered non-agricultural (*fei nongye renkou*).[15] This legal administrative designation concealed the numbers actually residing in the built-up town centers, but it did provide a useful baseline. Combined with data provided by informants, it is possible to estimate an adjusted level of urbanization for all of China, although the same is much more difficult for small jurisdictions such as Kunshan.[16] Data in the 1990 gazetteer does suggest, however, that Kunshan was probably about 12 to 15 percent urbanized on the eve of reforms in the late 1970s.[17] While the level of urbanization in Kunshan has increased from perhaps 12 to 30 percent in the first 20 years of reform from 1978, it is important to clarify the nature of this transition. First, approximately 60 to 70 percent of the urban population in Kunshan in 1996 resided in 19 small towns outside the largest central urban settlement. Second, from 1978 to 1996 these small towns, which grew on average from about 2,000 to 5,000 people, accounted for nearly 90 percent of the growth in Kunshan's "urban" population over the same period.[18] The level of urbanization, its rate of increase and the structure of urban settlement in Kunshan strongly suggest that rapid industrial growth here has not resulted in urban concentration during this period. This finding becomes even more significant when we consider that the 1998 per capita gross value of industrial output in Kunshan (RMB51,945) and per capita GDP (RMB25,675) were both substantially larger than the figures for Suzhou City (RMB42,206 and RMB18,426 respectively), which was at least 90 percent urbanized at the time![19]

It is striking that the lower Yangzi delta could retain its national prominence as China's premier agricultural producer region, while at the same time undergoing rapid industrial growth. While cities are commonly viewed as the nexus of economic growth, regional development in the delta over the 20 year period to 1998 appears to have been more complex than merely in terms of its purported dependence upon urban centered forces vigorously proposed by some.[20] The critical parameters and the vitality of regional development in the lower Yangzi delta were in fact centered within a multitude of "rural" localities, fundamentally challenging the conventionally perceived role of large cities. It would seem there are aspects of the delta's spatial economic patterns that are not fully captured in the conventional explanations of the dynamics of regional industrial expansion and urbanization.

One of the key practical outcomes in the 20 year period to 1998 has been the spatial proliferation of non-agricultural enterprises into all corners of the countryside. Motivated by the desire to generate extra budgetary revenues, every town and village administration in Kunshan sought to establish their own enterprises leading to the scattering of factories across local town and village jurisdictions. While a number of these enterprises were located in or near the town seats, most were built among the rice paddies, wheat fields and canola crops (see Plates 8.1 and 8.2). The locational distribution of town and village enterprises was closely linked to the structure of ownership and the territorial extent of the respective administrative jurisdictions. The most important group of enterprises in Kunshan included town and village level industries that together comprised 69.8 percent of the 2,205 industrial enterprises and 58.5 percent of the gross value of industrial output in 1996. Town and village level enterprises included collectives (396), village factories (745), domestic joint ventures and cooperatives (252) and Sino-foreign joint ventures (147) scattered throughout rural Kunshan. Of the 132 wholly foreign-owned industrial enterprises, which accounted for 31.0 percent of gross output value in 1996, 91 were located in the special economic and technological development zone just east of Yushan Town (see Figure 8.2). The 59 Kunshan-level state-owned enterprises in 1996 were located in or near the built-up core of Yushan, throughout several towns, and in the Red Flag Industrial Area. Most of the 470 private enterprises were established in Kunshan's 466 villages. Kunshan had four joint stock enterprises in 1996. These figures do not include 997 small scale household-based individual industrial enterprises that were listed separated in the official statistics at the time.[21]

Plate 8.1 Have your factory built in a day, rural Kunshan.

Plate 8.2 The new factory erected within a few weeks, rural Kunshan.

In addition to the development of broadly similar industrial structures across the region, this spontaneous and haphazard growth created enormous problems related to the provision of infrastructure, duplication and the waste of capital and land. Allusions to such conditions were captured in the local slogan: *cun cun dianhuo, chu chu maoyan* (in every village fires stir, and everywhere is belching smoke).[22] While such industrial development was "comprehensive" and relatively successful at the local scale, in regional terms (county level and higher) it remained "irrational" and spatially scattered. In conceptual terms, the diverse structure and spatial proliferation of industrial activities in Kunshan strongly suggested that the transformation observed here occurred largely as a response to intensely localized development imperatives. The result was a dense mixture of residential, industrial and agricultural land uses.

This is well illustrated in an examination of Dianshanhu town located in the southeastern most part of Kunshan well away from the administrative center of Yushan (see Figure 8.2).[23] The town borders Shanghai to the east and south and has nearly 25 kilometers of shoreline along Dianshan Lake from which it derives its name. In 1996 the registered local population of Dianshanhu was just under 27,000 residing in just over 8,000 households with approximately 4,500 residing in the town seat and the rest in small towns and villages.[24] Table 8.3 summarizes the data for rural industrial enterprises in the period between 1989 and 1996.

Total industrial output from these rural enterprises in Dianshanhu grew by an annual average of 33.5 percent over the seven years to 1996. Meanwhile, the value of exports from these enterprises listed at the bottom of Table 8.3 also grew at an astonishing rate. This is consistent with the importance of the

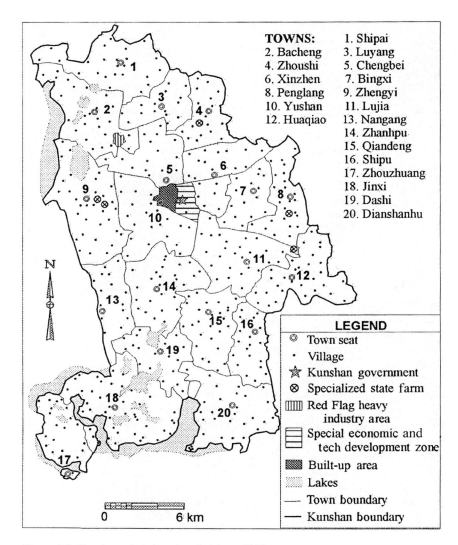

TOWNS:
1. Shipai
2. Bacheng   3. Luyang
4. Zhoushi   5. Chengbei
6. Xinzhen   7. Bingxi
8. Penglang   9. Zhengyi
10. Yushan   11. Lujia
12. Huaqiao   13. Nangang
                14. Zhanhpu
                15. Qiandeng
                16. Shipu
                17. Zhouzhuang
                18. Jinxi
                19. Dashi
                20. Dianshanhu

LEGEND

◎ Town seat
•   Village
☆ Kunshan government
⊗ Specialized state farm
▥ Red Flag heavy
     industry area
▤ Special economic and
     tech development zone
▩ Built-up area
░ Lakes
— Town boundary
— Kunshan boundary

0   6 km

Figure 8.2 Kunshan administrative divisions, 1998.

national level figures referred to earlier. What, if any impact did this growing internationalization of local enterprises have upon their spatial distribution and organization at the time?

Figure 8.3 illustrates the spatial distribution of industrial enterprises across Dianshanhu town in 1997. The proliferation of enterprises into all corners of the town by the late 1990s is clear. This is very much in spite of localized attempts to encourage the relocation of enterprises to take advantage of perceived opportunities of agglomeration and economies of scale. Under the direction of

Table 8.3 Dianshanhu town, Kunshan, rural enterprises, 1989–96

	1989	1990	1991	1992	1993	1994	1995	1996
TVEs (#)	138	127	102	83	81	79	55	57
Employees (#)	5,735	5,115	5,968	6,140	6,840	5,920	5,382	5,325
GVIO[a] (10^6 RMB)[b]	140.9	168.3	232.3	551.2	903.3	965.6	817.2[c] (584.1)	566.2
Exports (10^6 RMB)[d]	17.0	41.4	73.9	164.7	318.6	437.9	563.7	379.0

Sources: Adapted from Marton (2002), p. 32.

Notes
a gross value of industrial output.
b figures here are in 1990 constant prices.
c the method of calculating output changed in 1995. The amount in brackets and for the subsequent year indicates the total as calculated by the new method.
d figures here are in current prices for the year shown.

county-level officials, Dianshanhu had by 1997 implemented other measures to "force" changes in the management of local enterprises by renegotiating their links to local governments and experimenting with new types of ownership and corporate groupings.[25] Along with the reorganization and reduction of local government departments that was in full swing at the time, policies for a "unified land system" (*yi tian zhi*) were also introduced focusing on the development of specialized zones – especially among the small towns – to capture economies of scale at the local level.

One such town level special zone in Dianshanhu was a designated industrial development area located about a kilometer to the west of the town seat that was being heavily promoted by local officials. One of the few resident enterprises in the zone was a very large packaging and printing concern formerly based in one of the nearby villages. The general manager extolled the virtues of the enterprise's location within the zone and the various management and ownership changes linked to the desire to export to international markets. Interestingly, when pressed privately about enterprise expansion plans he admitted that local government "interference" was still a problem and that the new factory would be built back in the "home" village.[26] Thus, while local actors were quite aware of the pressures associated with internationalization, practical responses in the mid to late 1990s were still clearly being mediated by other exigencies and opportunities at the local level. The proliferation of successful and highly competitive enterprises seen in Dianshanhu was typical of Kunshan and characteristic of the wider lower Yangzi delta region away from the big cities.

This pattern is confirmed by the data presented in Table 8.4, which provides an indication of the local and relative value of economic activity across the six county-level units and one city in Suzhou Prefecture. While absolute values of industrial output were comparable to the city of Suzhou, average per capita industrial output in the county-level units was higher. Assuming that the figures were distorted somewhat by the dominance of relatively inefficient state-owned

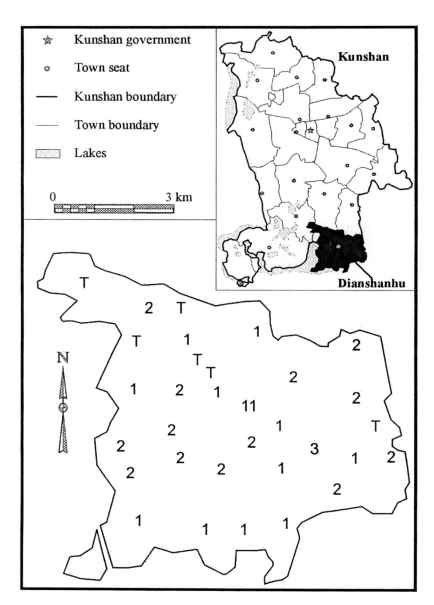

Figure 8.3 Location of rural enterprises: Dianshanhu town, Kunshan, 1996 (source: adapted from Marton (2000), p. 143).

Note
Numerals refer to the number of enterprises and their location. "T" refers to the town level enterprises located outside the town seat.

Table 8.4 Industry and GDP by region: Suzhou and Shanghai, 1998

Location	GVIO[a] (billion RMB)	Per-capita GVIO (RMB × 1,000)	Per-capita GDP (RMB × 1,000)	Per-worker GDP (RMB × 1,000)
Suzhou City	45.48	42.21	18.42	36.69
Kunshan	30.52	51.95	25.68	44.18
Changshu	40.78	39.14	19.70	34.21
Zhangjiagang	47.21	55.28	27.53	58.61
Taicang	24.04	53.45	26.81	48.96
Wuxian	38.07	39.24	16.99	32.19
Wujiang	35.51	45.93	28.60	40.43
Average for non-urban Suzhou	N/A	46.22	22.49	41.56
Shanghai[b]	584.78	39.94	25.19	55.05

Sources: Adapted from Marton (2002), p. 31.

Notes
a Gross value of industrial output.
b Figures here are for the entire municipal region including both urban districts and suburban counties.

enterprises in urban areas at the time, we might expect per capita and per worker gross domestic product to show the city in a more favorable light. This is not the case. Indeed, average values of GDP per worker and per capita for the county-level units are 13 and 22 percent higher than for the city of Suzhou. Figures for the city of Shanghai are provided for comparison. The key point here is that even at the point when globalizing influences were beginning to take hold there was still apparently a lot of relatively efficient economic activity occurring across rural regions outside big cities. Moreover, it is important to recall that this activity exists in a region where unit area yields of staple grains such as rice are among the highest in China. The next section examines the most recent phase of urban development and transformation in Kunshan from 1998.

Rural agglomeration to urban agglomeration post 1998

Perhaps the clearest spatial manifestation of rural agglomeration in Kunshan was the emergence of a large number of special zones and industrial parks (Figure 8.4).[27] Many of the 28 special zones in Kunshan illustrated in Figure 8.4 were a response to local efforts to take advantage of real or perceived benefits. However, the planned or desirable directions of developments in these zones revealed a profound lack of specialization and other problems associated with the dramatic growth in the number of such zones and their spatial proliferation into productive agricultural land. By the end of 1997 virtually every town in the lower Yangzi delta had some sort of a special development zone designed to attract foreign and domestic investment. Within Kunshan itself at least half of the 466 villages at the time also had areas considered as special development districts. Within the farming sector in Kunshan, the general response to the

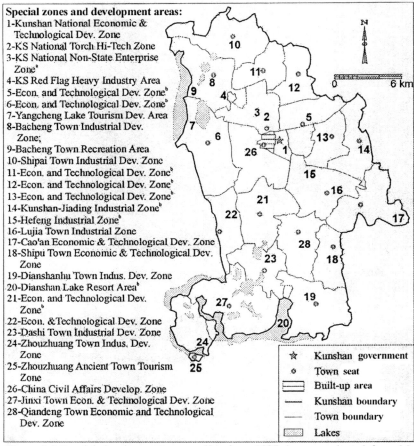

Special zones and development areas:
1-Kunshan National Economic &
  Technological Dev. Zone
2-KS National Torch Hi-Tech Zone
3-KS National Non-State Enterprise
  Zone[a]
4-KS Red Flag Heavy Industry Area
5-Econ. and Technological Dev. Zone[b]
6-Econ. and Technological Dev. Zone[b]
7-Yangcheng Lake Tourism Dev. Area
8-Bacheng Town Industrial Dev.
  Zone;
9-Bacheng Town Recreation Area
10-Shipai Town Industrial Dev. Zone
11-Econ. and Technological Dev. Zone[b]
12-Econ. and Technological Dev. Zone[b]
13-Econ. and Technological Dev. Zone[b]
14-Kunshan-Jiading Industrial Zone[b]
15-Hefeng Industrial Zone[b]
16-Lujia Town Industrial Zone
17-Cao'an Economic & Technological Dev. Zone
18-Shipu Town Economic & Technological Dev.
  Zone
19-Dianshanhu Town Indus. Dev. Zone
20-Dianshan Lake Resort Area[b]
21-Econ. and Technological Dev.
  Zone[b]
22-Econ. & Technological Dev. Zone
23-Dashi Town Industrial Dev. Zone
24-Zhouzhuang Town Indus. Dev.
  Zone
25-Zhouzhuang Ancient Town Tourism
  Zone
26-China Civil Affairs Develop. Zone
27-Jinxi Town Econ. & Technological Dev. Zone
28-Qiandeng Town Economic and Technological
  Dev. Zone

☆   Kunshan government
◊   Town seat
▤   Built-up area
—   Kunshan boundary
—   Town boundary
▨   Lakes

Figure 8.4 Special development zones: Kunshan, 1997 (source: adapted from Marton
(2000), p.152).

Notes
a. While this zone was spatially distinct, administratively it was part of the National Torch High
Technology Zone. b. These zones were affiliated (*peitao*) with the Kunshan National Economic and
Technological Development Zone, although they were spatially distinct and managed by the respective town level bureaucracies.

emergence of large numbers of non-agricultural enterprises was characterized by
the dual processes of preservation and specialization of agricultural land. Taken
together, these outcomes suggested that there was a deliberate effort to create
concentrations of particular types of land use captured in the notion of rural
agglomeration. However, in practice such efforts remained intensely localized as
virtually every administrative jurisdiction endeavored to construct its own recre-
ational, commercial and industrial space (see Figure 8.4).

In the period since 1998 there has been a radical change in the spatial pattern

Plate 8.3 Beginning of a new "special development zone," rural Kunshan.

Plate 8.4 The new zone open for business just a few months later.

of industrialization in Kunshan. First, there has been a trend towards economic specialization that seeks to reposition the profile of industrialization to develop and enhance local comparative advantages. This process of repositioning is discussed in more detail below. Second, there has also been a deliberate and sometimes highly controversial process to significantly reconfigure administrative boundaries and a commensurate reconstitution of institutional frameworks and bureaucratic responsibility. By the early 2000s in Kunshan these simultaneous processes revolved around development and expansion of the State Council sanctioned special economic and technological development zone (*kaifaqu*) pivoting on the central town and government seat of Yushan (item 1 on Figure 8.4; see also Figure 8.2). It is proposed here that the contours of this repositioning and administrative reconfiguration in Kunshan constitute a new urban form that seeks to rationalize agglomeration and land use at a scale rather larger and spatially more centralized than in the period prior to 1998, which has been characterized as rural agglomeration.

In terms of repositioning, Kunshan has had some success since 2000 in adopting a more deliberate strategy of functional specialization to develop and upgrade in key targeted industrial sectors – most notably IT along with other "pillar" industries of high precision machinery, refined chemicals and the production of household goods.[28] Several sources confirm that this strategy explicitly sought to move away from the duplication of investment into similar industries in adjacent regions in southern Jiangsu and Shanghai.[29] This appears to be part of deliberate policy on the part of Kunshan to develop an industrial strategy that, rather than compete with other industrial centers in the lower Yangzi such as Shanghai, is designed to complement and position the municipality in the evolving industrial structure of the region. By 2004 Kunshan city had become one of the major centers in China and, globally, for the production of information technology related output. At this time the estimated investment in this sector amounted to RMB42.2 billion (approximately US$5 billion) in more than 250 enterprises, half of which was concentrated in the *kaifaqu* in Kunshan.[30]

Furthermore, a key characteristic of the shifting industrial profile in Kunshan was the emergence of a large number of enterprises involved in the production of highly sophisticated inputs for these industrial processes. For example, in 2000 Praxair (Kunshan), a branch of the largest industrial gas supplier in North and South America, inaugurated its specialty gases plant in the Kunshan *kaifaqu* to provide specialty gases to local semi-conductor plants. The plant is a hub for supplying technology, customer service and other products to the micro-electronic industry.[31] A similar pattern of investment and location is also exhibited in other product sectors. In November 2004, Cooper Standard Automotive, a global supplier of high-tech control systems, announced that it had begun operations in the Kunshan *kaifaqu* to supply both Chinese and global manufacturers. The announcement emphasized that "the Kunshan location was chosen for its excellent logistics, the availability of qualified materials suppliers, as well as a pool of readily available workers."[32] While much of this investment was focused on the main State Council sanctioned *kaifaqu*, there was also a continuing development of smaller specialist industrial clusters in various towns in Kunshan. The emergence of such clustering is significant throughout this part of the lower Yangzi delta and has implications for the transforming urban industrial complex. Local planning

Plate 8.5 New high-tech factories and other buildings in the *kaifaqu*, Kunshan.

officials, for example, also confirmed that over 50 percent of the material and component inputs for enterprises in Kunshan were sourced from within the six county-level units of Suzhou Prefecture.[33]

Kunshan has become a favored location for foreign investment, which has been driving an import/export volume comprising 1.3 percent of China's total by 2004.[34] By early 2006, Kunshan accommodated 4,200 companies from 50 countries and regions.[35] Among them, the Taiwanese have become the largest group of foreign investors in Kunshan since the late 1990s. As of early 2006 Kunshan had attracted more than 11 percent of total accumulated Taiwanese investment in the mainland.[36] Large Taiwanese companies such as Uni-President, Cheng Shin Tire, Compal, Giant Group and Gloat Glass, and six of Taiwan's top ten laptop producers, have made major investments. There is now a sizable Taiwanese population estimated at between 30,000–40,000 in 2006 living in Kunshan, most of them concentrated in the vicinity of their company facilities in and near the main *kaifaqu*.[37] Taiwanese schools and shopping malls are being constructed to service this population and there is a very active Taiwanese business association with extremely close relations with the local government. Indeed, networks established since the late 1990s along with linguistic and cultural affinities have "helped to connect Taiwanese investors to Jiangsu and to make Jiangsu a favorable host location for Taiwanese investment."[38] In addition, both the provincial and Suzhou administrations have encouraged the Kunshan government actively to seek Taiwanese investment.

Deliberately focusing on investments in so-called pillar industries and the increasing internationalization of the local economy in Kunshan and elsewhere in the lower Yangzi delta has necessarily raised the importance of a host of other key factors that impact urban formation in such regions. The desire to upgrade into higher technology and high precision industrial sectors requires greater attention to issues of quality control in production, environmental quality and efficiency. WTO regimes and increasing integration into international trading systems also focuses attention on these issues. Evidence from Kunshan suggests that part of the response to these increasing pressures has been to leverage the restructuring of economic space by reconfiguring local political and administrative space. In practical terms in Kunshan since 2000 there has been a dramatic redrawing of town boundaries and administrative jurisdiction, including significant changes to the territorial extent of the central town of Yushan and the main *kaifaqu*.

The outcomes of this radical reclassification and reorganization of administrative jurisdiction in Kunshan are illustrated in Figure 8.5. Across Kunshan as a whole, the key change involved the amalgamation of 20 town administrations in 1999 to 15 by the end of 2001 and to just ten by 2005. There has also been a commensurate reduction in the number of village level administrations from 466 in 1997 to just 184 by 2005. Most villages were absorbed into town level administrations and reconstituted as "social areas" (*shequ*) within neighborhood committees, thereby losing their relative independence. The urban built-up area of Yushan town, the administrative seat of Kunshan, expanded from an area of five square kilometers in the early 1990s to just over 13 square kilometers by 2000.[39] Meanwhile, changes in administrative boundaries have resulted in the area of the entire central town of Yushan expanding from 54 square kilometers prior to 2003 to just over 116 square kilometers by the end of 2005.[40] The expanded jurisdiction has incorporated parts of other former towns, several villages near the centre of Kunshan that are now urban "neighborhoods" and parts of the main *kaifaqu* and "branch" zones (*peiqu*) in adjacent town jurisdictions that abutted the main zone. The *kaifaqu* itself, which is listed as a separate entity in the statistical yearbooks, has also undergone major changes in territorial extent and jurisdiction. The *kaifaqu* was originally established in 1984 on a 6.18 square kilometer parcel just to the east of Yushan town. By mid-1993, in the year following formal national designation by the State Council, the zone had slowly expanded to ten square kilometers, but then quickly doubled to 20 square kilometers by the end of 1995. By 2004 the administrative area of the *kaifaqu* had expanded to 57.34 square kilometers, expanding further still to 92.67 square kilometers by the end of 2005.[41] More importantly, the relatively autonomous management of the *kaifaqu* falls under the authority of the Kunshan municipal government, which explains why its boundaries (and administrative jurisdiction) also extend into and superseded town administrations (see Figure 8.5).[42] Combined with the reconfiguration and consolidation of town administrations, this has resulted in a substantial shift in political, economic and planning authority to the administrative and geographic – though largely redefined – centre of Kunshan.

The effects of this repositioning and administrative restructuring on the

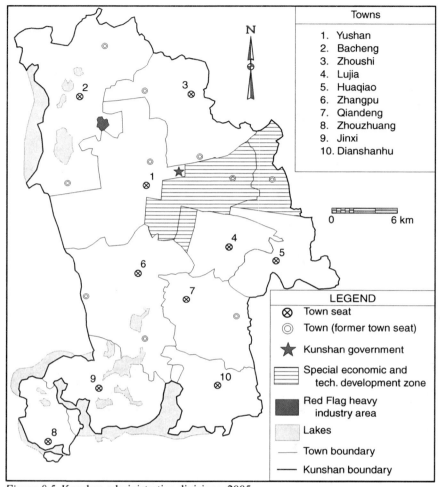

Towns

1. Yushan
2. Bacheng
3. Zhoushi
4. Lujia
5. Huaqiao
6. Zhangpu
7. Qiandeng
8. Zhouzhuang
9. Jinxi
10. Dianshanhu

0   6 km

LEGEND

⊗   Town seat
◎   Town (former town seat)
★   Kunshan government
     Special economic and
     tech. development zone
     Red Flag heavy
     industry area
     Lakes
──   Town boundary
──   Kunshan boundary

Figure 8.5 Kunshan administrative divisions, 2005.

urbanization of Kunshan since 1998 have been considerable. While, much of
the earlier industrialization that proliferated into towns and villages remains
and continues to expand, these more recent circumstances have enhanced the
development of a thriving industrial area in and around the centre of Kunshan
pivoting on Yushan town and the *kaifaqu* (see Figure 8.5). In terms of the residential location of population, estimates discussed earlier suggested that
Kunshan was about 12 to 15 percent urbanized at the beginning of the reform
period in the late 1970s. By the late 1990s this level of urbanization had
increased to perhaps 30 percent among the registered local population of about
580,000. However, 90 percent of the growth in urban population between 1978

and 1996 occurred in the 19 small towns away from the centre of Kunshan, where approximately 70 percent of the urban population resided at the end of this period (see Figure 8.2).[43] By the end of 2005 the profile of urban population had shifted dramatically. Across Kunshan as a whole the total registered local population had grown to more than 654,000, of whom at least 56 percent resided in urban built-up areas. Moreover, by 2005 nearly 69 percent of all this urban population resided within Yushan town and the *kaifaqu* (see Figure 8.5). If the adjacent towns of Lujia, Huaqiao and Zhoushi are included, this figure rises to more than 77 percent.[44] While part of this shift may be attributed to the redrawing of administrative boundaries and the reclassification of household registration, it is quite clear that there has also been some concentration of the urban population in and around central Kunshan. This rapid growth of the urban core has also benefited from improvements in urban infrastructure and other components of the urban environment as the city administration has sought to make Kunshan a clean and livable environment.

The concentration of urban population is mirrored in similar trends in the location of industrial enterprises and the large number of migrants that have moved into Kunshan. While the total value of industrial output has continued its rapid growth since 1998, there has also been a growing concentration of the proportion of industrial production located in central Kunshan. In 1998 approximately 60 percent of the total value of industrial output in Kunshan was attributed to township and village level enterprises located away from the built-up core of Yushan and the *kaifaqu*.[45] By the end of 2005, enterprises located in Yushan and the *kaifaqu* accounted for just over 72 percent of total industrial output by value. As with the population figures described above, if the adjacent towns of Lujia, Huaqiao and Zhoushi are included (see Figure 8.5), this figure rises to more than 84 percent.[46] These industrial developments have also created a large demand for labor that has led to substantial growth in the number of migrants (*wailai renkou*) in Kunshan.[47] According to the official statistics the number of residents from outside Kunshan numbered nearly 690,000. Well informed local informants suggest that the actual number is probably well over 800,000, not counting the several tens of thousands of foreigners – most of whom are Taiwanese.[48] Although figures for migrant residents were not officially reported in the statistical yearbooks before 2004, figures from other sources indicated there were already 400,000 migrants in Kunshan by early 2003.[49] Approximately 50 percent of these migrants live within central Yushan town and the expanded administrative jurisdiction of the *kaifaqu*, together comprising 23 percent of the total land area of Kunshan, with the remainder distributed across the other nine towns.

The processes and patterns of this urban formation in Kunshan are different from the conventional agglomeration and spread of the built-up area of large cities like Shanghai. If we assume broadly similar patterns of spatial economic transformation across the now 24 other county-level units in southern Jiangsu, including the concentration of population and industrial activities into and around central towns, its significance in relation to the changes in large cities nearby is clear.[50] What this means for reconceptualizing a "new model of urbanization" and urban transition in China's mega-urban regions is explored in the final section of this chapter.

Conclusion

This case study of Kunshan and the lower Yangzi delta raises many questions concerning the production of urban space in China. It would appear that the processes and mechanisms of "bureaucratic entrepreneurialism," that in the 1980s were focused on rural towns and villages, have been repositioned in an assemblage of new urban administrative jurisdictions in the lower Yangzi delta. The concept of the *urban echo* that was introduced in the title of this chapter is helpful in conceptualizing the resulting shift in the patterns and processes of this transition. The term is derived from local officials' perception of the need to develop strategies that create a positive "echo" of developments in Shanghai.[51] The Chinese term urban "echo" (*huying gouxiang*) carries the meaning of a positive mutual echo of the overall concept or "plot" of regional development. This chapter goes a step further to suggest that specific locally driven development strategies and policies – economic repositioning and political/administrative restructuring – and how they manifest themselves in spatial terms, explicitly seek to globalize places like Kunshan by leap-frogging places like Shanghai and Pudong by directly mobilizing international investment, production linkages and commodity chains. Parallel developments in much larger urban centers such as Shanghai are taken as opportunities in the case of places like Kunshan to revise and redirect local and foreign investment strategies, both to complement and leap-frog the bigger urban centers. From this perspective, local forces are seen as continuing to play a critically important role in regional and urban development in concert with growing international forces that have accelerated global interactions and interrelationships in places like Kunshan.

However, the urban echo concept is not merely the reflecting back of something originating in the cosmopolitan centers such as Shanghai. Nor is it an attempt to capture the overflow of investment from Shanghai and Pudong. Much of the recent investment in Shanghai in recent years has been in services while in southern Jiangsu the focus has been on manufacturing and industry – which partly explains why the region of Suzhou, including Kunshan, has received more foreign direct investment in value terms than Shanghai in recent years. The success of such areas in the lower Yangzi delta arises from deliberate local strategies to develop and respond to comparative advantages that seek to reposition places like Kunshan within wider regional and international spatial economic regimes.

The circumstances reviewed in this chapter confirm that the state-led urbanization project in Kunshan has had a dramatic impact on urban formation. These phenomena also present a challenge to the persistent idea that it is the location of such places on the perceived "urban margins" of large cities like Shanghai that explains the patterns and processes of spatial change in the lower Yangzi delta.

What is also clear is that the former pragmatic and largely endogenously driven "go it alone" strategies, which emphasized a narrow local view, have yielded to a desire to take advantage of increasing international opportunities at all administrative levels. As a result the transactional environment, as a form of social capital operating at the local level, has been changed over the seven or eight years to 2005, both by the extension of "urban" administrative jurisdictions into adjacent rural industrial spaces, and the reorganization and consolidation of town level administrations. The result has been an increase in functional specialization at the local level and some sense of spatial economic concentration despite the continuing growth of industrial activity in rural areas.

With Shanghai booming as the "dragon head" of the lower Yangzi delta it has been experiencing fast growth in selected manufacturing sectors and services, much of it located in a restructured urban core and in the immediate margins of these areas, such as the Pudong New Area. Here, there has been a deliberate comprehensive consolidation and professionalization of urban planning and governance applied to a large area with the blessing of the Shanghai municipal authorities and sanctioned by China's State Council.[52] This is distinguished from the often messy and largely informal bargaining between local actors across different administrative jurisdictions over smaller scale bureaucratic and economic space, which has characterized regional and urban development in the lower Yangzi delta – at least up till the late 1990s. This scaling down of the "state machine" over the 1990s in places like Kunshan resulted in complicated, uneven and spatially dispersed patterns of economic management and mixed land use.[53] Similar to the framework implemented in Pudong described above, the authorities in Kunshan have, since 1998, sought to break down and reconfigure the established administrative and bureaucratic hierarchies to invoke new planning and governance regimes less attached to small scale territorial jurisdiction. For example, through local branches of the Land Resources Management Bureau, all county-level units are now required to produce comprehensive plans that must, among other things, endeavour to rationalize patterns of industrial and agricultural land use.[54] Given the strong central government mandate behind this initiative, Kunshan has used these planning efforts to facilitate implementation of a range of measures to radically reorientate and reconfigure local administrative jurisdiction and bureaucratic space.

The key objective of these measures has been to create a rather less horizontal (often uncooperative) administrative and decision-making environment to "rationalize" the behavior of "bureaucratic entrepreneurs." While the short term impact on the spatial proliferation of non-agricultural enterprises and industrial location is still a work in progress, the overall aim in Kunshan is clear. Four main trends can be identified.

1   A shift away from a highly competitive "anything goes" approach to basic development, towards a "functional development" that seeks to fit into niches in the wider regional space economy especially in relation to Shanghai and Pudong.

2   A shift in the patterns of industrial activity away from the traditional Sunan model of disarticulated proliferation into the countryside to one based increasingly on industrial networks, and sub-contracting linkages. This does not necessarily imply intensive agglomeration, although there is evidence of this, but rather the creation of a kind of assemblage of connected urban spaces within the extended metropolitan region.
3   In practical terms these industrial strategies involve seeking investment in specific targeted sectors within planned project-driven initiatives.
4   Identifying and promoting investment in targeted sectors to orientate industrial production beyond regional and national markets to international markets.

It is possible to argue that key elements of the earlier phase of spatial economic development up to 1998 were a necessary precursor for these later developments. These circumstances have been leading more recently to an emerging extended metropolitan region that is beginning to develop industrial clusters and functional specialization between urban centers within the lower Yangzi delta. At the same time rural town and village level industrial production continues to be important, especially as it becomes increasingly linked to larger scale local enterprises. Thus, the urban echo in Kunshan is leading to a new urban formation through a process of localized urban agglomeration that is part of the wider set of process and mechanisms driving the emergence of mega-urban regions in China.

9 Divergent urbanization paths in the Shenyang–Dalian urban corridor, Liaoning Province

Introduction

In the late 1980s, McGee enlarged the Asian metropolitan region hypothesis by arguing that a new distinctive form of urban region was emerging in the margins of the city cores, the *desakota* region.[1] This work extended the concept of the metropolitan region to include a much greater spatial spread of urban activities into areas that were still characterized by rural activities. Research that built upon this idea revealed that many Asian extended metropolitan regions (EMRs) fitted this model, finding that they were typically large urbanizing regions, sometimes stretching over 100 or more kilometers and often located between and including two existing major urban centers. They are characterized by intense concentrations and flows of both people and commodities, highly mixed agricultural and non-agricultural activities, and an intense interaction between rural and urban areas.[2] In the early 1990s, a group of scholars conducted several case studies into Chinese EMRs, demonstrating the key features and dynamics of growth within them.[3] Wang's work during the 1990s identified the emergence of the Shenyang–Dalian (S–D) EMR as an urban corridor sharing many of the major characteristics of other Asian EMRs, including intensive rural–urban interaction and rapid development of non-agricultural sectors, not only in the margins of Shenyang and Dalian, but also the corridor between these two centers.[4]

However, since the mid-1990s two important processes have brought about radical changes to the economic patterns of the S–D EMR corridor. First, the reform of state-owned enterprises (SOEs) has dramatically reshaped this region. While other EMRs, especially in the Pearl River Delta and the lower Yangzi delta, have experienced rapid spatial reorganization resulting in more intensified rural–urban linkages, the S–D region's experience of SOE reform has led to unequal spatial economic development and rural–urban fragmentation in the corridor. While all parts of the S–D corridor have experienced economic problems as a result of the reform of SOEs, it is the northern node's urban cluster of cities based on Shenyang that experienced most economic problems. In the southern node of Dalian, EMR globalization has led to much more positive economic growth with high rates of foreign investment and successful adjustment to the decline in SOEs. These contrasting processes have led to an increasing divergence in the economic growth of the two urban poles of the S–D corridor and a breakdown in rural–urban integration in the region. This chapter focuses on how the S–D EMR has been transformed since the mid-1990s, reflecting the impact of social, economic and political processes and their effects on spatial patterns of the EMR. The first section of this chapter provides a background to the major social economic changes in Liaoning. The second section demonstrates the major transformations in the S–D region through the examination of the changes in rural and urban regions and changing rural–urban linkages. This is followed by a detailed discussion of a new spatial form of the S–D EMR. Finally this chapter concludes with the argument that economic reforms since the mid-1990s have impacted China's mega-urban regions in different ways, resulting in patterns of different regional restructuring leading to different spatial outcomes of transformation. It is argued that the SOE reform policies and different local government policies have affected different parts of the S–D region and explain the emergence of unique spatial patterns of urban transformation there. Thus, the patterns of urbanization in the S–D region support the argument that the urbanization process is experiencing different regional trajectories even within the coastal region, of which globalization has had the most impact.

Liaoning in trouble

Located in the southern part of northeast China, Liaoning Province and its major ports in the south are the only gateways for the largely landlocked northeast China. Liaoning is one of the key cradles of China's industrialization. It has been considered as one of China's most important industrial bases since the 1930s. Its economic profile and endowment of natural resources differ sharply from other mega-urban regions in China. For example, with limited natural resources, mega-urban regions such as Shanghai–Nanjing–Hangzhou, Guangzhou–Shenzhen and Beijing–Tianjin, act as reprocessing centers but crucially depend on the other provinces and international markets to supply raw materials. By contrast, Liaoning is the only industrialized region in coastal China with rich, natural mineral resources and its heavy industry (manufacturing and resource-based mining industry) is an important part of China's national economy.[5] For example, in 1978 Liaoning had the highest proportion of SOEs in industry units in China. This is important to the understanding of the economic change that has occurred since 1995.

The S–D corridor is located in the central and southern parts of the province. It is roughly 380 kilometers long and 100 kilometers wide and contains a large proportion of the main activities of the province's economic activity, foreign investment, population and large urban centers (see Figure 9.1). Of greatest significance is the fact that today, the S–D corridor contains China's largest heavy industrial centers. This manufacturing belt is located in the central part of the province, lying within a 60 kilometer diameter. It includes a number of heavy industrial cities, such as Shenyang (the capital city of the province and the

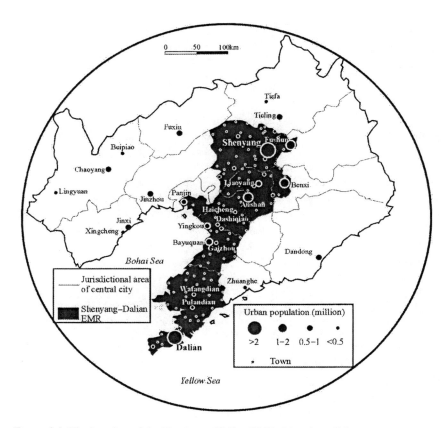

Figure 9.1 The location of the Shenyang–Dalian EMR, Liaoning, China.

major industrial city in China), the iron and steel city of Anshan, the coal mining city of Fushun and the coal and iron mining city of Benxi.[6] This belt also contains the iron-steel and petrol-chemical industrial city of Liaoyang and some industrial towns and districts. Chinese scholars refer to this belt as China's "Ruhr industrial zone." In the southern part of the S–D region, Dalian has become the most important port city in northeast China and produced the largest share of industrial output in Liaoning. For example, in 2004, 27.9 percent of urban industrial output in Liaoning was produced by Dalian city, compared to 21.6 percent by Shenyang city.

Liaoning's urbanization process and urban system are also very distinctive in China. In 2004, over 47 percent of its population was classified as an urban population, which was the highest among all of China's provinces, except the provincial level municipalities of Beijing, Shanghai and Tianjin. The S–D corridor is Liaoning's heartland – a centre of economic activity and of the population. The region has the highest concentration of large cities in China. For example, within 100 kilometers around the capital city of Shenyang in the centre of Liaoning Province, there are three large cities (Shenyang with 4.9 million population, Anshan with 1.4 million, Fushun with 1.3 million), two medium-sized cities (Benxi with 0.96 million population, Liaoyang with 0.71 million) and dozens of small cities and urban centers. In the southern part of S–D region, the urban system is dominated by the city of Dalian (with over two million urban population) and the rest of the urban centers include a dozen small cities and towns (see Figure 9.1).

The existence of these large cities in the S–D region makes Liaoning's urban system distinctive because it is dominated by large cities. For example, the urban population of those cities with a population greater than one million accounted for more than 56 percent of the total urban population, compared with 41 percent in China, 37 percent in Beijing–Tianjin, and 49 percent in Shanghai–Nanjing–Hangzhou. If a lower threshold size of those cities with a population greater than 50,000 was taken, then they accounted for more than 78 percent of total urban population, compared with 54 percent in China, 45 percent in Guangdong and 65 percent in Shanghai–Nanjing–Hangzhou. Laquian calls the large city-dominated urban system in Liaoning, China's "poly-nucleated urban region."[7]

Since economic reform began in 1978, the S–D region became one of China's coastal open economic zones, which were given priority by the Chinese government in terms of fostering economic growth, trade and foreign investment.[8] One of the government's first economic initiatives was the establishment of several foreign investment zones. In 1984, the city of Dalian was designated as one of China's 14 open coastal cities. Three national level special economic and technological development zones were also established in the S–D corridor in an attempt to encourage foreign investment and technology. They are the Dalian Economic and Technological Development Zone (in Dalian), the Shenyang Tiexi Economic and Technological Development Zone (in Shenyang, sometimes called Tiexi Industrial Transformation Zone) and the Bayuquan Special Economic Zone (in Yingkou, sometimes called Yingkou Economic Development Zone). These three new "open zones" were expected to act as a gateway to the global market for the hinterland of the whole northeast China.[9]

Up until the mid-1990s, in a similar manner to other coastal regions and open cities in China, Liaoning was one of the main growth engines of China's economic growth and had largely benefited from economic globalization, attracting a large share of foreign investment and exporting "made-in-China" products. In fact, Liaoning became one of those regions that had acquired much wealth by making their economies more export oriented. For example, in 1991, Liaoning was ranked second after Guangdong Province in both attracting foreign investment and exporting to overseas markets. However, Liaoning's situation changed radically in the mid-1990s with the introduction of widespread SOE reforms, which was the most influential factor putting Liaoning at a severe disadvantage in terms of economic growth compared to other provinces. Given its historically very high number of China's SOEs, the reforms have disproportionately impacted the development and transformation of the S–D EMR, producing different spatial outcomes from other EMRs in China. Reforms have not only impacted on SOEs and their workers, but also on those rural enterprises to which urban SOEs were strongly linked.

The rationale for SOE reform is well known. While they once held a pre-eminent position in the economy in the early 1990s, they had increasingly become a drag on China's financial resources due to low economic efficiency and overstaffing. Considering that increasing economic globalization forces were forcing China to restructure its economy in order to make its industry more competitive in the global market, it is not difficult to understand that the government's economic policies in the SOE sectors were directed to reduce the labor force and increase efficiency so that the remaining SOEs could compete internationally with transnational corporations after China's entry into the WTO.[10] The central government sought to achieve this by privatizing government-owned firms and enterprises, by "right-sizing government," and by reducing or eliminating subsidies (UNESCAP, 2000; Kahn, 1996).

The path taken by China to reform its large scale SOEs was radically different from that followed in other planned economies, which had pursued a "big bang" approach of abandoning previous industrial policies while undertaking sweeping privatization of the large scale state sector in an attempt to replace state planning, almost overnight, with market forces, and allowing the market to decide the outcome.[11] The strategy for reforming SOEs was to "grasp the large and let the medium and small go," which meant that China would allow its small and medium-sized SOEs to be privatized; at the same time it is attempting to merge its large SOEs to form a few giant SOE groups (referred to as "national teams") or to ensure the state as one of the large shareholders if a large SOE is privatized. It is expected that those "national teams" will become a group of globally powerful companies that can compete in international markets on the global level playing field.[12] The Chinese policy-makers believe that the outcome of economic competition between nations is largely a function of the competition between each nation's major corporations. Wu Bangguo, a member of the Chinese State Assembly described this position succinctly in 1988 when he said "Our nation's position in the international economic order will be to a large extent determined by the position of our nation's large enterprises and groups."[13]

This is a part of the rationale that has led to as many as 45 million workers in China being laid off.[14] The situation is even worse in northeast China, where from 1997 to 2002, one-in-four of the 34 million SOE workers were laid off in the region.[15] Several studies of the reform of SOEs in Liaoning argue that in China, they are some of the most problematic since the beginning of the SOE reform.[16] In 1995, official statistical data suggests that nearly half of its large and medium-sized SOEs were loss-making. This does not include those "hidden losses" reported by the Chinese media that refer to the heavy debts of these enterprises that had to be covered by the banks of the central government. The intensified SOEs' reform and industrial restructuring in the state sector has broken the social and spatial balance established in the cities during the planned economy period. Having served in the so-called "old economy" so many years, former SOE employees are now laid off. They have lost all protection from poverty provided by their work-units system, which had previously guaranteed life-long employment, cradle-to-grave social services and adequate living standards and welfare. Many former SOE workers have become a new urban poverty segment of the population, forming a massive and growing new urban underclass.[17] In China, the number of urban poor – defined as people with a monthly income lower than 130 yuan (US$1 is about 8.2 yuan in 2005) – increased from almost nil[18] in 1978 to 12 million in 1993 and reaching 30 million by 1996.[19] Between January 1997 and September 2001, the total number of employed urban persons in employment in China had fallen by 23.4 percent. In the state sector, there was a fall of 27.4 percent, while in the collective sector, the most severely affected, over half (52 percent) of the urban jobs had been lost.[20] These numbers do not include the rural-to-urban migrants (the commonly cited estimate of their number for the whole of China being 140 million in 2000); most of them who live in very poor conditions.

Liaoning adopted the central government's radical reform policies.[21] However, given that Liaoning has the largest number of China's SOEs, reforms have caused a disproportionate degree of distress compared to other areas of China. Owing to the fact that many SOEs in Liaoning were merged, privatized, downsided or closed down,[22] the number of SOEs dropped from 4,292 in 1995 to 937[23] in 2003. In 1995, Liaoning had 516 large SOEs employing 2.27 million workers, but these numbers dropped to 95 SOEs employing 0.88 million workers in 2003.

When many SOEs were merged, privatized or closed down, the state sector lost its dominant position in the regional economy. The share of both industrial output value and employment by SOEs in Liaoning has declined dramatically since the mid-1990s. For example, in the early 1990s, SOEs in Liaoning employed 62 percent of total workers but only 38 percent in 2003.

Not only did SOEs' shares in total employment, output and value, and the number of enterprises fall, but the absolute value number of SOEs' output also fell. For example, Liaoning's SOEs' output value declined from 204 billion yuan in 1997 to 97.3 billion yuan in 2003. This is different from other parts of the coastal region, such as Jiangsu, Shanghai and Zhejiang where SOEs' share in total output declined, but the absolute value of their SOEs' output remained the same (i.e. stagnation). This difference can be explained by the dissimilarity of their employment capacity of non-state sectors and the magnitude of laid-off SOEs. In other coastal regions, the non-state sectors are very prosperous, providing job opportunities for laid-off SOE workers. In Liaoning, its collective and private sectors provide limited job opportunities. Wang (2004) reports that laid-off workers in Liaoning complain that too many unemployed laborers (including laid-off workers) have been laid off and that there are limited opportunities provided by the non-state sector.[24] Overall, decollectivization (declining in both state and collective sectors) has disadvantaged Liaoning's laid-off workers to a greater degree than their counterparts in other coastal regions, making it more difficult for its workers to find jobs.

Another reason to explain the greater negative impact of SOE reforms in Liaoning and its higher unemployment rate is due to limited assistance from the central government. For example, the central government's policy of forming a few large SOE groups ("national team") with competitive advantages and/or which are strategically important to China, ensures that the nation's largest SOEs are granted special financial assistance. However, this policy has offered little opportunity for Liaoning's SOEs. Although Liaoning has the largest share of China's SOEs in terms of absolute number, only AnGang (Anshan Steel Complex in Anshan city) is on the list of large and strategically important SOEs.[25]

Regional transformation patterns

In the S–D region, the SOE reforms have marginalized not only the state sector, but also the regions with a large number of SOEs and reduced the rural–urban linkages, which will be discussed in the fifth section of this chapter. This section mainly examines the changing patterns of population and industrial growth. Wang (1997a) reports that up until the mid-1990s, most suburbs and rural areas of all cities had increased their share in population. But since then, the overall population distribution has changed little.[26] From 1992 to 2003, the cores, suburbs and rural areas of all cities had a similar share of the population (see Table 9.1). Only the sub-urban district of Yingkou had almost doubled its population share from 9.5 percent in 1992 to 18.6 percent in 2003. This was mainly due to many people migrating to the Bayuquan district, which became Yingkou's new port after it was designated as a new industrial zone.

In terms of the industrial growth pattern, several features can be identified in the post-1995 period. First, in the S–D region as whole, the share of industrial output value in the city cores had dropped from 93.7 percent in 1978, to

Table 9.1 Population distribution by city cores/suburban districts/rural areas in the Shenyang–Dalian corridor, 1992, 1995, 2003 (%)

Region	1992	1995	2003	Region	1992	1995	2003
Sub total	100.0	100.0	100.0	Anshan	100.0	100.0	100.0
city core	34.3	35.0	36.0	city core	39.3	39.9	9.0
suburbs	19.4	19.0	19.0	suburbs	10.7	10.3	8.3
rural	46.3	46.0	45.0	rural	50.0	49.8	50.8
Shenyang	100.0	100.0	100.0	Yingkou	100.0	100.0	100.0
city core	52.6	55.1	55.2	city core	14.3	18.1	18.5
suburbs	26.3	24.1	24.9	suburbs	9.5	9.8	18.6
rural	21.1	19.8	19.9	rural	76.2	72.1	62.9
Dalian	100.0	100.0	100.0	Liaoyang	100.0	100.0	100.0
city core	23.1	23.9	23.3	city core	23.5	27.1	27.2
suburbs	23.1	23.4	23.2	suburbs	11.8	11.7	11.4
rural	53.8	52.7	53.5	rural	64.7	61.2	60.7

Sources: Liaoning Statistical Bureau (1985, 1992, 1996 and 2004).

Table 9.2 Share of industrial output by city core/suburbs/rural area in major Shenyang–Dalian metropolitan regions 1978–2003 (%)

Region	1978	1984	1992	1995	2003	Region	1978	1984	1992	1995	2003
Shenyang	100	100	100	100	100	Yingkou	100	100	100	100	100
city core	97	94	74	48	41	city core	74	74	57	25	17
suburbs	2	4	20	39	45	suburbs	2†	4†	7†	45	21
rural	1	2	6	13	14	rural	24	22	36	30	62
Dalian	100	100	100	100	100	Liaoyang	100	100	100	100	100
city core	92	86	59	41	13	city core	96	95	76	21	26
suburbs	3	6	19	21	32	suburbs	1	1	1	3	8
rural	5	8	22	38	55	rural	3*	4*	23	76	56
Anshan	100	100	100	100	100	Total	100	100	100	100	100
city core	95	90	74	47	21	city core	94	90	68	25	27
suburbs	1	2	4	4	3	suburbs	2	4	15	47	38
rural	4	8	22	49	76	rural	4	6	17	38	44

Sources: Liaoning Statistical Bureau (1985), pp. 542–73; ibid. (1993), pp. 470–1.

Notes
* Dengta County only, Liaoyang data not available.
† only Gongchangling District. Definitions of city core, suburbs and rural areas are based on existing administrative boundaries.

68.4 percent in 1992, and to only 27 percent in 2003. Wang shows that from 1978 to 1992, the decline in the city core's share was due mainly due to rapid increases of the shares of suburbs and rural areas of total output, which is evidence to the process of "rural agglomeration."[27] However, the city core's absolute industrial output value continued to grow. In other words, an increasing share of industrial output in the surrounding sub-urban and rural areas during pre-1995 had not necessarily resulted in any industrial decline or stagnation in the city cores. Rather, the city cores still registered an annual growth rate of about 10 percent from 1978–92.[28] Since the mid-1990s, due to the ongoing SOEs' reform leading to the closing down of many SOEs in the city core, both the SOEs' output value and share in total regional industrial output dropped. Table 9.2 demonstrates a substantial decline of city cores' share in industrial output value. Most city cores have lost their leading role in regional economic growth. Questions on whether rural industry has gained significant growth and how the declining role of the city core has impacted rural–urban relations in this region will be the central issues for the next two sections.

Urban decline

In general, the urban centers of Liaoning's provinces (with the exception of Dalian) have suffered greatly during China's SOE reform, leading to a loss of their competitive advantage over other provinces. As Table 9.3 shows, the ranking of Liaoning's urban comprehensive development index among the Chinese cities dropped from third (after Beijing and Shanghai) in 1990 to ninth in 2000. Beijing and Shanghai retained their top ranking while all other top eight

Table 9.3 Ranking of urban comprehensive development index in selected province, China

Ranking of urban comprehensive development index (first to ninth): in 1990, Beijing, Shanghai, *Liaoning*, Guangdong, Tianjin, Jiangsu, Shandong, Zhejiang, Fujian; in 2000, Beijing, Shanghai, Guangdong, Tianjin, Jiangsu, Shandong, Zhejiang, Fujian, *Liaoning*.

The ranking of selected indexes from 1991 to 2003:

Export and import	Foreign investment	Output by large SOEs*	GDP	Urban per capita income
Liaoning 2nd→9th etc	Liaoning 2nd→6th	Liaoning 2nd→7th	Liaoning 5th→8th	Liaoning 11th→16th
Guangdong 1st→1st	Jiangsu 6th→1st	Guangdong 3rd→1st	Guangdong 1st→1st	Shanghai 2nd→1st
Jiangsu 5th→2nd	Guangdong 1st→2nd	Shandong 4th→2nd	Jiangsu 3rd→2nd	Beijing 4th→2nd
Shanghai 3rd→3rd	Shandong 4th →3rd	Jiangsu 5th→3rd	Shandong 2nd→3rd	Zhejiang 5th→3rd
Beijing 10th→4th	Shanghai 5th→4th	Zhejiang 10th→4th	Zhejiang 7th→4th	Guangdong 1st→4th
Zhejiang 6th→5th	Zhejiang 10th→5th	Shanghai 1st→5th	Heinan 6th→6th	Tianjin 7th→5th

Sources: Liaoning Statistical Bureau (1992, 2004); Yan and Lin (2004).

Note

Liaoning 2nd→9th means Liaoning was ranked second in 1991 but ninth in 2003.

provinces' cities upgraded or remained in top positions (Table 9.3). It should be noted that the comprehensive index is based on performance of the following five sets of indexes: export orientation (export/import), foreign investment, role of SOEs (output by large SOEs), GDP and living standard (per capita income in urban areas). Yan and Lin use them to reflect China's urban clusters' development during the period of 1990–2000.[29] Table 9.3 also shows that ranking of all five indexes in Liaoning dropped significantly. For example, Liaoning's ranking of second in export orientation, foreign investment and output value of large SOEs had dropped to ninth, sixth and seventh respectively. In 1980, Liaoning's industrial output was about 8.8 percent of the whole country while Guangdong's was only 4.5 percent. By 2002, however, Guangdong's GDP was more than triple Liaoning's GDP (Chen *et al.*, 2004b).

However, looking at individual urban districts, clear spatial patterns can be identified. In troubled central Liaoning, those major heavy industrial districts with large numbers of heavy industrial SOEs suffered greatly while a few other city districts performed well, especially those districts where high-tech parks and/or substantial foreign funded firms were located. For example, Dadong district in Shenyang city, Hongwei in Liaoyang city and Shuncheng in Fushun city have performed better. Another exception is Boyuquan district of Yingkou, where its special economic zone and new Yingkou port are located. The main reason for their exceptional performance is mainly due to the fact that they have been selected as sites for newly designated development zones. More capital (both foreign and domestic) has been invested in these districts. As will be discussed later, at municipality level, Dalian is exceptional. All of its urban districts and suburbs have a large proportion of foreign funded firms.

The overall decline of the urban state sector in the S–D region has led to the exclusion of the S–D region from the list of China's top EMRs since the mid-1990s in many Chinese government documents and by some scholars.[30] In other words, the ongoing SOE reforms and the resulting closure of many SOEs in the city core have made many city cores lose their leading role in regional economic growth. Questions are raised regarding whether rural industries have grown more rapidly in recent years and how the declining role of the city core has impacted rural–urban relations. These questions will be addressed in the next section.

Rural sector

Similar to the trend in the 1980s and early 1990s, the agricultural sector in Liaoning continues to diversify. This process is characterized by a decline in the cultivation farming sector and a rapid increase in animal husbandry and fishing sectors. Figure 9.2 shows a consistent increase in these two sectors, especially animal husbandry. In 2003, animal husbandry almost produced the same amount of output value as the farming sector.

In the S–D region, the non-agricultural sector is still an important source of income and rural employment. However, compared with the pre-1995 period, the post-1995 period has shown an overall slower pace of rural–urban integration.

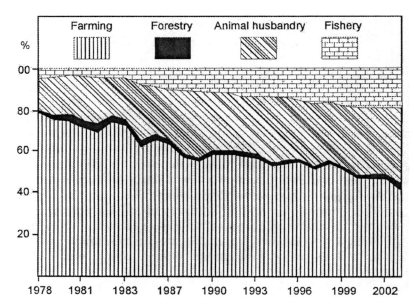

Figure 9.2 The Structure of Liaoning's Agricultural Output Value (1978–2003) (source: Liaoning Statistical Bureau (2004)).

Two main trends can be identified. The first one is that the pace of change to non-agriculturalization has been slowed down. The proportion of the economy represented by the non-agricultural sectors experienced a 20 percent increase (from 12.4 percent in 1978 to 31.6 percent in 1995) as compared to a 2.7 percent increase (31.6 percent in 1995 to 34.3 percent in 2003). The second trend is that the proportional share of rural laborers working in rural industry declined from over 10 percent in the 1980s to 8.4 percent in 2003.

There are several factors that help explain these previous patterns. First, the growth of TVEs slowed down due to the problems in the urban SOE sector. Up to the mid-1990s, the production linkages between TVEs and urban SOEs meant that increases in industrial output were associated with the growth of industry outside the major urban areas. This growth contributed to the "blending" of urban and rural activities along the S–D corridor. Like the other EMRs, the rural industry and other non-agricultural sectors remained the most important source of income and employment. In particular, those township and village enterprises established in the 1980s were linked to urban cores and could benefit from their urban partners. Up until the start of the SOE reforms in the mid-1990s, many rural enterprises received subcontracts from urban enterprises. This included partnerships between urban SOEs and rural industrial enterprises. Wang (1998) shows that subcontracting was a special form of rural–urban linkage based on the spatial division of labor.[31] Thus, on one hand, TVEs became responsible for routine production and the supply of manufactured parts and semi-processed materials by using cheap labor and land. Some rural enterprises also supplied local raw materials to urban SOEs. On the other hand, while urban-based enterprises provided capital, know-how (managerial, technical and technological), marketing skills and sometimes raw materials, urban SOEs were also responsible for searching the market for products. Rural enterprises manufactured parts or provided semi-processed materials for their urban SOE partners based on a subcontract agreement. For example, in 1992, Hunhebu village – near Shenyang city – had eight enterprises that acted as subcontractors for urban-based enterprises. Examples of this form of subcontracting included mini electric motors, electric wire, chemical engineering products and plastic products. Hunhebu village subcontracting enterprises were set up according to the urban enterprises' cooperative demands. These eight rural enterprises produced almost one-third of the total village industrial output.[32] However, since the SOE reform, all their SOE partners in Shenyang have either been closed down or downsized. As a consequence, most of these TVE subcontractors have also closed down. As a result, Hunhebu village lost almost one-third of its industrial income. Similarly, many rural enterprises in Liaoning either went bankrupt or struggled to survive mainly due to their urban SOE partners having been closed down, downsized or merged.[33] As can be seen, there is an intimate link between industrial restructuring occurring within cities, and changes occurring within the rural industrial sector in the hinterland.

Since the SOEs have great difficulty in surviving, those rural enterprises largely depending on their urban SOEs have been greatly affected. Those that can continue to survive after losing urban SOE partners often process local specialized products. For example, the rural areas in the Dalian region have been able to maintain their local rural industrialization. A good example is Houshi village lying along the coast of the Bohai Sea in the southern part of the corridor, located about 70 kilometers away from the metropolitan centre of Dalian. Since the mid-1980s, the village has had "agricultural-industrial-trade combines" (*nong-gong-mao lian-heqiye*). Basically, these combines link agricultural production and local natural resource exploitation with processing, storage and distribution facilities. The rural enterprises include: (1) fruit production and fishery products combined with canned food processing factories, fruit storage and cooler houses; (2) quarry limestone mining (limekiln) linked with prefabricated building materials processing and construction teams; (3) vegetable production units linked with the village transportation teams; (4) sweet potato plantations linked with sweet potato starch factories; (5) dairy farming linked with an ice cream factory; and (6) small and unsold fish production linked with raising martens.[34] Such forms of rural industrialization allow for maximum use of local resources, offer more jobs for local workers and create more value-added products. More importantly, they are not urban SOE dependent. While urban SOEs have suffered, Houshi village has still managed to keep its non-agricultural sector growing.

Another factor associated with the declining rural industry is related to the change in the industrial decentralization policy. Starting from the early 1980s, the provincial government attempted to stimulate the rural industry, especially in the middle part of the S–D corridor. It relocated some of the urban-based heavy industrial enterprises to the corridor between Shenyang and Dalian. The rationale behind this move to decentralize the urban industry from large cities of Shenyang, Anshan and Dalian was to limit congestion in the traditional urban-based industrial areas of these cities as well as to free up the former industrial land for other forms of commercial development. Consequently, new sites were chosen for the expansion of these industries, including the small towns and villages around Yingkou and Panjin, which lie about 100 kilometers away from Shenyang, and the rural areas around Wafangdian and Zhuanghe, which lie 50 to 100 kilometers away from Dalian (see Figure 9.3). These government policies gave new rural industrial enterprises a legal status and granted them more freedom to operate. Industrial growth patterns in the S–D corridor from 1980 to the mid-1990s were characterized by faster growth rates in non-urban areas than major urban centers.[35] For example, during the period of 1978 to 1992, the overall growth rate of industrial output value was much higher in the sub-urban

Figure 9.3 Direction of urban industry relocation in Liaoning (sources: Wang (1998) and also see www.dlpfi.com/jchtd/jch-04.htr).

and rural areas of the corridor (33.5 percent and 26.1 percent respectively) than in the city core areas (9.8 percent). The period of 1984–92 witnessed further movement of the urban industry to the suburbs and rural areas than the period of 1978–84. This is reflected in the 10 percent gain of industrial output share in rural and sub-urban areas for 1984–92, compared with just 2 percent during 1978–84.

This contributed to the rapid proliferation of rural growth as many TVEs were established with the direct assistance of urban-based state factories, as demonstrated by the Hunhebu village case above. Rural–urban links were sustained by subcontracting relationships with urban industries in the S–D region. For example, in 1990, Shenyang city had 484 urban processing enterprises, which had subcontracting relationships with rural enterprises in its surrounding areas. The output of these subcontracted rural industries amounted to 630 million yuan, which made up about 10 percent of the total rural industrial output.[36]

Lee offers an explanation for the general motives of urban industries in strengthening their ties with TVEs, including much lower land rents and labor costs, which reduce the costs of production.[37] Another consideration, less discussed, is that they wished to evade pollution-control expenses since environmental control has been weaker in rural areas.

However, since the mid-1990s, only Dalian has been able to continue relocating its industries to its surrounding rural areas.[38] Its city center has been converted into a commercial and service center and all major manufacturing enterprises have been moved to the surrounding areas. Due to a desire to improve the urban environment, Dalian has strived to become "the most livable city" in China. Today, it attracts the largest share of foreign investment in Liaoning and foreign funded firms contribute a larger share to its total industrial output than any other city in the region (see Plates 9.1, 9.2 and 9.3). The industrial cities in central Liaoning, such as Shenyang and Anshan, cannot afford to continue losing more enterprises in their city cores due to the overwhelming SOE closures and already existing high unemployment.

Therefore, different parts of the S–D EMR have experienced different transformations in the post-1995 period, leading to a fragmentation of the corridor. Dalian experiences continual economic growth and integration with its hinterland unlike other parts of the corridor, especially the region between Shenyang and Dalian. Such a contrast is reflected in the spatial pattern of foreign investment in this region. In 2003, Dalian and its surrounding regions received the largest share of foreign investment and had the largest share of industrial output value from foreign funded firms (see Figure 9.4). The remainder of the corridor has been left behind.

In response to this economic fragmentation of the S–D corridor and the challenge posed by the SOE reform, municipal governments in different parts of the corridor have acted separately. The Shenyang municipal government, with the support of the provincial government, has proposed the formation of the Shenyang Economic Zone as well as plans to unite the cities around Shenyang (such as Anshan, Fushun, Benxi, Liaoyang) to form an urban "club."[39] The members of this club are supposed to coordinate and cooperate with one another so as to

Plate 9.1 One of public squares in Dalian.

Note
Most public squares and parks in Dalian are well maintained with a lot of flowers and grassland.

Plate 9.2 Sign for Jinzhou economic development zone, Dalian.

protect themselves.[40] It should be noted that such a club does not give much attention to their rural areas even those directly under their jurisdiction. These cities are attempting to minimize the negative impacts of SOE reforms and pursue development opportunities. For example, in order to avoid competition among the similar manufacturing sectors in these "club cities," each member city is encouraged to identify its key sectors with competitive advantages. If

Plate 9.3 Jinzhou economic development zone in Dalian. Note: Many companies from Japan and South Korea invested in Jinzhou Economic Development Zone.

agreed, duplication of a similar industry in these cities can be avoided. In such a way, many SOEs may survive under this agreement.

Another development is that the provincial government has started to treat Dalian and Shenyang as being separate economic regions. The political explanation may be that the former governor of the province, Bo Xilai, was the mayor of Dalian before he took over the governor position in the late 1990s. His intention may have been purposely to separate the "problem region" – Shenyang region from his more prosperous Dalian. His dream for Dalian is "not the largest, but the best." Such a dream has been partially recognized by the UN, which identified Dalian as a "leading city in environmental improvement in the Asian-Pacific Region."[41] Therefore, many policies and plans, especially during Bo's governing period appear to avoid putting the more favored Dalian in the same category as the more troublesome Shenyang.[42] In contrast to such an approach, which fails to address essential development issues in the whole of the S–D mega-urban region, the recent development plans of the EMRs of Beijing–Tianjin, lower Yangzi delta and the Pearl River Delta have increasingly adopted a region-wide oriented approach. Such plans fulfill urban transformation and rural–urban integration needs whilst promoting the treatment of the EMR as a whole rather than separately.

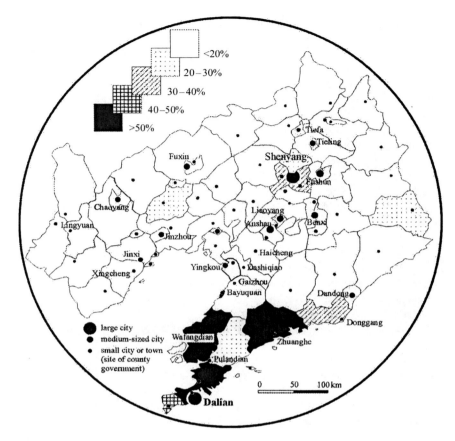

Figure 9.4 Proportion of industrial output value by foreign funded firms, Liaoning, 2003 (county-level data; %) (source: Liaoning Statistical Bureau (2004)).

Conclusion

It is clear that the SOE reforms introduced since the mid-1990s have not only marginalized the state sector but also the regions with a large number of SOEs. In fact, the closure of many SOEs in the cities of Shenyang, Anshan, Fushun and Benxi in central Liaoning has also impacted the rural industrial sectors especially those with strong linkages with urban SOEs. The S–D region is now experiencing similar problems of unemployment and work transitions to those experienced by other increasingly globalizing economies. Such negative consequences have caused the sub-regions of the S–D corridor to be affected to different degrees. On the one hand, diversification of the economy and employment in rural areas can be identified as a common characteristic in the region. On the other hand, rural and urban areas in the southern part of the region, where Dalian is located, are continually being integrated. Large foreign investment inflows and increased export orientation have ensured that the city core plays an important role in the economic growth of the EMR as well as its surrounding areas. In contrast, in the northern part of the S–D region, the cluster of cities centered around Shenyang are suffering job losses and the closing down of SOEs. As a result, many linkages between rural–urban sectors have been broken down. Therefore, the SOE reforms coupled with the FDI-led export-oriented development plan is leading to divergent outcomes in the S–D urban corridor. Such regional divergence indicates that economic globalization and China's industrial restructuring policy are closely linked and have significant spatial consequences. The spatial selectivity of globalization and SOE reform policies are producing an increasingly unequal spatial development of Chinese EMRs. Such spatial disproportion can also be seen on three geographic scales.

At the national level, China's EMRs identified by Zhou have followed different transformation paths.[43] As discussed in the previous chapters, in some of the EMRs, noticeably the Pearl River and lower Yangzi deltas, there have been increased linkages between the core cities and the surrounding areas, resulting in an emerging pattern of functional differentiation. In others, like the S–D region, rural–urban relations have become less integrated in the Shenyang node and more focused on the Dalian node. Thus, the S–D EMR has become more fragmented.

Spatial unevenness can also be identified within the S–D region. The corridor of the S–D EMR consists of two main parts: the Shenyang-centered northern circle and Dalian-centered southern circle, leaving the middle region between these two poles lagging far behind in economic development and rural–urban interaction. Dalian is becoming more attractive for foreign investment. This enables it to continue to play a leading role in the process of economic integration with its surrounding areas. Shenyang and its surrounding region in the central part of Liaoning, however, have moved towards adopting a more city-centered development strategy in an effort to survive, leaving the surrounding rural areas out of their urban agendas.

Such fragmentation can be further identified with metropolitan areas. For example, in the metropolitan areas of Shenyang, the districts designated as high-tech parks/zones or districts with a low number of SOEs perform better than districts contained in the traditionally rust belt SOEs.

The future development of the S–D corridor depends largely on the new campaign of the central government directed towards the revitalization of northeast China. At the sixteenth Communist Party Congress in November 2002, northeast China was put at the top of the central government's agenda. The aim was to rebuild the northeast region into a competitive industrial base for the production of essential equipment and raw materials. It is hoped that the northeast will once again become an important regional economic powerhouse of China, along with the Pearl River and Yangzi River deltas as well as the Bohai region.[44] Recently, the central government has been providing Liaoning, together with other parts of northeast China, with funds to invest in infrastructure projects. However, without further stimulation provided by other policies, economic growth in the S–D corridor will remain problematic. For example, the major driving force behind the economic take-off in the Pearl River Delta in the early 1980s was mainly due to an injection of investment from Hong Kong. The economic take-off in southern Jiangsu Province (or Sunan's TVEs) and Wenzhou in Zhejiang Province (a private economy) was mainly as a result of grassroot rural industrialization. In Shanghai, Pudong's success was a product of the central government's state urban projects. Without comprehensive policies and proper investment by the state into Liaoning, the state project to revitalize northeast China is unlikely to succeed. Thus far, it is unclear what privileges Liaoning will receive from the central government. It would seem that the S–D extended metropolitan region will need to have autonomy and special privileges granted by the central government if the EMR is to achieve the economic dynamism of the Hong Kong–Macao–Guangzhou and lower Yangzi EMRs.

10 Reviewing the case studies

Dimensions of scale in the Chinese urbanization process

> It would be something of a truism to say that social life is fundamentally scaled and issues of geographic scale are central to how social life is structured and played out.
>
> Andrew Herod and Melissa Wright (2002)[1]

Introduction

A reading of the preceding case studies offers the opportunity for a closer dissection of the process of the production of urban space in China than has been presented. But before we proceed to this synthesis we need to make some general comments on scale theory and the difficulties of scaling up data from the local level to regional and national levels that is often regarded as a central problem of social science research. In China it must be also emphasized that most of the research on scale has been focused on the reverse process of scaling down particularly with respect to fiscal and administrative decentralization. To begin with, it should be made clear, that when we use the concept of scale we are following Neil Smith's suggestion "that specific geographical scales can be conceived of as platforms for specific kinds of social activity."[2] Thus this idea of territorial scale includes the entire spectrum of human activities at the level of individuals, households, neighborhoods/villages, localities, regions, nations and the global scale. Central to our arguments concerning the production of urban space is the view that these different platforms reflect the constructed reality of the people, institutions and social practices that occur in these platforms that follows Lefebvre's triad of factors that produce urban space discussed in Chapter 2. Of course we recognize that these "platforms" are not spatially bounded and are linked through networks of political power, informational flows, kinship and economic transactions that leap-frog and fluctuate in intensity within and between these levels. Perhaps a more useful way of explaining the concept is by using the concept of a "domain," which carries with it the idea of political power and obligation being tied in a network that operates at the level of different platforms. The most complex research task is establishing how changes operating in one domain cause changes in another domain – for example the effect of world energy prices on the ability of national governments to deliver income improvement at the village level. Efforts to establish this connecting chain of causation are complex and often result in researchers focusing upon *in situ* change within one domain. By explaining what occurs in one domain the relationship to the other domain becomes clearer.[3]

In the case of China the post-reform era has seen a constant administrative rescaling of domains. One aspect of this has been the decentralization of responsibility for economic development downwards. Another more recent aspect has been the upward centralization of power to larger urban cores. Tang and Chung (2002) summarize this process as follows: "The reform measures introduced in the past two decades can then be deemed as measures to accentuate the role of towns and cities in the whole network of government extending across various geographical scales."[4] This issue is addressed in recent articles on China by Cartier (2005), Shen (2005), Ma (2005) and Hsing (2006) that discuss the consequences of this administrative rescaling.[5]

This administrative rescaling is a complex process particularly as it involves the negotiation of power relationships between different administrative levels. One aspect of the process is the active role of the central state in decentralizing fiscal and administrative powers to local governments that encourage initiatives in economic development, particularly industrial investment and its associated infrastructure needs. This process has encouraged a proliferation of industrial activity in the margins of many Chinese cities in the coastal zones. At the same time the changing urban status of the administrative centers (urban cores) increases their political power over the urban planning process and land management of which the proliferation of agencies concerned with initiating and overseeing development are an example. This process is creating two kinds of urban space. An "entrepreneurial urban space" in the city cores and their immediate adjacent areas in which meso-level agencies are vigorously promoting high-technology industry and services creating a built-environment that will be attractive to investors. Meanwhile in the *desakota* margins industry is introduced in two ways: first, implanted in industrial and enterprise zones and second, in the *in situ* growth of small and medium-sized industries focused on towns and villages that proliferate alongside rural activities that are becoming more commercialized. The reclassification of counties as municipalities, as for example in the case of Dongguan or Kunshan, has involved redefinitions of individuals, households etc., as urban participants even if in reality many still remain farmers or migrants. At the same time the fiscal and economic incentives are such that this process of redefinition was, and is, actively sought by local institutions so that there is a broad consensus about this process of rescaling of political power among the administrative entrepreneurial leaders at various levels although the process is characterized by negotiation, resistance and cooperation. In a sense the urban scale is being stretched into the rural as a strategy of repositioning urban space, actively pursued by national, provincial and municipal and township governments. This scaling up is at the expense of the rural, the powerless and the displaced farmers whose land is taken away often without adequate compensation or justice. There is not a day in China without some kind of resistance by peasants in rural areas to the transferring of their rural land defined as collective land (see Chapter 2) to some form of non-agricultural use. This resistance is also occurring in city cores as "enveloped villages" (*chengzhongcun*) and older urban neighborhoods (*hutongs*) are destroyed as part of the urban restructuring of the core cities.[6] There are also ongoing problems with the migrant populations, both within cities and their margins, with respect to their status within these urban areas that has caused them to be segregated both socially and spatially. Recent changes in the *hukou* system that allows the peasants to become official urban population in small and medium-sized cities and some large urban cities may go some way to alleviating this problem.[7]

This rescaling means that there is a form of contested space in the context of Chinese urbanization that is not an unfamiliar theme in the history of global urbanization. Often this process of "contestation" is portrayed as a result of the limited capacity that local civil society has to "resist" this reshaping of the territorial manifestations of Chinese urban expansion. But Hsing has shown the townships and the villages that they administer have managed to enlarge into what Hsing describes as an illegal process of land management.[8] As Hsing points out this process is associated in many cases with efforts on the part of township "administration" "to move into a town seat to help build-up a more urban like town centre, called *nongmin jizi jianchen* [peasants raise funds for town building]."[9] In this way townships hope that this will increase revenue from these "urban developments." It seems that the "urban centering activities" of bureaucratic entrepreneurs permeate all levels of administration both in urban and rural space.

The processes of urban formation in these wider urban regions are important because of the challenges they present to interpretations of urban formation that draw their stimulus from the experience of the urban transformation in the developed countries of the West. We have already discussed the theoretical arguments that support the view that the Chinese urbanization process exhibits distinct features, particularly in the peripheral zones of urban growth away from the urban cores. This is often captured by the idea that the process of urban formation in these zones is "emerging 'organically' as the product of a multiplicity of small scale-local circumstances."[10] This is sometimes referred to as local "typicality" (*leixingxing*) and is recognized as an important factor in all the cases studies.

Turning next to another kind of rescaling, which is use of data collected at the level of one platform to enable a better understanding of processes that are occurring at a national level. There are four main problems in using this data. First we have not sought to present the case studies so that they conform to some preconceived organizational framework. In this book because each of the drafting authors has been working in the site of their case study for many years, they have chosen features of the urban transformation in their site that they feel deserves prioritizing and best reflects the local context. Thus in Liaoning Province, the contrast is clearly demonstrated between Shenyang and its neighboring cities, where industrial restructuring of state-owned enterprises (SOEs) dominates, and Dalian where rapid development has occurred because of integration into global markets. In the case of Dongguan, the close connection with Hong Kong and Hong Kong investment as well as the persistence of "township" industrial activities has been identified as a crucial factor in the production of urban space. In Kunshan it has been argued that it is the institutional structure of the area facilitating local transaction networks that was a major factor in the creation of peripheral urban space in Kunshan Municipality. But in the late 1990s a process of metropolitanization focused on Shanghai facilitated by improved communication has led to growing functional specialization in the extended metropolitan region and an increase in industrial activity in the industrial parks adjacent to the administrative centre of Kunshan Municipality. In the case of Shanghai Municipality, administrative restructuring and reclassification and the drive to make Shanghai, a major national and global city, play a major role in the restructuring of the old city and facilitating the growth of urban activities into the surrounding margins. While this process is dominated by the need to integrate Shanghai into international and domestic markets and its growing regional importance as a service center within the lower Yangzi region and China, it is the ability of outer margin local governments to position their municipalities most favorably in processes of economic restructuring that is also important in the transformation of urban space in the margins.

Second, these case studies are presented and analyzed at various geographic scales (platforms) that means urban growth is explored at different political levels: Liaoning Province and Guangdong Province; Shanghai (a municipality of provincial status) and Dongguan and Kunshan municipalities (former counties that have become municipalities). This makes the comparison of the urban transformation at different scales of political and geographic space difficult but also enables more probing insights into the effects of urban growth on regional space. Third, there is the time dimension. Of necessity the authors have sought to present their material in a recent historical context with some emphasis on the period before 1998 but in the past seven years the sites of these case studies have begun to change dramatically as the coastal provinces of China (in particular) have been rapidly integrated into the global and national system of trade, investment and production. As the globalization imperative has sharpened in China these sites have had to adjust to the competitive wages, land prices and other local incentives from other parts of China as well as the regulatory requirements of accelerated globalization. This last five years need careful consideration in the discussion of the urban processes.

It must also be stressed that the case studies tend to focus on the urban processes using a comparative approach have tended to focus on cities and their immediate margins rather than larger urban areas.[11] The study of the urban margins of the Chinese cities that is the major focus of this book is an attempt not only to fill a lacunae in the literature but also because the authors see the urban margins as the zone of urban space that presents the most challenges to developing a successful urban policy for China.

Another important element in this situation is the meanings that are attached to the urban–rural relationship within these sites. The ideas that drove the urban and rural divide during the Maoist era are now increasingly less relevant, although there are continuing policy laments about the loss of agricultural land or the decline of rural occupations and conflicts over the transfer of rural to urban land use. What appears to be occurring in these sites is both an urban and a rural transformation. While rural space, in the sense that the majority of people are engaged in rural activities, remains on the geographical edges of the extended metropolitan regions of which the case studies are part, it is being metamorphosed in other parts of the urban periphery through processes of commercial intensification (including crop and animal husbandry changes) and the growth of non-agricultural employment at the household level. Urban transformation in the urban peripheries remains a process where the built-up urban area is reflected in a patchwork urban fabric, that can include older satellite cities (Shanghai) export and high-technology zones, residential and commercial growth in pre-existing towns and smaller scale industrial activity that coexists with intensive rural activities leading to the classic mixture of economic activities. This is sometimes presented in terms of the concept of "city–countryside integration" (*chengxiang yitihua*) that captures the idea of a distinctive form of spatial transition that was embodied in the concept of *desakota* (see Chapter 4). But in the period since 1998 within the coastal provinces that are the settings for the case studies there has been a huge growth of domestic and foreign investment, extension of the transport infrastructure, expansion of the built-up areas (especially in the urban cores), restructuring of industry with a growing importance of free export zones and economic and technological development zones (ETDZs). These developments are often located close to, or within, the administrative urban cores in the sites where administrative entrepreneurial elites are vigorously putting in policies that link their cities to the international export economy. This process raises intriguing question as to how these industrial changes are affecting the formation of urban space. Is it possible to suggest that in China conventional processes of urban agglomeration and external economies are now playing a significant role in urban formation in the urban cores but operate to a much lesser extent in the adjacent peri-urban areas? In these areas small and medium-sized industries (such as town and village enterprises (TVEs)) continue to be more closely linked to smaller towns of the outer periphery that coexist with rural activities.

In order to structure this exercise we have divided the discussion into several themes that encompass the temporal, spatial and contextual aspects of the urbanization process followed by a discussion of the implications of the rapidly evolving process of Chinese urbanization for the future.

Temporal aspects of the urbanization process

In earlier chapters we have suggested that the understanding of the urbanization process involves investigation of the long history of Chinese urbanization. But in the case studies of the preceding section we have focused on the urbanization process in the reform period that has been dominated by overlapping processes of decentralization, marketization and globalization. The case studies suggest a periodization common to all sites as follows. (1) In the period between 1978 and 1988 the major influence on the growth of urbanization was the growth of TVEs located primarily outside the urban cores. The three biggest city cores of the sites, Shenyang, Shanghai and Guangzhou all experienced industrial relocation, decline and restructuring and comparatively slow economic growth. (2) A second phase from 1988 that has been dominated by the creation of large scale ETDZs, high-technology parks and free trade zones that are often located on the edges of the city cores and designed to attract foreign investment and a rapid redevelopment of the city cores. These occurred before but the principal feature of this period is the acceleration in their number and importance of cities in the coastal zones. It has also been suggested by Webster *et al.* (2003)[12] that while this period was characterized by a potential for competition the surge of foreign investment was so large that internal competition was "relatively subdued" and there was enough economic growth to encourage an increase in local consumption and international demand to enable the TVEs to continue to flourish as well as the new industries. Finally in the period since 1998, Webster argues that national competition is accelerating as wage costs have begun to increase in south China and Shanghai. Thus the location of industry is being driven by "lower costs of production in Western and interior China" and in newly developed sites in the coastal zones (Kunshan or Liaoning and Shandong). The political leaders of these older city cores are thus forced to upgrade their investment environment by emphasizing the amenity advantages of their locale and to emphasize the role of the service sector including research and development.

Spatial aspects of the urbanization process

Building on the discussion of Chapter 4 we want to suggest that the patterns of urbanization that are occurring in the case studies sites can best be understood if they are positioned within a framework of spatial levels that are laddered from national, to regional, sub-regional and site specific examples. From the point of view of the case studies we argue that the best way to analyze the spatial change is at the regional, sub-regional and site specific levels since we have already dealt with the regional and national levels in preceding chapters. Within the coastal zone each of these sites is located in a region that has been positioned within the wider context of China in certain ways as outside investment and local development accelerated after 1978. Thus Liaoning Province forms part of the northeast region that also includes Beijing, Hebei, Shandong and Tianjin; Shanghai and Kunshan are located in the lower Yangzi River delta that includes Jiangsu and Zhejiang and Dongguan in the south China region that includes Fujian, Guandong and special administrative regions of Macao and Hong Kong. With respect to investment there, it is useful to compare the three regions by the main sources of foreign investment from Greater China (Taiwan, Hong Kong), the northeast (Korea and Japan) and the rest of the world. Thus the overall pattern of investment in China has moved from a situation in the 1980s when Hong Kong and Taiwan investment was the major source of FDI directed to southern China and was primarily directed to labor intensive industries that were located in peripheral zones of the urban cores. While in the other urban areas of the other coastal zones most development was characterized by domestic capital investment in TVEs. In the 1990s FDI investment has become more diversified with Japan and Korea dominating in the northeast and a wide global spread of investments in the lower Yangzi delta region. The type of investment is also becoming much more diversified with manufacturing becoming more capital intensive associated with a growth of quaternary services investment in real estate, insurance banking services, finance, etc., that is flowing to the core cities of these regions such as Beijing, Shanghai and Guangzhou (Hong Kong still remains important). At a regional level the period in which each region has been inserted into these global linkages is important to explain the developments in each of the sites. Thus the development of TVEs and the surge of Hong Kong investment was part of the first opening up of China that had been initiated by Deng after 1978. In the lower Yangzi, Kunshan was comparatively late within the Sunan (south Jiangsu) region in its growth of TVEs, almost coinciding with the opening up of the Sunan to foreign investment in 1985. The establishment of the Kunshan ETDZ in 1985 in the urban core of Kunshan county (Yushan) acted as a major incentive to FDI, which grew rapidly and has accelerated in the period since 1998 particularly in the electronic industry. On the other hand Shanghai really only began to grow economically and begin the policies of annexing the adjacent counties from 1988 on, once again actively encouraged by the national government. The combined efforts of the Shanghai government and national government to make Shanghai the "dragon head" of the regional economy of the Yangzi basin and one of the main global gateways to China have proved remarkably successful and are now reflected in the rapid development of the peripheral areas of the municipality. The most successful example is the creation of Pudong now the largest urban "district" of Shanghai. Finally Liaoning, as one of the major centers of heavy industrial production in China dominated by SOEs has experienced an uneven regional incorporation into the global system. While Dalian its largest port in the south of the province has been following a pattern of development that is a more modest version of Shanghai's development, Shenyang has had great difficulty in structurally adjusting with the need to reform its SOEs. It is only in the period since 2000 that it has begun to restructure the SOEs and attract foreign investment.

Within each of these regions each of these sites has also been positioned by its location in relation to the principal transportation arteries. With increased economic growth each of these regions is being rapidly transformed by the emergence of corridors of economic activity that influence spatial developments of the urbanization process that are linked to the main urban cores of the region. In Liaoning Province, the Shenyang–Dalian corridor; in Jiangsu, Kunshan is located strategically in relation to the Nanjing – Shanghai corridor and in Guangdong, Lin shows clearly how economic activity is relocating in relationship to the two main arterial routes between Guangzhou and Hong Kong.

Within the case study sites the shaping of urban space can be most effectively analyzed within the framework suggested by Webster *et al.*, defined as occurring in the following spaces:[13] (1) urban cores that are made up of the main city cores' districts. These may include the national municipalities such as Shanghai, administrative centers at the provincial level, Shenyang, Guangzhou, and administrative centers of counties that have been reclassified as municipalities such as Kunshan, Dongguan and Dalian. (2) Inner peri-urban areas that include adjacent districts often under the administrative control of the core city. (3) Outer peri-urban areas that include counties that have a dominance of industrial employment or mixed employment patterns in which towns are the main urban centers. (4) Rural districts in which more than 60 percent of the employment is still in rural activities.

A review of the case studies within this spatial framework reveals the following trends. (1) Restructuring of inner cores with the growth of administrative functions, and increase in other service functions such as retailing and a "cleaner" capital-intensive high-technology industry. This is associated with increased household income that is leading to the growth of a "middle class" that forms a growing market for residential accommodation, household durables and luxury items such as cars. New streets of specialized retailing are emerging and shopping centers have begun to proliferate. (2) Similar trends are observable in the inner peri-urban areas that are often the location of high-tech zones. There is an expansion of the built-up area and new residential complexes are emerging. This does not lead as yet to the complete elimination of agriculture but this is the zone in which there is the greatest loss of agricultural land. (3) The outer peri-urban zones are the area where TVEs form the major sector of industrial activity. Much of the urban growth occurs in towns that exhibit the same features of the built-environment of the larger towns but without high-tech developments. Intensification of agriculture continues in these areas but there is still a decline in grain crops. In this zone there is a form of "embedded industry" that is facing severe problems of adjustment due to competition and structural adjustment. Nevertheless a classic form of the *desakota* landscapes still persists. (4) On the edges of these sites rural districts become increasingly marginalized, characterized by income inequality and service shortfall. Thus the process of urbanization as indicated by the case studies emphasizes increasing spatial internal differentiation and functional specialization. (5) The issue of the spatial integration of these urban regions as shown by increasing functional specialization and agglomerative trends are still incipient. This seems to be more an indication of the power of local development that still asserts control over economic activities. This issue will become of increasing importance as the Chinese national space becomes more integrated and developed.

Contextual aspects of the urbanization process

One unifying theme of the case studies is the emphasis on the context in which the production of urban space occurs in each of the sites. By context we refer to the particular mélange of historical paths, geographic settings, people and institutions that exists at any point in time in a given territorial unit of space. Thus while the coastal zone of China has experienced common processes of urban administrative reclassification, economic change and exposure to the processes of local development and globalization, the particular manner in which these processes have worked their way out in each site is not identical. This fact has been recognized in a recent article by Smart and Lin (2006) that delineates three overlapping localisms that operate in "scaler shifts" associated with development. These are "local capitalisms" that subordinate global forces to local economic and social forces, "local citizenship" that sees entitlement and exclusion as being accomplished locally and "translocality" as being those influences that operate in the case of place of birth and ethnic or business ties that operate between other places and the local place.[14] Examples of this interaction of localisms abound in the case studies. In Liaoning Province the scaler shifts that involved the restructuring of state operated enterprises in the old industrial heartland centered around Shenyang (including Anshan, Fushun, Benxi and Liaoyang) led to slower urbanization both in the urban cores and peripheries than in many other parts of the coastal zone. In this situation many TVEs in rural counties linked to the SOEs have lost their contracts and been forced to close down. It is only in the last few years that local and national initiatives have began to lead to a reversal of this trend. At the same time Dalian the main port began to develop much earlier attracting new industries and expanding its urban area under the influences of globalization in which both local capitalisms and translocality played an important part. In Kunshan in the lower Yangzi delta the 1980s and 1990s were dominated by the growth of TVEs in the periphery, which was driven by local bureaucratic entrepreneurs. Since the early 2000s there has been an acceleration of FDI in Kunshan, particularly from Taiwan focused in electronics industries based near the municipal government seat in which translocal influences have been of paramount importance. This has actively been encouraged by the Suzhou Prefecture and the provincial governments. Shanghai Municipality exhibits a different pattern that is characterized by the movement of industrial units out of the urban core, the vigorous promotion of Shanghai as national and regional service centre and the establishment of technological zones in the inner margin of the urban area. That is part of a deliberate national policy to develop Shanghai as a national financial center and gateway between the Yangzi River valley and global markets. But again local bureaucratic capitalism has been important in shaping the cities, spatial dimensions. Dongguan, which, at one time still appeared to be embedded in the earlier phase of TVE dominance is now exhibiting some of the features of Kunshan with the growth of the electronic industries in the industrial zones adjacent to the city core.

These economic patterns are reflected in the labor markets of the three regions. In Liaoning the closure of SOEs and economic restructuring led to considerable unemployment and low rates of in-migration. But in the last few years unemployment has been reduced and active programs of industrialization have led to accelerated urbanization in Dalian and the Shenyang–Anshan cluster of cities. In Kunshan, much of the TVEs, demand for unskilled labor was met locally but in the late 1990s the influx of foreign investment and growing presence of a large number of Taiwanese (30,000) in Kunshan city has led to an increased demand for migrant workers that today make up a significant proportion of the urban population. In Shanghai, the growth of industry had led to a demand for unskilled labor while its growing role as a national service center increased the need for professional workers. But in Dongguan in Guangdong Province there is a continuing demand for unskilled labor that is reflected in the high proportion of the labor force that are made up of unskilled migrants. It does appear that as urbanization patterns are becoming more diverse in China labor markets are becoming more responsive to wage levels. Thus there is now a situation where this is becoming a major problem in areas such as the Pearl River Delta where a labor shortage is beginning to develop as the cost of living increases and wage levels fall behind places such as Shanghai and Beijing. In this situation low wage locations such as the Shandong peninsula and the Chongqing–Chengdu mega-urban region become more attractive for both foreign and domestic investment. These labor force problems are also a reflection of China's recent rural policy, which is attempting to increase productivity in rural areas. The government is also attempting to improve the conditions of rural life, especially its reduction of agricultural tax and "green for grain" program in inland China (peasants are encouraged to plant trees and in receive financial subsidies and support including in kind (grain)).Thus it is hoped that peasants will find that staying at home in increasingly productive farming will be able to generate increased income. This is certainly the intention of the major focus of the Eleventh Five Year Plan that is discussed in Chapters 3 and 11.

Conclusion: implications for the urban future. Repositioning the Chinese urban transformation

To conclude we want to discuss the implications of this fine grained discussion of "grounded urbanization" to the explanation of the ongoing Chinese urban transformation. This provides the introduction to the final chapter that discusses the challenges of Chinese urbanization, its relevance to the global context and the future patterns of urbanization.

In another context Oakes has written about a process in China where "local identity is being scaled-up to match … the discrete space within political boundaries."[15] We would argue that in a similar manner local places are being scaled up to conform to national goals for an urban China. The national and provincial states play a crucial role in this process, but local forces are also highly important, emphasizing the particular economic and other incentives of their "place" that will be attractive packages for investors, both local and foreign. At this level the process is being led by the "growth coalitions" of core urban areas that are most active in developing strategic plans designed to achieve these objectives. These growth coalitions can be broadly grouped into the following six groups: (1) Government at all levels. (2) Developers and investors including service companies in the private sector, for example, Kunshan Municipality recently signed a contract with a bank in Shanghai to provide financial services to the municipality. (3) Research agencies including universities. (4) Individual actors: the role of dynamic "movers and shakers" is important, for example, the former Mayor of Dalian, Mr. Bo Xilai, who initiated and mobilized Dalian's development. (5) Labor availability: in this respect the role of migrants in the labor force has been particularly important in the coastal areas enabling labor costs to remain low for several decades because their *hukou* are still in rural hometown. A typical life cycle for migrants is that after working in coastal area for several years, they return home but introduce their villagers/friends/relative to replace them with the same salary and same living conditions. The creation of skilled labor forces in the newer high-technology and innovation industries draws upon a much larger national market. (6) Institutional factors: while the general thrust of writing about Chinese urban development places great emphasis upon the fragmented and competitive nature of the urban development process there are indications that China is attempting to develop alliances and growth coalitions at the regional level that involve meetings between the mayors in a region and an inter-city cooperation agreement that is operating in the Shenyang centered clusters of cities in Liaoning. As Chinese national economic space becomes more integrated this will become increasingly important.

Thus we might suggest at the local level that while the role of core urban areas is increasing both economically and administratively in the promotion of the urban transition, it would be a mistake to present this as some inevitable consequence of the dynamics of globalization. Local urban administrations and local investors are using their distinctive regional contexts as an incentive to global investment and negotiating their urban paths.

To take this argument another step. While the case studies certainly support the view that urbanization in the coastal zones is beginning to assume some of the spatial and economic features of the developed countries there is still a persistence of what one of the authors of the book had described as "dual urbanization" (Lin). This is characterized by the growth of "modern" urbanization in the city cores (most obviously Shanghai) and surrounding built-up areas alongside a persistence of "town-based" organic urbanization with a prevalence of small and medium-sized enterprises in the outer periphery and growing marginalization of rural activities in the outer margins. This urban pattern is occurring in Liaoning, Jiangsu and Guangdong and is supported by a number of studies from other coastal provinces.

In summary the case studies provide ample evidence of the rapid urban transformation of coastal China. At present the major tendency is for a continuation of "dual track urbanization" with the central city core governments in combination with private development companies playing an increasingly important role of creating "entrepreneurial urban space" with the associated needs for urban infrastructure (roads, energy, public services etc.) and a built-environment that is needed for the "entrepreneurial city" (office buildings, high-technology estates, shopping complexes, apartment housing etc.). This is facilitating an expansion into the adjacent peri-urban areas particularly along the major transport corridors: Hong Kong – Guangzhou, Shenyang–Dalian and Shanghai – Nanjing. As investment competition between cities increases this process is also characterized by the need to create more livable cities and attractive cities. For example this has become an important part of Shenyang's efforts to revitalize their city. Within these corridors municipalities such as Dongguan and Kunshan (located conveniently close to major cores, Hong Kong and Shanghai) are also vigorously promoting "entrepreneurial urban spaces" in a similar manner to the core cities. This has meant that in the period since 1998 a large proportion of capital investment is occurring in these core cities. At the same time while there is some investment in the outer peripheral areas particularly in the towns this is very small and is leading to an increasing inequality in income, investment and the provision of services. The shortfall of the latter in the periphery is particularly alarming because of the dangers for the environment and implications for public health.

At this point it would seem that the process of urbanization in coastal China is also beginning to exhibit growing functional differentiation between city cores and their outer urban–rural peripheries. While the city cores are becoming more fully integrated into national and global systems of trade, investment and communication the urban peripheries are sharing unevenly in this process, with TVEs adjusting from a previous economic phase that emphasized labor intensity and cheap wages that makes them vulnerable to competition from cheaper locations in other parts of China (e.g. Chongqing–Chengdu corridor). Evidence from Lin and Marton suggests that some small and medium-sized enterprise managers are able to remain competitive by a number of strategies among which the ability to utilize both Chinese and foreign markets is an important factor in the ability of these TVEs to survive. For example the practice of linking production processes through subcontracting that is described in Liaoning. The rapidity of development throughout these urban regions is accentuating the ecological and economic vulnerability of the margins of Chinese cities that has important implications to the future pattern of Chinese urbanization in the light of overall population distribution that is dominated by the high proportion of total and urban population in the coastal zone and the significant proportion of population residing in the urban margins.

Three possible scenarios for the future are suggested by these cases studies. First, that the present pattern of "dual urbanization" will continue in which the majority of population increase occurs in the margins and economic activity based on restructured TVEs is able to remain competitive along with more productive commercial agriculture. This would broadly conform to Marton's ideas of "rural agglomeration" or McGee's ideas of *desakota*. From the point of view of the urban system this model suggests that a majority of the urban increase will be based on the towns of the margins although the core cities will continue to grow and expand. A second scenario assumes that the urban activities in the margins become increasingly uncompetitive and are relocated closer to the urban cores. This would mean the movement of the margins population to the city cores in a similar manner to that experienced by the developed countries in the earlier phases of their urbanization transition. This also assumes the operation of agglomeration and economies of scale and the continued growth of urban city cores and the immediate peripheries which, because of the volume of population, will create even larger mega-cities than are already predicted. A final scenario assumes that economic activities of the outer margins are able to adjust to competition by closer integration with economic activities in the city core area through subcontracting, increased capital intensity, information and labor linkages. This would lead to an ongoing dispersal of industrial and service activities throughout the urban margins and an upgrading of services and infrastructure in these areas. In this way the margins would be "leap-frogged" into a phase of development that is more characteristic of the so-called "post-industrial societies" of the developed countries. This would also lead to an ongoing pattern of population growth based on city cores and dispersed population growth based on small and medium-sized towns within a wider extended metropolitan region.

From a policy point of view we suggest that the third scenario offers the most viable path for policy-makers but it does create an imperative for creating greater integration within these urban regions that is designed to break the path of increasing dis-articulation between urban cores and their margins that we have observed. As Webster *et al.* have suggested. "In the longer run a more 'level playing field' for investment in peri-urban areas, across China may be desirable, not least to better enforce environmental regulations"[16] but this would mean the involvement of all levels of government and careful management of the urban transition. In the final chapter we will discuss these challenges to the future of Chinese urbanization.

11 Conclusion

Rewriting China's urban future

Whatever China today takes from outside she undoes and refashions in her way, as the Romans of old pulled Chinese silk to shreds and wove it afresh into fine gauze for the ladies.

Francoise Geoffry Deschaume (1967) China Looks at the World[1]

Introduction

The message of this book is straightforward. China, the world's largest country in terms of population with 21 percent of the world's population in 2001[2] is firmly embarked upon a development trajectory that will lead to an urbanized society. While rural life will remain important in China it will be the urban spaces of China that are, and will remain, the *locus* of most of the significant social and economic change that will occur in the country. It will also be the urban spaces that are the focus of most of the major political, environmental and social challenges of China's future.[3] One purpose of this study has been to show the difficulties of analyzing the demographic, social, economic and political dimensions of this urban transition. In a similar manner to every state in the global system the "facts" of urbanization are "cultural constructs" that have to be given "meaning" by researchers from within and outside the country who are familiar with the political economy of the state in which these "facts" are collected. For example, the very commendable efforts of the United Nations Population Division's biannual charting of the statistical dimensions of global urbanization, record that in 2001 42.5 percent of China's population were "urban." However, if the proportion of population recorded as engaged in "non-agricultural" occupations was utilized to indicate the urban proportion it would be of a much lower order of 33 percent. The 2000 Chinese census figure for the urban population of China was 36.9 percent.

If this lower level of urbanization of these three figures is more reflective of the real level of urbanization in China then it has important implications to China's urban future because it suggests that the numerical increase of urban populations will be very large over the next 30 years. For example, the United Nations estimates that the total population of China will grow from 1.2 billion in 2000 to 1.5 billion by 2030 while the urban population will increase from 463.6

million to 892.9 million in 2030 at which time China will have an urbanization level of 59 percent.[4] This projection assumes an average yearly increase of 14.3 million. If, however, the lower estimate of 33 percent urban were utilized (which is closer to the 2000 census figures) and the same level of urbanization predicted by the UN were accepted, a not unrealistic assumption in view of the decline of more than 200 million in the numbers of rural population in China, this would then suggest an increase of the urban population of 583 million and an average yearly increase of 19.4 million. Thus China will experience a yearly growth of urban population that exceeds the total population of most the contemporary world's nations in 2000. This sustained growth in the numbers of urban population within one country has not been seen before in human history and will probably be only approached by one other country, India. What is more, most of this increase in urban space will be occurring in the coastal region of China where the density per square kilometer is many times larger than that of European states and the USA at rather similar stages of the urban transition. This means that the pressure on available resources such as land, water and energy is very much higher than at comparable stages in the European experience of urbanization (see Table 11.1). Thus this increase in urban population poses immense challenges to the creation of sustainable urbanization.

The preceding discussion of the book has emphasized that this growth of urbanization in China is best understood as a project planned, guided and implemented by the central state in conjunction with the participation of other levels of government, quasi-government agencies, the private sector and foreign investment. This assertion flies in the face of a prevalent view that the Chinese urban transition is being led by increasingly strong market forces in which foreign direct investment is seen as a major influence. It is our view that the Chinese urbanization process must be seen as essentially state driven in a manner that frames the urbanization process so that it can be as facilitative to market forces as the existing political economy will permit. The fostering of urbanization, as we have argued, is central to the state modernization project.

Table 11.1 Population density of China's coastal provinces (2004) and selected developed countries at the end of the nineteenth century (persons/square km)

Country	*Population density*
Belgium	206
England and Wales	192
Netherlands	139
Italy	107
Japan	107
Germany	92
France	73
USA	8
China's coastal provinces	*215*

As we have explained this urbanization project is not just a top-down exercise, for at times (for example in the 1980s) local level initiatives have moved much faster than the central state's intentions. The urbanization project in China is one that involves constant negotiation and resistance with, and against, the central state often in the margins of urban areas that are less controlled by the central and provincial governments. But a broad consensus on the need to create an "urban China" reinforces the pace of the urban trajectory.

At the same time the urbanization process poses many challenges to the creation of a sustainable society in China that are in many ways similar to other developing countries where 80 percent of the world's urban growth will occur over the next 30 years. Given the size of China's urban increase and its growing importance in the global system it is imperative that the management of the urbanization process in China should be accomplished in such a manner as to avoid the worst of these problems. In this book we have argued that the Chinese urban experience will lead to new ways of thinking about the urbanization process that involves critically evaluating assumptions about the urbanization process that has relevance to other developing countries. It will also force the adoption of innovative and experimental policies within China that will form a learning experience for other developing countries that are at earlier stages of the urbanization transition. This approach involves deconstructing the urbanization process in a manner that we have introduced in the earlier chapters, presenting the challenges that are posed by the process and the policy responses that are possible. For this purpose this chapter explores China's urbanization within the context of its global trends in the urbanization and urban policy. First we present the main ideological debates concerning urbanization. Second we describe the main demographic features of urbanization as it is occurring at an Asian and global scale in relationship to China. The third part of the chapter analyzes the major reasons for the acceleration of the processes of urbanization in developing countries in terms of the concept of the telescoping of urban, economic, transport and environmental transitions. The next section deals with the challenges of the Chinese urban transition that include issues relating to economic, social, environmental, infrastructural and management challenges that are being presented by rapid urbanization. The final section deals with urban strategies that are needed to create sustainable urbanization.

The ideology of urbanization debates

Debates concerning the urbanization transition, particularly in developing countries, are not new and an anti-urban and pro-urban rhetoric is a prevailing trope of debates on the subject. Writing in 1971 one of the authors of this volume had this to say:

> Two visions haunt the intellectuals who view the urbanization process in the Third World. In the first vision the cities are seen as "enclaves" surrounded by a hostile peasantry. In these enclaves foppish elites play luxurious games

with the power and wealth they have inherited or created since Independence. In other visions the cities are seen as "beach-heads," centres of modernization which act as the catalysts of economic growth, the centres from which the benefits of modernization flow outwards to revitalize the stagnating agricultural sector.[5]

But today after more than 30 years during which urbanization in developing countries has accelerated these debates have become more complex reflecting the neo-liberal biases of the ideologies of globalization and different views on the role of "cities" and views concerning the relationship between urbanization and sustainability. Broadly it is possible to distinguish three positions in this debate. First there are a group of writers who essentially adopt a techno-economic position who argue that cities and in particular mega-urban regions are crucial to the emergence and effective functioning of the national and global economy. For example Alan Scott says this about mega-urban regions: "They function as territorial platforms for much of the post-Fordist economy that constitute the dominant leading edge of contemporary capitalist development as important staging posts for multinational corporations."[6] In addition they are major nodes in the transactional geography of the global economy and important contributors to the economic growth of their countries. The contribution of the four mega-urban regions of China to the GDP reported in Chapter 4 certainly support this claim. Another thread of these arguments is that these mega-urban centers are constantly in competition to capture a greater proportion of the global flows of labor, capital, commodities and goods. This competition is bringing about increasing functional specialization that is captured by the idea of the "global city." Sassen suggests that London, New York and Tokyo are the financial centers of this global hierarchy of mega-urban regions.[7] But within Asia there are many cities such as Shanghai, Singapore and Seoul that seek to become such global centers. The Chinese urbanization strategy is certainly designed to promote the larger Chinese cities of the coastal region to reach this status.

A second position in the debate on the urbanization process can be labeled the ecological approach.[8] Here the principal uniting theme is the idea that cities are a threat to global sustainability. At least one element of this concern is the belief that the sheer size of urban regions is a threat.[9] For the writers who embrace this approach the urban regions are voracious consumers of the resources of their hinterlands and are destroying ecosystems that have developed over long periods of time. The outputs of these urban regions cause environmental deterioration in the form of air pollution, decline in water quality, loss of valuable agricultural land and problems of waste disposal. While many of these writers recognize that as urban regions become richer their environmental problems may be managed more effectively they still argue that increasing global urbanization, particularly focused on an automobile mode of transport and energy demands will be a threat to global sustainability that requires ongoing policy intervention. While Chinese planners clearly understand these problems the pace of change is so rapid and their capacity to respond so restricted that the implementation of a comprehensive environmental strategy can only be incremental. Certainly one can make the argument that transformation in the urban administration that has been discussed in the preceding chapters is motivated at least in part by the goal of making the management of the urban environment more livable as an important part of a strategy to attract investment.

Finally there are a group of writers who point to the increasing social volatility these urban regions. Friedmann and Wolffe,[10] for example, argued that the social processes in the large urban centers of developing countries were creating a new form of urban poverty in which large numbers of people were being excluded from access to basic urban needs such as adequate employment, health, water, housing etc. This has been further exacerbated in the 1990s by neo-liberal policies designed to reduce subsidies on these services or privatize them; policies that have become an important component of World Bank requirements for loans to developing countries. Another facet of this social volatility is that the increased numbers of rural–urban migrants, laid-off workers from the state operated enterprises and the urban poor are creating social tension especially in situations where job opportunities are limited. In a recent article Dorothy Solinger (2006) argues that these groups together with other low income populations who eke out a living in the informal sector make up a new urban underclass in China who have "been estimated to number somewhere between 15 and 37 million depending upon whether income or expenditure is used as the standard of poverty."[11] Their plight is further exacerbated by limited access to education, health and other services. Thus the state is faced with a challenge of developing policies that can respond to these problems. Finally volatility in the global financial system can cause major social and economic problems in the urban centers. For example, the social impact of the financial crisis in Thailand was much more severe in urban areas than in the countryside.[12] There are growing pressures on the Chinese government to revalue its currency as it becomes more integrated into the global financial system. These demands together with structural adjustments required by membership of the WTO create potential problems of unemployment and social unrest.

The demographic realities of the urbanization process: setting the Chinese urbanization process in context

Long-term United Nations projections estimate that the world's population will grow from 6.06 billion in 2000 to 8.27 billion by 2030.[13] The single component of this increase that attracts the most attention is the fact that most of the predicted increase will occur in urban areas, which will grow from 2.86 billion to 4.98 billion. Of equal importance is the fact that almost all of this urban increase will occur in developing countries. It is also important to note that this huge increase in the urban population of developing countries will still only reach a level of urbanization of 56.4 percent by 2030 compared to the contemporary figure of more than 75 percent in the developed countries.

From the point of view of our discussion on China it is important to recognize that a major part of the global urban increase will occur in Asia. Thus between 2000 and 2030, 58 percent (1.3 billion) of this global increase in urban areas is based in Asia of which almost 80 percent is concentrated in the so-called population giants of India, Pakistan, Bangladesh, China and Indonesia where the levels of urbanization are at present quite low. China will experience the largest urban increase of all these population giants increasing between ten and 19 million a year until 2030 at which time it will still be only 59 percent urbanized. Potentially there will still be a large growth of urban population before it reaches the 75 percent level of developed countries today. Thus looming over all discussion of Asian urbanization trends is the demographic fact that a largest volume of population in the history of global urbanization will be involved in this urban shift in Asia.

There are dangers in using statistics such as these at the macro-level, for they fuel the ideology of anti-urbanists who see this demographic explosion of cities as the cause of the problems of management, environmental deterioration, energy consumption and social problems. This view is reinforced by the persistence of the ideas that rural society (as opposed to urban society) should be reinforced and conserved as a spatial block of societal good as opposed to urban evil. For any number of reasons ranging from political gerrymandering, to goals of national food security and belief in the morality of rural society the state is often a supporter of these ideologies. China's recent history and political economy introduces an ongoing ambivalence with respect to these arguments that leads to policy fluctuations such as the decision to freeze the conversion of rural land to urban land in 1998. But while these policies may be understandable they are clearly based upon a set of assumptions that are increasingly outmoded in contemporary China as the preceding chapters of this book show. The policies are outdated because they assume that the model of rural–urban differences is still applicable when there is increasing evidence that the rural–urban divide is being broken down through rural–urban mobility, the increase of urban activities in rural areas and the growth in information access in rural areas. Increasingly households in rural areas are sourcing their income from non-farm employment and remittances from migrants in urban areas. This is facilitated by a transactional revolution in communications that enables increased mobility and interaction between urban and rural areas. Second this assumption of rural–urban differences is based upon statistical definitions that are unable to keep pace with the changing spatial dimensions of the urbanization process. Even though, as we have argued in preceding chapters, the Chinese government has been extending the spatial extent of such urban administration it is still a long way from capturing the "invisible urbanization" processes occurring in rural areas. In particular it is the large urban regions based upon core mega-cities in China where this process of rural–urban collapse is most well developed. Of course at a national level there still remains a significant spatial divide between the areas of western China and middle and eastern China in this rural–urban dichotomy.

This creation of large mega-urban regions is now occurring at a global level at an accelerating rate. The United Nations estimates that urban agglomerations of more than ten million in size will grow from one in 1950 to 21 by 2015 of which eight will in China. A majority of these will be located in the coastal zone.

As we have shown in the earlier parts of the book it is difficult to analyze the real growth of the cities in China at a detailed statistical level because of the different systems of statistical collection as well as the under-bounding of urban activity. This means that many arguments concerning the relative importance of the different city size groupings as component of the urbanization process are bedeviled by statistical misunderstandings. Thus UN statistics show that the relative proportion of urban residents in the less developed countries in urban settlements of below 500,000 will only decline slightly from 51.2 percent to 49.0 percent by 2015. At the same time the proportion of population resident in urban settlements of above five million will grow from 14.6 percent to 16.8 percent. This leads to an assertion that large urban regions are given undue emphasis in the popular literature and that more attention should be paid to the smaller urban settlements, in part because they may act as a counter-magnet to the growth of population in larger urban areas where urban problems are said to be more severe. While the need to improve the urban livability of smaller urban settlements is important and is recognized in China we would argue that their importance is statistically over-emphasized and unlikely to slow down the growth of the large urban areas. By the year 2020 there will be 70 to 100 cities over one million in size making up 30 percent of the national population and making up more than 60 percent of the urban population. Many of them will be part of clusters of cities that are part of major mega-urban regions.

Convergence and divergence in the Chinese urbanization process: the significance of telescoping transitions

From our perspective it is more important to focus attention on the urbanization process within the framework of broader theories of societal transition that can be described in terms of the modernization transition from traditional to modern societies, the demographic transition from low growth to high growth and then to low growth societies, the urban transition from low to highly urbanized societies, the environmental transition and the transportation and information transition. All these theories suggest that as societies become wealthier and more urbanized their actions become more influenced by global forces as they become more integrated into the global economy. Most of these transition theories include assumptions that transition involves a series of stages over relatively long periods of time and are sequential. But in fact as Peter Marcotullio and Yok Shu Lee point out with respect to the theory of the urban environmental transition the unique feature of our present era is that there is a compression of the time frame in which transitions are occurring.[14] Their focus is on the environmental transition but we would argue that their arguments could be applied more broadly to the urbanization process. We have illustrated the effect of this telescoping urban transition on the urbanization process in the accompanying Figure 11.1, which shows the changes in the level of urbanization between England and Wales, Mexico and China at various points in their urbanization process. As is clear from this diagram China will take only half the time to reach the same level of urbanization as England and Wales and Mexico. But this will involve a much larger volume of population increase.

Marcotullio and Lee further argue that the various transitions are now overlapping in a "telescoping" of transition processes that is occurring in a much shorter time frame in developing countries than earlier transitions in the developed societies.[15] We find this concept of the "telescoping transitions" very helpful in explaining the processes of urbanization that are driven by a transactional transition that involves fundamental changes in the flows of people, commodities, capital and information between and within countries. Most obviously the flows of capital and information occur almost instantaneously in time and space (unless there are institutional or technological restraints) while the movement of people and commodities has become much faster over the last 50 years. The international components of this transactional revolution are generally referred to as part of a new era of globalization in which the role of transnational corporations is seen as increasingly important. The role of localities in this process is important for, increasingly, their development relies upon buying into this transactional revolution.

Most planners argue that this transactional revolution is leading to a greater centralization of the urban systems, not only in terms of large urban regions but also in the territorial configurations and functional specializations of these urban clusters.[16] Now they spread along transport corridors, as is the case with the Tokyo–Osaka urban corridor, or leap-frog outwards from the city core in a series of poly-nucleated cities, which form a large amorphous urban region.

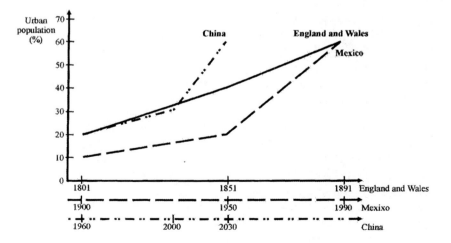

Figure 11.1 Telescoping transition: urban growth through time.

Sometimes they can even cross international boundaries as is the case in the Singapore Growth Triangle.[17] While Asian governments, including China, have at times adopted national policies that supported development away from such regions, developmental goals and emerging market forces have tended to reinforce concentration of economic activity in large urban regions.

This is most obvious in the development of transport systems that have encouraged the increasing use of auto-centered transport systems including private cars, motorbikes and various forms of public transportation such as buses and minibuses. Barter, Midgley and Kenworthy and Laube[18] have all shown that while Asian countries still have much lower vehicle/population ratios than the developed countries these ratios have been increasing rapidly in the last two decades with little change in the ratio between wealthier Asian countries and the lower middle-income countries. Public transport remains much more important in Asia than the OECD countries although data also indicates a fall in the proportion of public motorized transportation in terms of number of trips in the last two decades. China has firmly embarked upon this auto-dependent trajectory as is indicated by a statement on the automobile industry by Chen Quingtai, deputy director of the Development Research Centre of the State Council who says "The industry will have a profound impact on all aspects of Chinese cities."[19] Estimates of the increase in the number of automobiles over the next two decades suggest that the number of vehicles will increase to 140 million by 2020 and will be expected to reach the current level of the USA shortly after that date. This will occur despite the fact that many large cities are building subway systems.[20] This development will be further reinforced by the rapid growth of a national road system and the ongoing city-based policies of freeway development.

From the point of view of our earlier argument concerning the forces that create urban regions these auto-centered systems encourage the outward spread of urban-based activities (residential, work and leisure) in these mega-urban regions. What distinguishes the automobile from most other types of consumer goods is that it requires a great deal of space that leads to the outward spread of urban activity. These auto-centered systems include "an extensive material infrastructure of roadways, service and repair facilities, storage spaces, and an extensive social infrastructure of elaborate bureaucracies"[21] to control the system. The auto-dependent city is also supported by a culture of *automobility* that is encouraged by the car manufacturing industry, through advertising and the desire of the middle and upper income classes to own automobiles. The development strategy of China fosters the growth of a national car building industry often in conjunction with international car manufacturers. In fact national development strategies that encourage the spread of manufacturing create a road infrastructure that links industrial estates with transport nodes (airports, seaports) that eventually will serve a dual function for commuting by car and the transport of manufactured goods. Another aspect of the urban transition in China relates to the changing structure of energy consumption in China. In recent years as Gates and Yin (2004)[22] report roughly 60 percent of residential and commercial use of energy is made up of coal and wood and corn stalks. While much of this consumption occurs in rural areas or industrial activity the prevailing trend in the larger urban areas is for increasing consumption of oil, gas and electricity forms of energy. If for example China would follow the example of Korea it would reduce its reliance upon coal to almost 7 percent by 2060 and increase its use of oil, gas and electricity. Undoubtedly this would lead to cleaner cities and reduce the problems of ambient air pollution but it will also create huge demands for these alternative sources. China is already engaged in developing the west to east gas pipeline from Xinjiang to the Shanghai area as well as the Guangdong and Fujian liquid natural gas projects. The development of the Three Gorges Project and the reworking of electricity grids to provide more power to urban areas are examples of China's response to growing urbanization. This growing Chinese demand for oil and gas it has been argued is one of the many reasons for the increase in oil prices in 2004–05 and is likely to increase pressures on world supply.

A second hinge of this process of mega-urbanization is the tendency for the global space economy to become more integrated. Allen Scott describes these developments as follows:

> While most of economic activities and transactions still occur within the national boundaries an increasing amount of economic activity (input–output chains, migration stream, foreign direct investment by multi-national corporations, monetary flows etc.) now occur in the spaces that occur between nations.[23]

He goes onto argue that these developments have created a new "social grammar of space" in which "the whole edifice reposes upon a geographic foundation that can best described as a mosaic of city regions constituting the economic motors of the global economy."[24]

It must be stressed that the global economy is also telescoping as the global search for cheap labor and markets that involves the movement of manufacturing assemblies from OECD countries to the cheaper labor destinations in the developing world continues in which the cheaper labor locations of China and India assume increasing importance. At the same time financial flows from OECD countries also assume growing importance both as direct foreign investment and portfolio investment. It was the latter that was an important element of the financial crisis that occurred in several Asian countries from 1997. Most recently there has been a phase in which domestic markets have become more open (in part because of WTO requirements) and domestic markets are characterized by increasing domestic and cross-border mergers. The discussion of the merging of state-owned enterprises (SOEs) in Chapter 9 delineates this process very well. This is leading to a further concentration on the mega-urban regions that are the nodes in the circulation of this capital (see Chapter 3).

What we are describing here is an intensely competitive system in which mega-urban regions of China, like those in other parts of the world, are competing to capture some portion of these transactions generated at both national and international levels. Thus, there is growing pressure on the governments at both national and city level to create a favorable environment that will increase the flow of transactions to their mega-urban region. International expositions, Olympic games, major spectacle sites such as Disneyland, new airports, convention centers, multi-media corridors, urban renewal and industrial estates in peri-urban areas are all part of the packages that are designed to make these urban regions more attractive. This has involved governments giving priority to the use of public resources and they have less capacity to respond to the environmental and social problems of these regions.[25] Today China is in a frenzy of this form of development including preparations for the Beijing Olympics in 2008 and a major international exposition in Shanghai in 2010. While many policy-makers argue that this "spectacle" form of investment can help create more competitive economies in urban regions it also has the capacity to generate countervailing forces within the city regions in the form of socially progressive civil societies advocating livable city regions especially in the more developed Asian societies such as Japan, Korea and Singapore. But at present this is occurring slowly in China. For example the Beijing municipal government announced in 2004 that the Beijing Olympic Games would require an investment of US$2000 billion over the next five years.[26] Undoubtedly this form of expenditure creates an ongoing tension between growth oriented policies and those directed towards developing more livable urban regions. This tension also has a spatial dimension because the conflict between growth and livability are often reflected in the contrasts between the core cities and their margins.

The transactional revolution is causing contradictory processes of detachment of the central cores and the inner and outer margins. At the same time there is increasing functional integration emerging in larger mega-urban regions. There is also increasing detachment in the sense that city cores are increasingly sourcing their resources such as food from global and wider national markets and integration as the resources of the outer zones such as land and water are needed as the population of the inner parts of the mega-urban region increase. There are also important differences in the development of these two areas. In the core the built-environment is being transformed to make it more attractive to the forces of globalization. This involves major investments of public and private capital in the enticing infrastructure of globalization. For example in a national meeting held in 2005 Wang Guangtao, Minister of Construction, criticized these strategies. He reported that 183 cities have vowed to build themselves into international metropolises with so-called "show off projects" such as huge squares, luxury office buildings and airports. A report by the State Development Corporation estimates the total debt borrowed by local governments equals one trillion yuan (US$123 billion).[27] On the other hand the urban margins are being under-supplied with services and public and private investment is smaller and more focused on industrial estates, gated communities and road systems. At times it seems that the globalization processes are so technologically powerful and ubiquitous with the creation of industrial estates, freeways international airports, etc., that the integration with the global economy seems to be more important than livability.

A second issue that effects the growth of urban areas is urban–rural relation that has two components. The first is the growing income inequity between rural and urban areas that has become a major concern of the Chinese government. In 2005 annual incomes in rural areas were only 30 percent of those in urban areas. They have responded to this concern by focusing the Eleventh Five Year Plan from 2006–10, that was adopted by the People's Congress in April 2006, on building a "new socialist countryside that abolishes agricultural taxes on farmers, increasing the budget for rural development to $42.4 billion on rural development which compares to 35 billion on defense."[28] A second component of rural–urban relations that is more central to this book may be described as the urban–rural interface that as cities spread outwards particularly in the Asian context involves the expansion of urban activities into zones of intense rural–urban activity.[29] One aspect of this expansion emphasizes that the outer margins form a hinterland that functions as a resource pool providing water, food, building materials, land, labor, recreation space and waste disposal sites for the urban core. In the Chinese context as in other countries of the developing world there is particular concern with the loss of arable land to urban expansion, which is seen as affecting the security of national food supply. Atkinson points out that "this functional analysis of cities and their hinterlands focuses attention on resources which remains significant as an issue in ecological sustainability."[30] Thus the issue of city–hinterland relationships has been replaced by a scale of interaction that has become more spatially extended and more intense at the local level. What is more this interaction is occurring in the urbanizing regions of China where in the past there has been a multiplicity of administrative entities often set up in the past to administer districts in which rural activity dominated. The influx of urban activities and migrant populations further exacerbate the administrative difficulties and increase resource competition. In the Chinese context the response to this situation has been to extend administrative control over these marginal areas. This creates a political environment in which core city governments can attempt to create a more orderly and efficient environment for economic growth. Thus Webster, whose recent writing on this subject focuses on China, places much more emphasis on the driving forces that are creating urban margin regions, such as government policy, foreign investment particularly in manufacturing and the increase in land prices, encouraging speculation. In Webster's view the city cores of Chinese cities are assuming more service functions and the knowledge economy is growing in importance.[31]

This is forming a social structure that is dominated by middle and upper income groups whose demands for housing are being responded to by the growth of apartment and condominium units, which leads to social and spatial segregation between middle and upper income and lower income groups most prominently migrant workers. Some researchers argue that over time the growth of well-educated professionals and white collar workers in urban areas who make up the middle class will grow substantially from an estimated 19 percent in 2003 and lead to a change in transformation of society from the "onion" styled structure to an "olive" structure. They will fuel the consumption in Chinese cities with demands for up-market housing, household consumer goods and automobiles.[32] But over the next few years of high urbanization growth the majority of the core city populations will continue to live in crowded walk-up tenements while housing for low income groups is in short supply. Increasing integration into the global system creates demand for hotels and offices for both business and tourism. The internal morphology of these city cores assumes a poly-nucleated pattern and the development of automobile and public transport systems will further accentuate these developments with an increasing spread of the cities. At the same time some previous components of the cities, built-environment remain in the form of historical and cultural precincts and areas of housing where low income residents live sometimes still in "illegal settlements." Thus there are sharp distinctions in the social landscape of the city cores.[33]

In the inner rings of the mega-urban regions of China that are incipient commuting zones, residential housing is quite diverse ranging from row housing for lower to middle income dwellers to gated communities of large houses set in big lots often adjacent to golf courses and country clubs that form part of such developments. These housing developments are primarily populated by residents who have moved from the city core although some worker housing also exists in these areas. These zones are almost entirely serviced by motorized transportation and commuting is facilitated by expressways radiating outwards from the inner cores to the new zones of industrial growth in the outer margins. Mega-mall development close to the expressways is beginning to emerge in China. These inner rings, which were often the first location of industrial estates based on cheap labor, are increasingly threatened by the development of new industrial estates in the urban margins. This is a zone where agriculture has undergone the greatest transformation with the growth of capital-intensive agri-business and specialized cash crops such as fruit and animal husbandry. This process is described very well in the chapters on Dongguan and Kunshan.

Finally there are the outer margins into which urban activity continues to spread in the form of industrial estates and residential developments. This is the zone of fastest population growth characterized by the movement of internal migrants from other parts of China and residents from other parts of the mega-urban regions. While residential developments typical of the inner zone are occurring and migrants often rent housing from rural farmers, these are regions in which the competition between agriculture and urban activity is now most pronounced and the land use is highly mixed with the juxtaposition of these different uses causing major environmental and social problems that are the subject of the next section.

It is against this backdrop of these "demographic imperatives" of the Chinese urban transition and the very rapid economic growth of the last two decades particularly focused on the coastal region that the issues of urban growth and sustainability have to be positioned. Many commentators suggest that China is showing an inevitable convergence with the patterns of urbanization experienced in the developed countries such as the USA. But we would argue that the divergent historical path of China's development has laid the foundation for institutional and policy responses for managing the urban transition that enable the framing of divergent responses that offer innovative solutions to the challenges of Chinese urbanization that are discussed in the next section.

The challenges of the Chinese urban transition

On the face of it the preceding discussion suggests a rather gloomy prognosis for China's urban future. The large numbers of population that will have to be absorbed into urban areas is the first fact that will have to be faced. Second, there will need to be building of an adequate urban infrastructure that will provide this population with the basic services of transport, housing, education, health, energy, food, water and waste disposal. Third, the urban areas will have to create facilitative frameworks for the encouragement of economic activity and employment generation. Fourth, China will have to move even further in the reform of the *hukou* system and develop more effective policies to manage the movement of rural migrants into the cities. Already there have been some policy changes in this respect with some migrants being permitted the same benefits as urban dwellers in small and medium-sized cities and some large cities.[34] An important part of this challenge is the need to give these rural migrants the same access to public services, such as education, as urban residents. City governments have avoided these costs in the past by treating migrants as "temporary residents" who were not entitled to these benefits. As we have indicated China's rural population will continue to grow for some decades and the potential volume of rural–urban migrants is very large. Fifth, these urban areas will have to be managed and governed in a way that will ensure that the needs of the urban populations are provided so that the problems of the urban areas of other developing countries can be avoided. Finally these challenges will have to be faced in the context of a social, political and economic transition that has proved volatile in other transitional socialist countries. But despite these challenges there are grounds for optimism that China can manage this urban transition successfully.

Basically these challenges can be presented in terms of the contrast between a trajectory of economic modernization for China of which growing urbanization is seen as both a driver and product of economic growth and the challenges to national sustainability that this growth poses. As we have discussed in Chapter 3 since the Tenth Five Year Plan the Chinese government has accepted that urbanization will be the locomotive of economic growth. Influential senior economic planners go even further arguing that the growth of city clusters in the Yangzi River delta, the Pearl River Delta and the Bohai region should be further encouraged because of the greater economic efficiency and productivity of such regions and the contribution they make to national wealth. Already there are plans to create a new city district of Binhai New Zone in Tianjin on the model of Shenzhen and Pudong. Binhai New Zone is expected to be China's third growth pole after Shenzhen and Pudong, which would drive further economic growth and global linkages in north China. Such development will also hasten the process of the city-region planning approach and will involve further annexation of surrounding counties by municipalities of Beijing and Tianjin.

The central challenge relates to the pace of urban change that has gone beyond the capacity all levels of government to respond to in the short term. The "overheated" character of the current Chinese urban transition is raising many problems. First the rapid growth of urban population and urban construction is creating growing infrastructure demands. One authority has suggested that "Most of urban China has been built in the past 25 years, at a rate of 150 million square meters per year, often on large projects. This rate of urban expansion is unprecedented and is contributing to serious environmental degradation."[35] Chinese cities are suffering electricity "brownouts." There is growing traffic congestion and problems of automobile pollution. In many cities water provision is becoming a problem particularly in the Beijing–Tianjin mega-urban region. In 2004 almost two-thirds of the cities were short of water and almost 15 percent had a severe shortage. More generally the State Environmental Protection Administration claims that more than two out of three cities failed to reach national residential ambient air quality standards. This has important consequences to the health of the urban population exposing them to health risks such as chronic bronchitis, pulmonary disease and lung cancer.[36] The removal of waste and sewerage is an ongoing problem. They are further exacerbated by the spread of cities and the shortfall in infrastructure and services in the outer margins of cities. As we have commented the solution to these problems involves both adopting national programs (e.g. environmental protection), the enforcement of them at the local urban level and the investment in improving and creating the infrastructure. One estimate of the annual costs of Chinese urbanization is between 300–500 billion yuan (US$37 billion to 62 billion) which is roughly 2–4 percent of China's GDP in 2004. Economic planners in China argue that because of the considerable revenue being generated through land conversion and other local taxes local governments should have the capacity to provide much of the capital that is necessary for this infrastructure investment. But it will certainly involve some balance of investment between growth and sustainability. As urban governments are finding in the developed countries, investment in sustainable infrastructure and creating clean and attractive cities is making them more competitive as cities and increases their service base.

A second problem of the dominant urbanization trajectory relates to the issues of rural–urban relations. The most obvious example of this has been the large movement of rural migrants into the cities of coastal China. While this movement has provided increased income to migrants and their rural households there are ongoing problems in the migration that relate to access of migrants to urban services in urban areas and more particularly to fluctuations in labor force demands that causes unemployment. As of June 2005 it was estimated that 8.5 million were unemployed in Chinese cities and towns, which internationally was a comparatively low percentage of 2 percent. But undoubtedly this underestimated numbers. The inequality between rural and urban incomes will continue to motivate rural migrants into the cities and place great pressure on the provision of service and jobs. Many commentators have linked the growth in migrant numbers to increased crime and some cities such Shenzhen and Beijing have begun to restrict migration to their cities. More generally it seems that the Chinese government will have to recognize that urban poverty is an emerging feature of Chinese cities and the marketization of housing is making access difficult for some segments of the population. This suggests that low income housing policies will have to be an important part the responsibility of city administrations. There are other demographic and social issues that will become more important in Chinese cities of the future. First, while the "one-child policy" has been more successful in urban areas than rural areas in reducing population increase it has important welfare implications for the urban families of the future. As the proportion of Chinese urban population that are growing older increases the dependency burden will grow and this is unlikely to be met by family care that was typical of the extended family.[37] In this respect Singapore's experience is of particular relevance to the future of Chinese cities although as the rural–urban migration accelerates Chinese cities will not be able to limit these numbers as has Singapore and this will place growing pressure on social infrastructure needs. Another social trend that is likely to have implications for the future Chinese city is likely to be inter-generational differences particularly in consumption and savings values that is already reflected in the consumption landscapes of Chinese cities. These demographic and social developments that are so closely linked to increasing integration in the global economy also raise important issues of social vulnerability that surfaced in the currency crisis of some Asian countries of 1997 and had their major impact on the most globally integrated part of these societies–the urban areas. While China avoided this event the global pressure for it to revalue the yuan and open up its financial systems to the global financial system suggest that China might not be isolated in the future.

This discussion of the challenge of China's urban future is very skeletal but it suggests that China will have to develop broader responses to the urbanization process than just to facilitate the economic components of the process. We turn to this discussion in the next section.

Policy alternatives: economic growth and sustainabilty in China

These emerging urbanization trends raise many policy challenges. There are three assumptions that underlie such policy discussion. First, that there is a need to recognize that the urbanization process in China poses serious challenges to ecosystems of which they are part. In this discussion we will refer only to the local features of the ecosystem but it must also be recognized that the urbanization process creates broader problems to global sustainability by increasing the output of carbon gases into the ozone that increase global warming etc. Second, there is a need to accept the fact that policy intervention is a necessary prerequisite for sustainable urbanization. This means there is a need to investigate critically the scale of policy intervention that ideally must combine national and regional integration with local initiative. Third, there is a need to think of the vulnerability of urbanization that presents risks and advantages for both the population that lives in them and global society.

The policy implications of regarding the urban spaces of China as part of ecosystems demand further clarification of this concept. While there are many definitions of ecosystems we believe the one that best fits the urban context is the idea of the ecosystem that includes the dynamic interaction between people and the environment. Of course the social, economic and political institutions of which the people are part mediate this interaction. In this system the ecosystem provides such services as food, water and energy that provide the constituents of well-being. These ecosystems are capable of being changed by people and causing changes in human well-being. This vision of ecosystems sees large urban places as functioning as partial ecosystems that are generally supported by biophysical processes that occur elsewhere.[38] These urban spaces because they are significant nodes of energy and material transformation and consumption are more demanding of ecosystem services than non-urban areas. These demands can often affect the quality of the air, the availability of clean water, waste disposal and other aspects of the ambient environment and have been well documented.

The crucial part of this approach is that it recognizes the spatiality of the urbanization process arguing that the different linkages between urban systems and spatial parts of the urban regions produce a different mix of results both within urban areas and in relations with non-urban adjacent areas in the urban margins where the demand for water, land and waste disposal sites is most aggressive. The implications of understanding of the urban spaces as part of an ecosystem to the scale of policy intervention are considerable. In 1995 Robinson and McGee had argued that the central policy requirement of the large urban regions in Southeast Asia (that were generally construed as presenting the main demands upon ecosystems) was the need to create an institutional response at a regional level.[39] The myriad of administrative units with different responsibilities that characterize the typical mega-urban region are ill-equipped to respond, for example, to the challenges of environmental deterioration that are caused by river pollution from another part of the mega-urban region. But in the period since this argument was presented, the idea that regional planning can somehow provide a rational response to the policy requirements of the large urban region has increasingly been discarded, as neo-liberal thinking has developed its agenda of deregulation, privatization and decentralization. These neo-liberal ideas that have become part of the policy agenda of developed countries have now been transferred into the policy agendas of developing countries of Asia and have often been made the prerequisite of loans by international agencies. In some cases these ideologies clash with the modernist top-down projects of governments in developing countries that are still concerned with achieving development (see Chapter 3). This neo-liberal policy agenda brings about a fragmentation of policy responses in the mega-urban regions that is added to the intense political fragmentation. For example, waste disposal in the upper income housing developments in the urban margins has become the responsibility of the developer while low income dwellers have no waste disposal service. Thus as Atkinson points out "The mega city regions pose an insuperable problem for the theorists of a reasonable planning process ... whilst recognizing the major problems both in the inner cities and the extended regions focus attention on contingent solutions, rather than confronting the problematic as a whole."[40]

Thus the policy solutions for mega-urban regions in China will need some way of combining the regional vision that is needed for preserving the ecosystem; the sub-regional intervention at the level of city core, inner and outer margins and contingent solutions at the local level. This means there is a need to reconfigure power and management relations in urban and regional space. In fact this is already occurring in some developing countries with the emergence of new networks of civil society.[41] These developments create a complex managerial environment in which the myriad of polyarchic decision-making units comes into conflict with the transformative elements of the higher levels of government resulting in a decisional congestion that exists in the many urban regions of Asia. The accompanying diagram that is based upon a decisional framework attempts to identify the major problems (see Figure 11.2).

However, the rethinking of the methods of governance that this decisional congestion raises is very challenging. Broadly any institutional response at the level of the urban region would seem to involve a twofold interpretation of governance as incorporating the exercise of political will and power within a defined urban space and, second, the management of urban spaces that are designed to make them more livable. Such a vision does not exclude the possibility of city–region, public–private–government–civil society coalitions being formed. In fact the administrative spread of urban governance that has been

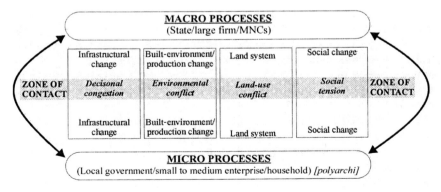

Figure 11.2 Hypothetical model of urban site.

occurring in China's urban spaces that has been one of the focuses of this book represent a potentially highly innovative and positive response to the need to develop livable urban spaces. This, of course, requires the continuation of the regional visioning of urban space that is evidenced by the formation coalitions of mayors in mega-urban region that aims to formulate regional solutions to economic duplication, transportation planning and environmental deterioration. An even larger vision is evident in the formation of the Pan Pearl River Delta grouping (nine plus two) that seeks to promote the role of the Pearl River Delta in the greater region of Guangdong, Fujian, Guangxi, Hunan, Yunnan, Sichuan, Jiangxi, Guizhou, Hainan and Hong Kong and Macao. At this point it remains largely a marketing device.[42] A form of regional visioning is needed that can when necessary, adopt region-wide policies. In this respect Brenner's carefully articulated review of metropolitan regionalism has relevance. He describes metropolitan regionalism as "including all strategies to establish institutions, policies or governance mechanisms at a geographical scale which approximates that of existing socio-economic interdependencies within an urban agglomeration."[43]

It can be suggested that reconfiguring of policy mechanisms would involve at least three levels of intervention: first, at the sub-city level through agreement between governments and local populations; second, at the city level where there is more need for negotiation between private and government interests; third, at the urban region level where planning and control of the use of resources can be monitored and managed and region-wide solutions implemented. For example, the issue of solid waste disposal is a major issue in Asia today. A recent report estimates that the urban areas of Asia now spend about US$2.5 billion on solid waste management per year and that this figure will increase to US$25 billion by 2025 generating 1.8 million tons per year. The report indicates that municipal governments are usually the responsible agencies for solid waste collection but the magnitude of the problem is well beyond the capacity of most municipal governments. The disposal of solid waste presents one of the more intractable conflicts within urban regions because in many of these regions solid waste collection systems are quite diverse but the most common means of disposal are landfills on the urban margins. This suggests that it is very important to implement spatially differentiated systems of waste management. For example the financially better-off core cities can afford relatively expensive incineration systems similar to those of Japan. But in the poorer outer margins of the urban region the local governments should encourage local communities to use recycling that can be implemented so as to have the least environmental impact. As part of this process there would have to be agreement between various authorities at the regional level designed to mediate the impact of the dumping of waste from city cores into their hinterlands. Similar problems exist with the loss of agricultural land that is caused by urban expansion policy concerns about food supply to the growing urban populations.

The third policy challenge relating to the urban space is the issue of vulnerability. Because urban regions are so important as centers of economic growth (typically generating 40–60 percent of national GDP) and are so reliant upon the ecosystems beyond the core they become particularly vulnerable to fluctuations in the supply of these services such as water and electricity. In many urban regions of developing Asia there are constant brownouts in power supply and the supply of clean water is inadequate. As Krauss points out "One major influencing factor is growing urbanization, and above all mega cities are particularly prone to supply crisis, social disorganization, political unrest, natural and man-made disasters due to their highest concentration of people and extreme dynamics of development."[44]

Another aspect of the vulnerability of these mega-urban regions relates to the considerable social fragmentation that is emerging in these areas. As the population of mega-urban regions grows the competition for access to ecosystems grows. In such a situation it is the poor who are most affected and deprived. Particularly, it is the urban margins that become the location of most of the urban poor. The poor often consist of recent migrants who are forced to live in inadequate poorly serviced housing. In addition the effects of environmental deterioration are most serious affecting the health and well-being of these poor populations. Within the city cores despite the growth of the middle and upper income populations there are large numbers of migrants who survive in the informal sector or low income occupations servicing the richer population. As the wealth of these city cores increases they also become attractive locations for international migration involved in domestic service or the construction industry. In this situation there are often sharp differences between the social complexity and volatility of the different parts of the urban region.

Conclusion

It is often difficult to relate the abstract theme of the processes of urbanization to the real world, but the first step in the assessment of the challenges of the urbanization processes, particularly in a region such as China, is to clarify the dimensions of the process of urbanization. Our analysis has suggested that while the growth of urbanization is often presented from an ideological perspective as a threat to global and national sustainability, when the process is deconstructed into its various spatial, ecological economic and social dimensions it is possible to be more constructive about managing the process so as to avoid adverse consequences.

Thus we have shown that an understanding of the techno-economic, spatial, ecological and human dimensions of the urbanization process in China enables more effective policy formation. This involves the recognition that the transactional revolution of globalization and the prevalence of the auto-centered mega-urban region are crucial drivers in the urbanization process; the spatial variation between city cores and their adjacent built-up areas and urban margins are central to the reconfiguration of the political and administrative systems of urban spaces; the understanding that urban areas are parts of broader ecosystems that need to be managed so that the conservation of ecosystems is given priority; and finally the need to place the issue of the vulnerability of cities and particularly the most vulnerable populations at the center of policy concerns.

The implications of this understanding are fourfold. First, because of the importance of the urbanization process in China with almost 22 percent of the world's population and a majority of mega-urban regions, the need to develop effective management of the mega-urbanization process is a major priority. Second, this will involve governmental commitment to continuing the administrative reorganization that reflect the realities of the urban spaces' internal differentiation and the different policy interventions that can be developed for increasingly differentiated urban spaces. As many writers have commented there are few working models of this type of governance and most are to fit the particular cultural and economic context of individual countries. They are therefore not easily transferred.

Third, the management of the urbanization process will involve adherence to the idea of preserving ecosystems of which the urban spaces are part. For many the auto-dependent city is seen as one of the principal causes of ecosystem deterioration and undoubtedly policy interventions that attempt to increase the role of public transport and reduce polluting effects of gas consumption are important in this respect. The theory of the urban environmental transition in developed countries certainly suggests that localized environmental problems decline as the wealth of cities increase. But these can only have a partial effect as the spatial *locus* of these problems shifts as the city becomes spatially more spread. Finally, policy solutions to the problems of urbanization will need to become more people based. The process of policy formation must become more incorporative of the various social components of urban regions including governments, the private sector, NGOs and community-based groups. As yet civil society has been slow to develop in Chinese urban spaces but as China's global integration continues its role will increase. This will be encouraged by the increasing involvement of international organizations such as the WTO and the requirements of international loan and aid agencies.

There is another dimension of policy formation that is significant. This is the need to create information bases at the urban scale and its various spatial components. Recent developments in demographic research have emphasized the need to redefine the territorial units of the national census to capture the reality of the mega-urban regions.[45] Ultimately of course the provision of information can only be effective if their means to use it is to inform public policy. Thus the development of databases must be linked to the kind of institutional changes that have been listed above. This will involve constant experimentation at all urban scales as our introductory quote points out and sharing of the results of these policies between urban spaces and the national state. It is vital to engage these issues in China at this point if the inevitable urban transition is to be managed so as to create a sustainable, livable and economically productive society. China, because of the size of its population, the volume of its projected urban increases in the urban transition and potential to develop innovative responses, is the crucial model for the future of world urbanization. As we have argued earlier in this book the key to understanding the processes of urbanization in China is not the blind acceptance of models of urbanization from other parts of the world. China is developing its own response to urbanization that represents as we have suggested a form of hybridity that is a result of the interaction between global, national and local forces that drive the urbanization process. A key to this "hybridity" is the endogenous "adaptability" that China is capable of applying to the challenges of urbanization. For example, it has been shown that in the 1980s China largely avoided the problems of unemployment and widespread social unrest that accompanied the movement of rural populations to urban areas that characterize other developing countries in the early phases of the urban transition. Now at the beginning of the twenty-first century China is engaged in another experiment in managing the urban transition through the extension of the urban administration over the "urban spaces" of China, while at the same time there is "leap-frogging" of urban activities into the largely rural margins of cities. This "dual track" process of urbanization creates the opportunity to facilitate economic growth and reorganize urban space to take steps to minimize the problems of the urban transition. As yet China is still lagging in developing an effective institutional structure to manage these "new urban spaces" preferring a slower incremental approach to changing institutional governance. But as China has shown already, its people and governments at all levels have the capacity to innovate "hybrid" solutions that may well show the other countries of the developing world how to manage urban transition which is the major transformational global process of the contemporary era.

Notes

Preface

1 See Brook and Frolic (1997); Goldman and Perry (2002); Yeh and Wu (1998) pp. 165–252; Chung (1999c); Solinger (1999); Logan (2002); Zhang (2002b) pp. 64–76; Zhang (2002a) pp. 303–23; Ma and Wu (2005a); and Friedmann (2005).

1 Introduction

1 Lefebvre (1991) p. 416.
2 Chinese statistical yearbooks do not report data from these SARs because of their special status.
3 See Wang *et al.* (2002) pp. 113–42.
4 In 1984, the first 11 economic and technological development zones were established in 11 coastal cities. By the mid-1990s, another 21 economic and technological development zones were established. Meanwhile 52 high-tech industrial zones were set up with different names, such as High Tech Park, High and New Tech Park, High Tech Experiment Zone or International Industrial Zone. For detail, see Gu and Zhao (1998).
5 See Cartier (2001b). Also Wang and Meng (2004) pp. 181–96.
6 See Lin (1997); Wang (1998); Marton (2000); Zhu (1999); and Gulden (1997).
7 See Zhu (1998) pp. 267–84; Zhu (2000) pp. 413–34; Zhu (2002) pp. 9–22; and Zhu (2004) pp. 207–28.
8 See Sit and Yang (1997) pp. 647–77; and Hsing (1998).
9 Wang (2002a) pp. 23–9.
10 Feuchtwang (2004) pp. 3–30.
11 Ma (2005) p. 478.
12 Guthrie (2000) pp. 727–49.
13 See Harvey (1985); Wu and Ma (2005) pp. 260–79; and Smart and Lee (2003) pp. 163–71.
14 In particular the work of Zhou Yixing, one of the leading urban geographers of China, is an exception to this generalization. See Zhou (1991) pp. 89–112.
15 For example, the term city is included in the title of three of the more important collections of papers about urbanization in China. See Chung (1999c); Logan (2002); and Ma and Wu (2005b).
16 See Xu and Yeh (2005) pp. 283–308.
17 See, for example, Gaubatz (1995) pp. 79–86; Gautbatz (1999) pp. 1495–521; Sit (1995); Hook (1998); and Zhou (1998) pp. 429–36.

2 The political economy of Chinese urbanization

1 Ma and Wu (2005b) pp. 1–20.

2 This argument that the urbanization process in developing countries has some different features from the developed countries is drawn from the "dependency theorists." For a summary of these arguments see Armstrong and McGee (1984).

3 See Nee (1991) pp. 663–81; Nee (1992) pp. 1–27; Nee and Cao (2000) pp. 1175–95; Nee and Swedburg (2005); Lefebvre (1991); and Harvey (1982). While there is by no means agreement between the writers who are engaged in the "new economic geography" they share a common interest in the role of culture, institutions and the social embedding of economic activity in place. See Barnes (2001) pp. 546–65; Olds and Poon (2002) pp. 535–55; and Yeung (2002a) pp. 250–2.

4 In particular on this point see the valuable assessment by Guthrie (2000) pp. 727–49.

5 This issue is discussed in Yeung and Lin (2003) pp. 107–28. Also see Lin (2002b) pp. 1809–31.

6 See McGee (1991a) pp. 3–25; McGee (1991b); Zhou (1991) pp. 89–112; Lin (1994) pp. 1–23; Lin (1997); Wang (1998); and Marton (2000).

7 Ma (2002) pp. 1545–69.

8 See Yeh *et al.* (2002). Also see Leung (1993) pp. 272–302; and Smart and Smart (1991) pp. 216–33.

9 Kelly (1999) pp. 379–400; and Yeung (2002b) pp. 285–305.

10 See the discussion of the impact of globalization on Southeast Asia cities for a comparative perspective. McGee (2002) pp. 8–27; and Dicken (2003).

11 See Hall (1966); Friedmann and Wolff (1982) pp. 309–44; Sassen (1991).

12 See Scott (1988).

13 Ohmae (1995).

14 Knox (1996) pp. 115–17.

15 Ibid. p. 116.

16 See French and Hamilton (1979) pp. 1–22; Murray and Szelenyi (1984) pp. 90–107; Demko and Regulska (1984) pp. 90–107; and Szelenyi (1996) pp. 286–317.

17 See Andrusz *et al.* (1996).

18 See Szelenyi (1996) and Andrusz *et al.* (1996).

19 Szelenyi (1996).

20 Armstrong and McGee (1985).

21 Dick and Rimmer (1998) pp. 2303–21.

22 Ibid. p. 2318.

23 Ibid. p. 2317.

24 Ibid. p. 2319.

25 Ma and Hanten (1981); Whyte and Parish (1984); Chan (1994b) pp. 243–81; and Pannell (1990) pp. 214–36.

26 Lin (2002b).

27 Wu (2003b) p. 1337.

28 Ibid. p. 1337.

29 Yeung and Lin (2003) p. 120.

30 Webster (2002).

31 See Oi (1992) pp. 99–126; Oi (1999); and Oi and Walder (1999).

32 Chung (1999b) p. 105.

33 See, for example, Kellie Tsai's superb study of the formation of private capital outside the formal banking sector that shows the way the private sector operates in a transitional environment characterized by a situation in which the formal sector banks are reluctant to give loans to small entrepreneurs in the private sector. See Tsai (2002). See also Hsu (2006) pp. 1–39.

34 See Zhou (2000) pp. 1135–74, who argues for the state and market sector as two interpenetrated spheres of activity. This idea echoes earlier ideas of Milton Santos who introduced the idea of the two circuits of formal and informal activity as interpenetrated and reliant upon each other in the context of developing urban areas.

Santos (1979). In the Chinese context also see Li (1998a) pp. 393–7; Dickson (2003); and Hong (2004) pp. 23–42.

35 See Harvey (1989b); Logan and Molotch (1987); Stoker (1995); Kotlar *et al.* (1990); Ashworth and Voog (1990); Loftman and Nevin (1996) pp. 991–1019; and Hiller (2000) pp. 439–58.

36 Jiang Xu and Anthony Yeh have a perceptive discussion of the meaning of entrepreneurialism in China arguing that bureaucratic entrepreneurialism in the transitional economy is different from that in fully developed market systems. Until recently "risk-taking" was carried out in a different fiscal environment in which it was assumed the state would cover loans if the borrower was unable to pay them. In another words the "risk taking aspects" of the market economy were not a factor. See Xu and Yeh (2005) pp. 208–308.

37 For earlier discussions of the role of entrepreneurs in China see Goodman (1996) pp. 225–42; and Pearson (1997).

38 See Naughton (1995b) pp. 61–89.

39 Lin (2002a) pp. 209–316.

40 See Wu (2000a) pp. 1359–77.

41 Lin and Ho (2005) pp. 411–36; Ho (2001) pp. 394–421; see also Smart (1998); Unger and Chan (1999) pp. 44–7; Li (1997) pp. 321–35, Wu (2001) pp. 273–9; Zhang (2000) pp. 187–99; Yeh and Wu (1996) pp. 330–53; Ho (2001) pp. 394–421; and Yeh (2005) pp. 59–79.

42 Lin and Ho (2005), p. 431.

43 Ibid. p. 431.

44 Ibid. p. 423.

45 See Kornai (1986) pp. 3–30; and Kornai (1992).

46 Naughton (1995b).

47 Harvey (1982).

48 Nee (1992) p. 22.

3 "Seeing like a state": the urbanization project in post-1978 China

1 Scott (1988) p. 5.

2 Ibid. pp. 4–5.

3 Ibid. pp. 4–5.

4 Chung (1999a) p. 1; for a more recent analysis see Chung and Lam (2004) pp. 945–64.

5 Naughton (1995b) pp. 61–89.

6 Chung and Lam (2004).

7 Wheatley (1971) p. 179; Wright (1977) p. 41.

8 Chang (1977) pp. 75–100; Wheatley (1971); Wright 1977.

9 Weber (1951) pp. 13–20; Wheatley (1971) p. 217; Naughton (1995b) p. 64.

10 Wright (1977) pp. 49–57.

11 Chang (1977) p. 77.

12 Wheatley (1971) p. 178.

13 Ma (1971) pp. 91–5.

14 Chang (1977) p. 99.

15 Elvin and Skinner (1974) p. 3; Naughton (1995b) p. 64.

16 Murphey (1974) pp. 17–71.

17 Wright (1977) p. 73.

18 Quoted in Friedman (1979) p. 35.

19 Ma (1976) pp. 114–18; Lo (1987) pp. 440–58; and Pannell (1990) pp. 214–36.

20 Pannell (1977) pp. 157–72; Ma (1979) pp. 838–55; Kwok and Parish (1981); Lo (1987).

21 Ma (1976) and (1979); Whyte and Parish (1984); Buck (1984) pp. 5–26; Lo (1987); Pannell (1990).

22 Fisher (1962) pp. 251–65; French and Hamilton (1979); Demko and Regulska (1987) pp. 289–92; Forbes and Thrift (1987); Szelenyi (1996) pp. 286–317.
23 Whyte and Parish (1984) p. 358.
24 Kirkby (1985); Pannell (1990); Chan (1992) pp. 275–306; Lin (1998) pp. 98–116; Ma (2002) pp. 1545–69.
25 Ofer (1977) pp. 277–303; Kirkby (1985); Chan (1992); Lin (1998).
26 Cheng and Selden (1994) p. 662.
27 Chan (1994a); Chan and Zhang (1999) pp. 818–55.
28 Naughton (1995b) p. 73.
29 Chan (1996) pp. 134–50; Solinger (1999); Elvin and Skinner (1974); Smart and Smart (2001) pp. 1853–69; Fan (2002) pp. 104–204.
30 Naughton (1995b) p. 82.
31 Liang and Ma (2004) pp. 483–84.
32 Chan (1996) p. 137.
33 China had 295 officially designated cities in 1984, of which 286 had comparable data for 1984–96. Data are for the urban districts (*shiqu*) and do not include sub-urban counties.
34 Li (2000) pp. 593–4; Ho and Lin (2004a) p. 87; Ho and Lin (2004b) p. 768.
35 Two of the cities in 1984 and nine of the cities in 1996 had no data on built-up areas.
36 In the current land market, urban redevelopment in the inner-city is much more costly than urban frontier expansion into the farmland in the sub-urban area. It was reported that the cost of land requisition and demolition in the inner-city of Beijing within the second ring road was 20 million yuan per *mu*, which was 120 times higher than the cost of the expropriation of farmland in the urban fringe of Beijing (100,000 to 150,000 yuan per *mu* for rice fields and 200,000 to 300,000 yuan per *mu* for vegetable land. In the city of Xi'an, the cost of land requisition and demolition was 900,000 yuan per *mu* in the inner-city within the second ring road but only 300,000 yuan per *mu* in the urban fringe outside of the second ring road. See Farmland Protection Investigation Team (1997) pp. 4–5; See also Zhou and Ma (2000) p. 219.
37 Kirby (1985) p. 250.
38 Ho and Lin (2004b) p. 766.
39 Li (1998b) pp. 9–12; Ho and Lin (2004b); Lin and Ho (2005) pp. 411–36.
40 Lin (2004a) pp. 18–44.
41 Ibid. p. 32.
42 Gaubatz (1999) pp. 1495–21; Lin (2004a).
43 Zhou and Ma (2000); Yeh (2005) pp. 59–79.
44 Ma and Xiang (1998) pp. 546–81; Zhang *et al.* (2003) pp. 912–37.
45 Gaubatz (1999) p. 1510.
46 Qian and Wong (2000) pp. 113–25; Wu (2004a) pp. 401–23.
47 Chan (1996); Solinger (1999); Smart and Smart (2001); Fan (2002).
48 Ma and Wu (2005b) pp. 1–20.
49 See Tang (1998) p. 351.
50 Lin (2004b) p. 147.
51 Ma (2005) p. 498.
52 Organization for Economic Co-Operation and Development (2005).
53 Ma (2005) p. 482.
54 Marton (2000).
55 See Ministry of Civil Affairs MOCA website.
56 Ma (2005).
57 Shen (2005).
58 For a critical review of this data base, see Montgomery *et al.* (2003).
59 Zhou and Ma (2003) p. 184.

60 The term urbanization is not used often in official Chinese government documents with the term "urban and town development" (*cheng zheng hua*) used more frequently. The term urbanization was first used in the Eighth Five Year Plan.
61 State Council of PRC (2001). This section is a summary of pages 41–42 in the plan.
62 Under this reorganization, the former Ministry of Geology and Mineral Resources, State Land Administration, State Oceanic Administration and State Bureau of Surveying and Mapping was merged to form the Ministry of Land and Resources.
63 Ma and Wu (2005b).
64 Castells (1996).
65 Appadurai (1990) p. 5.
66 Wakeman (1995) pp. 108–38; and Woodside (1998) pp. 121–34.
67 Vogel (1979).
68 See Pieterse (1995); Piertse (2001) pp. 219–45; and Hannerz (1996).
69 Goldstein-Gidoni (2001) pp. 21–38.
70 Appadurai (1990).
71 Lin (2000) pp. 455–72; and Ma (2002).
72 Summarized from Chung and Lam (2004) pp. 957–62.
73 Wong and Zhao (1999) pp. 113–26.; Cartier (2001b); and Lin and Ho (2005).
74 See Chan (1996); Fan (2002).
75 Dear and Flusty (1998) pp. 50–72; Nijman (2000) pp. 135–45.
76 Ma and Lin (1993) pp. 583–606; Lin (2002a) pp. 299–316; Shen *et al.* (2002) pp. 674–94.
77 Ho and Lin (2003) pp. 681–707; Yeh (2005); Lin and Ho (2005).

4 Representing urbanization in China: official and unofficial readings of the urban process

1 Champion and Hugo (2004) p. 3.
2 Dolphijn (2005) p. 21.
3 China State Council Population Census Office (2002).
4 United Nations Population Division (2002). There is, however, much debate about the validity of the census definitions of urban in China, which has fluctuated over the last 50 years. In the last 20 years efforts have been made to arrive at a more accurate definition of urban. See Zhang and Zhao (1998) pp. 330–81.
5 United Nations Population Division (2002), Table A.4, pp. 48–9.
6 Marcotullio and Lee (2003) p. 331.
7 For an excellent summary of this literature on North America see Bourne and Simmonds (2004) pp. 249–67.
8 Scott (2001). For a persuasive argument on the economic benefits of large cities' growth in the case of China see Zhao *et al.* (2003) pp. 265–78.
9 China State Statistical Bureau (2004).
10 See Naughton (1995a).
11 See the discussion of this process put forward in Chapters 2 and 3.
12 The recent rapid expansion in the number of urban places makes it very difficult to compare the changes in the period between 1984 and the present day.
13 It has been well documented that investment from Hong Kong and Taiwan in the first decade of the post-reform era tended to concentrate in Guangdong and Fujian provinces because of geographic proximity and cultural affinity. See Lin (1997); and Hsing (1998).
14 Lin (1999) p. 680.
15 Mumford (1961).
16 See McGee (1964) pp. 159–81.
17 In this section the terms Interlocking Metropolitan Region (IMR) and Extended Metropolitan Region (EMR) are used interchangeably. See Zhou (1991) pp. 89–112.

18 Gottmann (1961).
19 Zhou (1991) pp. 98–9.
20 Xu and Yeh (2005) pp. 283–308.
21 Yeung and Zhou (1988 and 1988–89). Yao (1992); Yeung and Hu (1992); Yao (1997); Tang (1997) pp. 1–65; Wang (1998); Zhou and Chao (1999) pp. 8–15; Gu *et al.* (1999) pp. 50–1; Zhu and Yau (2000) pp. 20–9; Hu *et al.* (2000); and Sit (2005) pp. 407–41.
22 See Yau and Chen (1998) pp. 271–80. Marton (1995) pp. 9–42; Marton (2000); Marton and McGee (1998) pp. 258–70; Cherod Ltd (2001); Webster and Mulle (2001); Webster (2002); and Webster (2003).
23 See, for example, Sit (1995); Hook (1998); Laquian (2005).
24 For Pearl River Delta, see Sit and Yang (1997) pp. 647–78; Sit (2001) pp. 199–238; Johnson (1992) pp. 185–220; Lin (1997); Lin (2001b) pp. 56–70; Yeung and Chu (1998); and Yeh *et al.* (2002).
25 See Zhu (1998) pp. 267–306. Zhu (1999); and Zhu (2002) pp. 9–22.
26 See Wang (1997a) pp. 229–50; Wang (1998).
27 Personal Communication from Dr. Ma Li, Research Scholar, Chinese Academy of Science. April 2006.
28 This data is taken from Sit (2005) Table 5 (p. 442) and Table 6 (p. 428) and Wang, M. Y. L. (2006) unpublished data analysis of the Shenyang – Dalian core region, Liaoning Province, China. Care should be taken in utilizing the data presented in these two analyses because of the delineation of the three main zones that is used in the two studies. The innovative choice of Hong Kong as the core of the Pearl River Delta and the two cities of Shenyang and Dalian in the Shenyang–Dalian EMR offers the opportunity for more accurate assessments of the differences between the main zones and the four EMRs but both authors are aware the delimitation of these zones and indeed the boundaries of the EMRs is very much in its infancy in China.
29 McGee (1991a) pp. 3–25. The term *desakota* is taken from two Bahasa Indonesia words: *desa* (village) and *kota* (town). When they are joined together they have the meaning of mixed rural and urban landscapes that are a dominant features of the margin of Chinese cities.
30 See Chan (1993) pp. 205–8; Dick and Rimmer (1998) pp. 2303–21; and Rimmer (2002) pp. 1–8.
31 Tang and Chung (2000); and Tang and Chung (2002) pp. 43–62. As the reader will recognize this book is essentially a response to that critique.
32 Guldin (1997) pp. 47–67.
33 McGee (1991a) Figures 1, 2, p. 13.
34 Webster *et al.* (2003).
35 See, for example, Yeh and Li (1997) pp. 195–222; and Seto *et al.* (2002) pp. 1985–2004. Seto and Kaufmann (2003) pp. 106–21.
36 See Sui and Zeng (2001) pp. 1–16; Heikkala *et al.* (2003) pp. 239–54; Xie *et al.* (2005) pp. 238–52; Xie *et al.* (2006) pp. 1297–309).
37 Naughton (1995a) p. 83.
38 Atkinson (1999).
39 For example, Kunming, the capital of Yunnan Province, is being rapidly developed as the focus of tourism for both domestic and international tourists. See Yeung and Shen (2004).
40 See Zhang (2000) pp. 123–25.

5 City core and the periphery: the emerging Hong Kong–Guangzhou metropolitan region

1 See Walder (1995) pp. 963–79; Lin (1999) pp. 670–96.
2 See Lardy (1987); Yeh and Xu (1996) pp. 219–67; and Lin (1997).

3 The four Special Economic Zones are Shenzhen, Zhuhai, Shantou and Xiamen. In April 1988, Hainan Island, originally a prefecture in Guangdong Province, was separated from Guangdong and designated as both a new province and the fifth Special Economic Zone.

4 The 14 Open Coastal Cities are Dalian, Qinhuangdao, Tianjin, Yantai, Qingdao, Lianyungang, Nantong, Shanghai, Ningbo, Wenzhou, Fuzhou, Guangzhou, Zhanjiang and Beihai. Almost all of these open port cities were the Treaty Ports established in the mid-nineteenth century. The three Open Economic Regions are the Pearl River Delta, Minnan Delta and Yangzi Delta.

5 See Yeung and Hu (1992); Lo (1989) pp. 293–308; Fan (1995) pp. 421–49; and Veeck (1991).

6 The total population of Guangdong includes 58.64 million local population and 25 million migrants (*wailai renkou*) who hold an official household registration elsewhere (23 million have lived in Guangdong for six months or longer and another two million have resided here for less than six months). See China State Council Population Census Office (CSCPCO) (2002) pp. 10–11 and 14–15. The land area is from the national land census undertaken in 1996. See Liu (2000); and Lin and Ho (2003) pp. 87–107.

7 See Cheung (1994) pp. 207–38; Johnson and Woon (1997) pp. 731–51; Lin (1999).

8 See Yeh (1997) pp. 25–39; Eng (1997) pp. 26–43; Lo (1992); Sit (1989) pp. 103–15; Taylor and Kwok (1989) pp. 309–22.

9 See Thoburn *et al.* (1990); Vogel (1989).

10 China State Statistical Bureau (2000) pp. 604–09.

11 See Hong Kong Census and Statistics Department (1972) p. 86; ibid. (1996) p. 32.

12 See Guangdong Statistical Bureau (2000) pp. 86 and 127.

13 For detailed discussions, see Lin (1997) pp. 86–125; So (2002) pp. 205–307.

14 For the importance of pre-existing kinship ties in the process of export-led industrialization in the delta region, see Smart and Smart (1991) pp. 216–33; Leung (1993) pp. 272–302; and Hsing (1998).

15 In 1984, the state allowed peasants to move to towns for permanent settlement and for doing non-agricultural jobs provided that they could look after their own needs for food, housing, medical care and other urban services (*zili kouliang renkou*). In 1985, the state further relaxed its control over rural to urban migration by permitting migrants to become "temporary urban residents" (*zanzhu renkou*). Although these migrants are officially treated as "agricultural population" and excluded from the provision of the benefits reserved for the urban "non-agricultural households," they are now allowed to enter the city and find their own living. For detailed discussions, see Lin (1993) pp. 327–338; Ma and Lin (1993) pp. 583–606; Lin and Ma (1994) pp. 75–97.

16 In the 2000 national population census, the state changed the definition of temporary population by shortening the period of stay from one year to less than six months. For discussion of the *zanzhu renkou*, see Chan (2003) pp. 1–12; Zhou and Ma (2003) pp. 176–96.

17 These are calculated on the basis of the unpublished data from Guangdong Province Population Census Office (1991) pp. 30–44. See also Lin (1997) p. 99.

18 See Guangdong Province Population Census Office (1988) pp. 546–53. See also Ma and Lin (1993).

19 Ma and Li (1993) p. 595.

20 For discussions of rural industrialization, see Byrd and Lin (1990) and Ho (1994).

21 See Xu and Li (1990) pp. 49–69.

22 For a discussion of the measurement of the urban population, see Kirkby (1985); Ma and Cui (1987) pp. 373–95; Zhang and Zhao (1998) pp. 330–81; and Lin (2002a) pp. 299–316.

23 For a detailed discussion of the special role played by Guangzhou in the national economy, see Johnson and Peterson (1999) pp. 3–18.

24 See Lin (1997) p. 67.
25 See Lo (1994) p. 134.
26 See Yeung and Hu (1992).
27 Guangzhou Statistical Bureau (2001) p. 24.
28 See Gong (2002) p. 95.
29 Guangzhou Statistical Bureau p. 116.
30 Ibid. p. 125.
31 See Lin (1997); Sit and Yang (1997) pp. 647–77.
32 Several studies have consistently shown a trend of a relative decline of Guangzhou as the largest economic center in the Pearl River Delta region since the 1980s. This revealed pattern is not contradictory to the finding of this study that Guangzhou has regained certain lost capital investment and production capacity in the last few years as a consequence of China's entry to the WTO. Lin's study covers the 1980s and Wong and Shen's study covers the period of up to 1998, both did not reflect on the impacts of China's WTO accession. See Lin (1997); Wong and Shen (2002).
33 Ho and Lin (2004a) p. 87.
34 Ho and Lin (2004b) p. 766.
35 See Gaubatz (1999) pp. 1495–521; Wu and Yeh (1999) pp. 377–94; Lin (2004a) pp. 18–44.

6 Urbanization of the Pearl River Delta: the case of Dongguan

1 See Guangdong Population Census Office (2002) pp. 50–1.
2 See Dongguan Yearbook Editorial Committee (2001) p. 185.
3 See Smart and Smart (1991) pp. 216–33; Leung (1993) pp. 272–302; Lin (1997); and Hsing (1998).
4 Vogel (1989) p. 176.
5 Dongguan Yearbook Editorial Committee (2001).
6 Interview notes, Dongguan, 3 September 2002.
7 Dongguan Statistical Bureau (2003) pp. 278–9.
8 Ibid. p. 64.
9 Gottmann (1961).
10 Garreau (1991) p. 4.
11 See CHH Asia Pacific (1988). For detailed discussions, see Ho and Lin (2003) pp. 681–707 and Lin and Ho (2005) pp. 411–36.
12 Lin and Ma (1994) p. 80.
13 Harvey (1989a) pp. 3–17; Hubbard and Hall (1998).
14 Logan and Molotch (1987); Stone (1989); Lin (2002a) pp. 299–316.
15 Dongguan Statistical Bureau (2003).
16 It should be noted, however, that the official statistics of exports for Dongguan may have underestimated the actual situation because some of the goods manufactured in Dongguan were exported through the ports in Shenzhen and therefore classified as Shenzhen's exports. It was also in the financial interests of exports contractors to under-report the goods processed because the processing fees to be paid by the overseas contractors were calculated on the basis of the value of the goods processed.
17 See Jessop (2000) p. 341.
18 Ma and Wu (2005b) pp. 1–20.

7 Manipulating the margins: the case of Shanghai

1 Wang (1997a) pp. 229–50.
2 Harvey (1982).
3 Brenner (1997) pp. 273–306.

4 All these urban districts were defined as rural counties in the Maoist period. After 1978, they have been gradually upgraded to urban districts.
5 Wang (2002a) pp. 23–9.
6 Shanghai Statistical Bureau (2000b).
7 Atash (1990) pp. 245–57. Yeung and Sun (1996).
8 White (1981) pp. 241–68.
9 "Five small plants" refer to small scale plants for production of iron and steel, fertilizer, cement, coal, hydroelectric power and machine building, see Perkins (1977). Murphey (1980).
10 Unpublished document obtained from field trips in 2001.
11 See also Yeh and Wu (1999) pp. 167–252.
12 Unpublished document obtained from field trips in 2001.
13 Wu (1999b) pp. 2263–82.
14 Two levels of government and two levels of management refer to municipal and district/county government. For detail see Zhang (2002a) pp. 303–23.
15 The term "themed zone" refers to the distinctive theme or functional specialization that was planned for each zone.
16 See Cartier (2001a) pp. 445–69.
17 The seven centrally designated and nine municipally designated development zones are well known. See also official website of Shanghai municipal government, available online at: http://www.shanghai.gov.cn/gb/shanghai/node2314/index.html. However, the numbers of development zones designated by local governments are derived from various sources; the data presented here was collected from personal interviews with officers in the Shanghai Department of Urban Planning in a field trip 2001.
18 Wu and Radbone (2005) pp. 275–86.
19 Shanghai Statistical Bureau (2006).
20 Ibid.
21 See Shanghai Construction Commission, available online at: htttp://202.109.112.226/zhtj/zhtj25.htm.
22 Wu (2002a) pp. 1591–615; Han (2000) pp. 2091–112.
23 Yang (2000).
24 Wei *et al.* (2002) pp. 191–204.
25 Shanghai Statistical Bureau (2005).
26 Shi *et al.* (2001) pp. 411–27.
27 He and Wu (2005) pp. 1–23.
28 Shanghai Statistical Bureau (2006).
29 Ibid.
30 The concept of floating population or temporary population is widely used in China to refer to migrants not living in the place of official household registration. The data here taken from the 2000 census includes all Chinese people who lived in Shanghai for a period of less than six months for job, business or social service purposes but did not hold Shanghai's household registration.
31 Wu (1999c). See also Wu (2005) pp. 222–42.
32 This policy was abolished after 2002.
33 Shanghai Statistical Bureau (2000a).
34 See Wu and Webber (2004) pp. 203–13.
35 *China Daily*, 11 December 2002.
36 *21st Century Economic News*, 1 July 2002 (in Chinese).
37 Shanghai Statistical Bureau (2006).
38 The implementation of policies designed to make Shanghai a global city have been the focus of much research. See Olds (1997) pp. 109–23. Wu (1999a) pp. 207–16. Wu (2000b) pp. 349–61; Yusuf and Wu (2002) pp. 1213–40; Wu (2004b) pp. 159–80.

39 *Xinming Daily*, 28 November 2000 (in Chinese).
40 Data calculated from Shanghai Statistical Bureau (2006).
41 Xia and Sun (2000) pp. 39–44.
42 Shanghai Statistical Bureau (2006).
43 Shanghai Statistical Bureau (2004).
44 These developments in Shanghai should be contrasted with carefully implemented and regulated plans of Hong Kong developed during the British administration where industry and population were moved from the urban cores of Hong Kong and Kowloon to a number of satellite towns linked by an efficient transport system that created a more orderly landscape in the urban margins.

8 Rural agglomeration and urbanisation in the lower Yangzi delta: the *urban echo* in Kunshan

1 These informants included Liu Junde, Professor of Geography and Director of the Administrative Divisions Research Centre at East China Normal University in Shanghai, and Mr. Zhu Hongcai, formerly Deputy Director of the Land Resource Management Bureau in Kunshan, Jiangsu Province.
2 Marton (2000) p. 191. The term "rural agglomeration" is discussed in more detail below and was first introduced (in English) in Marton (2000) pp. 184–6.
3 This is discussed extensively in Marton (2000).
4 Marton (2002) p. 36.
5 Ibid. p. 37.
6 Interview notes. The term was used by informants in Kunshan during field visits in early 2006.
7 Kunshan Statistical Bureau (2006); China Economic Net (2005) 20 October 2005, Top 10 richest counties of China released. Available online at: http://en.ce.cn/national/Local/20050920_4733255.shtml (accessed 30 October 2005); Xu (2006) p. 4.
8 Calculated from: Shanghai Statistical Bureau (1998) p. 9; China State Statistical Bureau (1997) pp. 26–7; ibid. (1998), pp. 22–3. Growth rates for rural industrial output for Shanghai could not be accurately determined since the relevant data was not provided in constant values. However, it was possible to estimate the average growth in rural industrial output between 1981 and 1997 for China at about 20 percent based on growth in the collective sector. See: ibid. (1998), p. 433.
9 This part is adapted from a more detailed discussion in Marton (2000).
10 Calculated from: Suzhou Statistical Bureau (1995), p. 15; ibid. (1999), pp. 14, 80. Several sources, including the local Kunshan statistical yearbooks, persist in reporting an area for Kunshan of 927.68 square kilometers: Kunshan Statistical Bureau (2006), p. 18.
11 Suzhou Statistical Bureau (1999), p. 48.
12 Calculated from: Jiangsu Statistical Bureau (1949–89), pp. 317–8, 393–4; Kunshan Statistical Bureau (several years), Preface.
13 Jiangsu Statistical Bureau (1999), p. 427.
14 Ibid., p. 429.
15 China State Statistical Bureau (1993), p. 330.
16 Zhang and Zhao (1998) pp. 376–7. They show an adjusted time series that suggests that China was 33 percent urbanized in 1995.
17 Kunshan County Gazetteer Editorial Office (1990), pp. 131–41; as with other estimates based on the official statistics for non-agricultural population, this value needs to be placed within the context of shifting definitions and mass campaigns that often dramatically affected urban and rural populations at the local level. The official non-agricultural population in Kunshan comprised between 16 to 18 percent of the total from 1949 to 1960 after which it declined gradually, reaching 10 percent in the late 1960s and where it remained until the late 1970s.

18 Calculated from the same figures used above to estimate the true level of urbanization. Interview notes; and Kunshan Statistical Bureau (1991), p. 14; ibid. (1996), p. 31.
19 Calculated from: Jiangsu Statistical Bureau (1999), pp. 363–7, 384–5.
20 Kwok (1992) p. 73; Pannell (1992) p. 36.
21 Kunshan Statistical Bureau (1996), p. 115.
22 Qinghua University Urban–Rural Development Research Group (1995) p. 85.
23 This discussion of Dianshanhu is adapted from Marton (2002) pp. 31–2.
24 Kunshan Statistical Bureau (1996), p. 31; Interview notes. Only 2,605 people held urban registration (*hukou*) in the town seat at that time.
25 Interview notes.
26 Ibid.
27 The discussion here is adapted from Marton (2002) pp. 33–5.
28 Xu (2006).
29 Wu and Sun (2003); Interview notes; more research is needed to show this empirically.
30 Kunshan Statistical Bureau (2005).
31 Business Wire (2005).
32 PRNewswire (2004).
33 Interview notes.
34 Ding (2004) p. 51.
35 Xu (2006).
36 Ibid.
37 Interview notes.
38 Wei (2002) p. 1742.
39 Kunshan Statistical Bureau (2000), p. 13.
40 Kunshan Statistical Bureau (2006), p. 18; Kunshan "city" is often marked on maps with a point that coincides with the administrative seat in the central town of Yushan. It is important to be clear that Kunshan "city" refers to the entire county-level municipal region, including ten towns and the *kaifaqu* in 2005. Furthermore, Yushan town has its own town level government and a separate administrative seat.
41 Marton (2000) pp. 151–2; Kunshan Statistical Bureau (2006).
42 Confirmed in interviews with key informants in July 2006.
43 Marton (2000) pp. 88–9.
44 Calculated from Kunshan Statistical Bureau (2006), p. 47; the proportion actually residing in urban built-up areas is based on the figures for the legally registered non-agricultural population. While the usual ambiguities and suspicions of the official statistics apply, it is quite clear that there has been a major shift in the profile of urban residential location since 1996.
45 Marton (2000) p. 111–13.
46 Kunshan Statistical Bureau (2006), p. 135.
47 The statistical yearbooks and local officials prefer to use this term (better translated as "outsiders") rather than the older more pejorative term of "floating population" (*liudong renkou*). This is in part a growing recognition of the essential and positive role of such outsiders in local development and their more lengthy (often permanent) residence in Kunshan.
48 Interview notes, July 2006.
49 Wu and Sun (2003) p. 2.
50 Similar to the restructuring of administrative divisions that occurred at the town level in Kunshan, there has been a radical reconfiguration of county-level units in southern Jiangsu from 35 in 1997 to just 25 in 2005; Jiangsu Statistical Bureau (various years).
51 Zhu and Wang (2002) pp. 298–303.
52 Marton and Wu (2006) p. 226.
53 Wu (2003a) p. 1692.
54 Interview notes, July 2006.

9   Divergent urbanization paths in the Shenyang – Dalian urban corridor, Liaoning Province

1   See McGee (1989) pp. 93–108; McGee (1991a) pp. 3–26; McGee and Robinson (1995).
2   Webster (2001); Jones (2001); Kelly (1998) pp. 35–54; Zhou (1991) pp. 89–112; Lin (2004a) pp. 18–44; Marton (2000); Wang (1998); Wang (1997a) pp. 229–50; Wang (1997b) pp. 1–18.
3   See Zhou (1991); Lin (2004a); Marton (2000); Wang (1998, 1997a, 1997b).
4   See Wang (1998).
5   Ibid.
6   Here, urban population includes non-agricultural population in urban districts.
7   See Laquian (1989) pp. 20.
8   See Yeung and Hu (1992); Ho and Huenemann (1984); Johnson (1992) pp. 85–220; Also see Liaoning Statistical Bureau (1992).
9   See Japan–China Northeast Development Association (1991).
10   For new urban poverty see Wang (2004) pp. 117–39; for WTO and its impacts, see Webber *et al.* (2002).
11   See Kelly (1998).
12   See Satterthwaite and Tacoli (2003).
13   Wu Bangguo's speech in August 1998 (a member of Chinese State Council).
14   According to the Labor and Social Security Ministry, reforms are expected to cost some three million jobs a year until 2006.
15   See Hong Kong Trade Development Council (2004).
16   Smyth and Zhai (2003) pp. 173–205; and Ding (1998) pp. 112–19.
17   See Wang (2004).
18   Before 1978, there were poor people in urban areas and their living standard was generally low. However, urban poverty was not problematic because of the widespread urban work-unit-based welfare system (which guaranteed lifelong employment, cradle-to-grave social services and adequate living standards and welfare) that was allocated to urban workers.
19   According to other sources, the rural poverty population in China had decreased from 250 million in 1978 to 125 million in 1985, 80 million in 1990 and 50 million in 1997. For detail, see Yang (1998) pp. 10–15, 37. This number further dropped to 42 million in 1999 and 22 million by the end of 2000. For detail, see Sheng (1999) pp. 1–8; also see Yang and Wang (2001) pp. 5–11.
20   Wang (2002b).
21   Song and Shen (1988).
22   Smyth and Zhai (2003); Mok *et al.* (2002) pp. 399–415.
23   Meanwhile, the ownership of many large and medium-sized SOEs has been changed. The shares of many SOEs were sold to private and foreign owners, leaving the state as one of the major share holders of these so-called state-controlled enterprises.
24   Wang (2004).
25   China's "national team" of large industrial firms included AVIC in the aerospace industry; Sinopec and CNPC in oil and petrochemicals; Sanjiu, Dongbei and Shandong Xinhua in pharmaceuticals; Harbin, Shanghai and Dongfang in power equipment; Yiqi, Erqi and Shanghai in automobiles; Shougang, Angang and Baogang in steel; and Datong, Yanzhou and Shenhua in coal mining; and China Mobile and China Unicom in telecommunications.
26   See Wang (1997a, 1998).
27   Wang (1995).
28   Wang (1998).
29   Yan and Lin (2004) pp. 437–45.
30   In Jing *et al.* (2006), the EMRs of Beijing-Tianjin, lower Yangzi delta and Pearl River, even Chengdu-Chongqing EMR and Wuhan mega urban region are discussed

but not the Shenyang–Dalian region. Also see Wang and Bai (2003) pp. 36–46; Sit and Cai (2003) pp. 531–40; also see newspaper: *China Economic Report* (2004) pp. 46–7; and *Enterprise Report* (2003) pp. 20–1.
31 See Wang (1998, 1995).
32 Ibid.
33 Yu *et al.* (1999) pp. 61–7.
34 A marten is a small, furry, weasel-like mammal having thick, soft fur ranging in color from golden brown to blackish-brown. It eats fish and its length ranges up to 80 centimeters, including the tail. Its fur is made into coats, stoles and other materials used for trimmings. For details see Wang (1995).
35 See Wang (1998).
36 Yue (1992).
37 See Lee (1991) pp. 137–56.
38 Song (2002) pp. 184–6.
39 Lin (2004b).
40 Feng (2004).
41 For detail, see www.dalian-gov.net.
42 Roy (2006) pp. 48–53.
43 Zhou (1991).
44 See Hong Kong Trade Development Council (2004).

10 Reviewing the case studies: dimensions of scale in the Chinese urbanization process

1 Herod and Wright (2002) p. 4.
2 Many authors have suggested that a more effective approach is to emphasize the networks of exchanges that transcend the different political scales and levels. See Smith (2000) p. 725. There is, of course, much debate concerning this issue of scale among social scientists. In particular this debate has centered on the validity of the global–local division that has become a central part of the globalization rhetoric; Castells (1996) echoes this idea of a network with his concept of the "space of flows." Herod and Wright (2002) have edited an indispensable collection that summarizes many of these debates. But in addition they have indicated that the evaluation of scale involves decisions on its ontological status, its validity as a research tool and the issues of rescaling that are implied by administrative restructuring, the division of labor and the spatial reorganization of power that are implicit in, for example, the decentralization of budgetary control. See also Brenner (2000) pp. 361–78.
3 McGee (1986) pp. 655–64 and de Walt and Pelto (1985).
4 Tang and Chung (2002) p. 45.
5 See Cartier (2005) pp. 21–38; Shen (2005) pp. 39–68; Ma (2005) pp. 477–97; Hsing (2006) pp. 103–24.
6 Tang and Chung (2002).
7 Wang (2002a) pp. 23–9.
8 Hsing (2006) p. 109.
9 Ibid. p. 114.
10 Liang (1992) pp. 336–43.
11 An excellent use of a structured comparative approach to the study of Chinese cities is Chung (1999c). Other examples of comparative methodology are Yeung and Hu (1992). Yusof and Wu (1997); Hu *et al.* (2000); and Gaubatz (1999) pp. 1495–521.
12 Webster *et al.* (2003).
13 Ibid.
14 Smart and Lin (2007).
15 Oakes (2000) pp. 667–72.
16 Webster *et al.* (2003) p. 38.

11 Conclusion: rewriting China's urban future

1 Cited in Buchanan (1970).
2 The 2005 population estimates for China indicate that the population was 1,303,313,000 compared to the next largest India with a population of 1,080,000,000.
3 As readers will have noted from the preceding chapters the term urban space does not equate with either the demographic or administrative definition of "urban" used in China. Rather it refers to the parts of the Chinese territory that have a majority of urban activities within them.
4 United Nations Population Division (2002). In fact Chinese population estimates suggest a much faster rate of urban growth. For example using data from the 2000 census the population census office under the State Council estimated that the urbanization level could be as high as 50.5 percent by 2010 and 61.4 percent by 2020. This would mean an even greater volume of population increase in urban areas. See China Council for International Cooperation in the Environment and Development (2005).
5 McGee (1971) p. 13.
6 Scott (2001) p. 4.
7 Sassen (1991). For an earlier statement of the concept of "world cities" see Hall (1966); and Friedmann (1986) pp. 69–83.
8 See for example Rees (1992) pp. 21–30. For a recent thoughtful critique of this approach see McManus and Haughton (2006) pp. 113–28. Also see Hardoy *et al.* (2001); and McGranahan and Satterwaite (2002) pp. 213–26 for a broader picture of the problems of sustainable urbanization.
9 The issue of the effect of urban size on development is contentious. One school of thought argues that as urban areas become larger they become more dysfunctional economically, politically and socially and this has fueled a powerful planning ideology promoting the growth of small and medium-sized cites. These policies do not seem to have been very successful. See Hamer (1994) pp. 172–91.
10 Friedmann and Wolfe (1982) pp. 309–44. This argument echoes earlier writing that drew attention to the growth of the urban poor in developing countries. See McGee (1971).
11 Solinger (2006) p. 179.
12 See McGee and Scott (2001).
13 United Nations Population Division (2002).
14 Marcotullio and Lee (2003) pp. 325–54. See also Marcotullio (2003) pp. 219–48.
15 Ibid. p. 331.
16 See Simmonds and Hack (2000).
17 Macleod and McGee (1996) pp. 417–64.
18 Barter (1999); Midgley (1994); Kenworthy and Laube (1996) pp. 279–308.
19 *China Daily* (2004) 7 October.
20 Westbrod (1999) pp. 89–100.
21 Freund and Martin (1999).
22 See Gates and Yin (2004) pp. 351–71.
23 Scott (1999) p. 4.
24 Ibid. p. 7.
25 See Douglass (1999) pp. 9–67.
26 *People's Daily* (2004a) 19 April.
27 Zhang (2005).
28 Ewing (2006).
29 See Atkinson (1999).
30 Ibid. p. 2.
31 See Webster (2002).
32 *People's Daily* (2004b). See also Davis (2000).
33 See Tang and Chung (2002) pp. 43–62.

34 Wang (2002a) pp. 23–9.
35 Carter (2003) p. 2.
36 Sustainable Development Research Group (2005).
37 Chen *et al.* (2004a).
38 We rely for these definitions on the comprehensive analysis presented in the Millenium Ecosystems Assessment Review published by the United Nations.
39 See McGee and Robinson (1995).
40 Atkinson (1999) p. 14.
41 See for example Douglass and Friedmann (1998).
42 See Yeung (2005a) pp. 75–9 and Yeung (2005b).
43 Brenner (1999) pp. 431–5.
44 Kraas (2003) pp. 6–15.
45 See Montgomery *et al.* (2003).

Bibliography

Andrusz, G., Harloe, M. and Szelenyi, I. (eds) (1996) *Cities after Socialism: Urban and Regional Change and Conflict in Post-Socialist Societies*. Cambridge, MA: Blackwell.

Appadurai, A. (1990) Disjuncture and difference in the global cultural economy. *Public Culture* 2 (2), pp. 1–24.

Armstrong, W. R. and McGee, T. G. (1985) *Theatres of Accumulation: Studies in Latin American and Asian Urbanization*. London and New York: Methuen.

Ashworth, G. J. and Voog, D. (1990) *Selling the City*. London: Bellhaven.

Atash, F. W. (1990) Satellite town development in Shanghai, China: an overview. *Journal of Architectural and Planning Research* 7 (3), pp. 245–57.

Atkinson, A. (1999) *Principles and Components of Strategic Environmental Planning and Management for the Peri-Urban Interface*. Discussion Paper of the Peri-Urban Research Project Team. London: Development Planning Unit, University College, University of London.

Barnes, T. (2001) Re-theorizing economic geography: from the quantitative revolution to the "cultural turn." *Annals of the Association of American Geographers* 91 (3), pp. 546–65.

Barter, P. (1999) *An International Comparative Perspective on Urban Transport and Urban Form in Pacific Asia: Challenges of Rapid Motorization in Dense Cities*. Perth: Perth Institute for Sustainability and Technology Policy, Murdoch University.

Bourne, L. S. and Simmonds, J. (2004) The conceptualization and analysis of urban systems: a North American perspective. In Champion, T. and Hugo, G. (eds) *New Forms of Urbanization: Beyond the Rural–Urban Dichotomy*. Aldershot and Burlington, VT: Ashgate, pp. 249–67.

Brenner, N. (1997) State territorial restructuring and the production of spatial scale. *Political Geography* 16 (4), pp. 273–306.

—— (1999) Globalization as reterritorialization: the re-scaling of urban governance in the European Union. *Urban Studies* 36 (3), pp. 431–51.

—— (2000) The urban question as a scale question: reflections on Henri Lefebvre, urban theory and the politics of scale. *International Journal of Urban and Regional Research* 24 (2), pp. 361–78.

Brook, T. and Frolic, B. M. (eds) (1997) *Civil Society in China*. Armonk, NY: M. E. Sharpe.

Buchanan, K. (1970) *The Transformation of the Chinese Earth: Perspectives on Modern China*. London: G. Bell & Sons.

Buck, D. (1984) Changes in Chinese urban planning since 1976. *Third World Planning Review* 6 (1), pp. 5–26.

Business Wire (2005) Praxair opens specialty gas plant in Kunshan. Available online at: www.highbeam.com/library/docfree.asp (accessed 20 October 2005).

Byrd, W. A. and Lin, Q. S. (eds) (1990) *China's Rural Industry*. Washington, DC: World Bank.

Cao, Y. and Nee, V. (2000) Comment: controversies and evidence in the market transition debate. *American Journal of Sociology* 105 (4), pp. 1175–95.

Cartier, C. (2001a) "Zone fever," the arable land debate, and real estate speculation: China's evolving land use regime and its geographical contradictions. *Journal of Contemporary China* 10 (28), pp. 445–69.

—— (2001b) *Globalising South China*. Oxford: Blackwell.

—— (2005) City-space: scale relations and China's spatial administrative hierarchy. In Ma, L. J. C. and Wu, F. L. (eds) *Restructuring the Chinese City: Changing Society, Economy and Space*. London and New York: Routledge, pp. 21–38.

Carter, J. (2003) Aspects of urban planning and sustainability in Mainland China. Available online at: www.ias.unu.edu.proceedings/icbs/ecocity03/papers/carter/paper/html (accessed 13 July 2005).

Castells, M. (1996) *The Rise of the Network Society*. Oxford: Blackwell.

Champion, T. and Hugo, G. (eds) (2004) *New Forms of Urbanization: Beyond the Rural–Urban Dichotomy*. Aldershot and Burlington, VT: Ashgate.

Chan, K. W. (1992) Economic growth strategy and urbanization policies in China, 1949–1982. *International Journal of Urban and Regional Research* 16 (2), pp. 275–306.

—— (1994a) *Cities with Invisible Walls*. Hong Kong: Oxford University Press.

—— (1994b) Economic growth strategy and urbanization policies in China since 1982. *Modern China* 20 (3), pp. 243–81.

—— (1996) Post-Mao China: a two-class urban society in the making. *International Journal of Urban and Regional Research* 20 (1), pp. 134–50.

—— (2003) Chinese census 2000: new opportunities and challenges. *China Review* 3 (2), pp. 1–12.

Chan, K. W. and Hu, Y. (2003) Urbanization in China in the 1990s: new definition, different series, and revised trends. *China Review* 3 (2), pp. 49–71.

Chan, K. W. and Zhang, L. (1999) The hukou system and rural–urban migration in China: processes and changes. *China Quarterly* 160, pp. 818–55.

Chan, K. Y. (1993) Review of "The extended metropolis: Settlement transition in Asia." *Urban Geography* 14 (2), pp. 205–8.

Chang, S. D. (1977) The morphology of walled capitals. In Skinner, G. W. (ed.) *The City in Late Imperial China*. Stanford, CA: Stanford University Press, pp. 75–100.

Chen, A., Liu, G. C. and Zhang, K. H. (eds) (2004a) *Urbanization and Social Welfare in China*. Aldershot and Burlington: Ashgate.

Chen, S. R., Liu, X. B. and Shi, H. (2004b) Revitalise northeast: I am proud of you, *People's Daily* (overseas edition) 9 August.

Cheng, T. and Selden, M. (1994) The origins and social consequences of China's hukou system. *China Quarterly* 139, pp. 644–68.

Cheung, P. T. (1994) The case of Guangdong in central-provincial relations. In Jia, H. and Lin, Z. M. (eds) *Changing Central–Local Relations in China*. Boulder, CO: Westview Press, pp. 207–38.

CHH Asia Pacific (ed.) (1998) Land management law of the People's Republic of China, Article 10. Originally adopted 25 June 1986, revised 29 December 1988, and further revised and promulgated 29 August 1998. In CHH Asia Pacific (Ed.) *China Laws for Foreign Business 3*, North Ryde, Australia: CCH Australia Ltd., pp. 18354–99.

China Council for International Cooperation in the Environment and Development. (2005) China's sustainable urbanization. Issues paper prepared for the 2005 CCICED Annual General Meeting. Available online at: www.harbour.sfu.ca/dlam/ Issues%20Paper%202005.htm (accessed March 2006).

China Economic Net (2005) 20 October 2005. Top 10 richest counties of China released. Available online at: http://en.ce.cn/national/Local/20050920_4733255.shtml (accessed 30 October 2005).

China Economic Report (2004) (*Zhongguo jingji daobao*) Vol. 12 (in Chinese).

China State Council Population Census Office (2002) *Zhongguo 2000 nian renkou pucha ziliao* (*Tabulation on the 2000 Population Census of the People's Republic of China. Volumes 1–3*). Beijing: State Statistical Press (in Chinese).

China State Statistical Bureau (1988) *Zhongguo 1987 nian 1% renkou chouyang diaocha ziliao: Quanguo fence* (*Tabulations of China's 1% population sample survey of 1987: National volume*). Beijing: China Statistical Press.

—— (1999) *New China's Cities Fifty Years*. Beijing: Xinhua Press.

China State Statistical Bureau (various years) *Huadong diqu tongji nianjian* (*East China Statistical Yearbook*). Beijing: State Statistical Press (in Chinese).

—— (various years) *Zhongguo tongji nianjian* (*China Statistical Yearbook*). Beijing: State Statistical Press (in Chinese).

China State Statistical Bureau (1984–2006) *Zhongguo tongji nianjian* (*Urban Statistical Yearbook of China*). Beijing: China Statistics Press (in Chinese).

China's Ministry of Construction (1993–2001) *Chengshi Jianshe Tongji Nianbao* (*Almanac of Urban Construction*). Beijing: Internal Publication.

Cherod Ltd (2001) *Urbanising Regions in China's Yangtze Basin: Summary Report Prepared for the East Asia Urban Sector Unit*. New York: World Bank.

Chung, J. H. (1999a) Recipes for development in Post-Mao Chinese cities. In Chung, J. H. (ed.) *Cities in China: Recipes for Economic Development in the Reform Era*. London and New York: Routledge.

—— (1999b) Preferential policies, municipal leadership and development strategies. In Chung, J. H. (ed.) *Cities in China: Recipes for Economic Development in the Reform Era*. London and New York: Routledge, pp.105–40.

—— (ed.) (1999c) *Cities in China: Recipes for Economic Development in the Reform Era*. London and New York: Routledge.

Chung, J. H. and Lam, T. (2004) China's "city system" in flux: explaining post-Mao administrative changes. *China Quarterly* 180, pp. 945–64.

Cox, K. (1995) Local/global. In Cloke, P. and Johnston, R. *Spaces of Geographical Thought*. London: Sage, pp.175–98.

Davis, D. S. (ed.) (2000) *The Consumer Revolution in Urban China*. Berkeley, CA: University of California Press.

de Walt, B. R. and Pelto, P. J. (eds) (1985) *Micro and Macro Levels of Analysis in Anthropology: Issues in Theory and Research*. Boulder, CO: Westview Press.

Dear, M. and Flusty, S. (1998) Postmodern urbanism. *Annals of the Association of American Geographers* 88 (1), pp. 50–72.

Demko, G. J. and Regulska, J. (1984) The city in the transition to socialism. *International Journal of Urban and Regional Research* 8, pp. 90–107.

—— (1987) Socialism and its impact on urban processes and the city. *Urban Geography* 8 (4), pp. 289–92.

Dick, H. W. and Rimmer, P. J. (1998) Beyond the third world city: the new urban geography. *Urban Studies* 35 (12): 2303–21.

Dicken, P. (2003) *Global Shift: Transforming the World Economy* (4th edn). London: Sage.

Dickson, B. J. (2003) *Red Capitalists in China: The Party, Private Entrepreneurs and Prospects for Political Change.* New York: Cambridge University Press.

Ding, I. (2004) Kunshan's investment pull. *China International Business* 205 (December), pp. 49–53.

Ding, Y. (1998) *Xiagang – jinri Zhongguo di remen huati* (Layoffs – China's hot topic today). *Dangdai Zhongguo yanjiu* (*Modern China Studies*) 1, pp. 112–19 (in Chinese).

Dolphijn, R. (2005) Welcome to photoshopolis. *International Institute of Asian Studies, Newsletter*, 39, p. 21.

Dongguan Statistical Bureau (1998–2003) *Doungguan tongji nianjian* (*Dongguan Statistical Yearbook*). Beijing: State Statistical Press (in Chinese).

Dongguan Yearbook Editorial Committee (2001) *Dongguan nianjian 1997–2001* (*Dongguan Yearbook 1997–2001*) Beijing: China Book Press (in Chinese).

Douglass, M. (1999) The future of cities on the Pacific Rim. *Comparative Urban and Community Research* 2, pp. 9–67.

Douglass, M. and Friedmann, J. (eds) (1998) *Cities for Citizens: Planning and the Rise of Civil Society in a Global Age.* New York: John Wiley.

Elvin, M. and Skinner, G. W. (eds) (1974) *The Chinese City Between Two Worlds.* Stanford CA: Stanford University Press.

Eng, I. (1997) Flexible production in late industrialization: the case of Hong Kong. *Economic Geography* 73 (1), pp. 26–43.

Enterprise Report (*Qiye daobao*) (2003) *Bijiao Zhongguo sanda dushiquan* (Comparison of China's three large city-regions). *Qiye daobao* (*Enterprise Report*) Vol. 3, pp. 20–1 (in Chinese).

Ewing, K. (2006) China goes back to the land. *Asia Times*, 9 March.

Fan, C. C. (1995) The origins and patterns of regional uneven development in post-Mao China. *Annals of the Association of American Geographers* 85 (3), pp. 421–49.

—— (2002) The elite, the natives, and the outsiders: migration and labor market segmentation in urban China. *Annals of the Association of American Geographers* 92 (1), pp. 103–24.

Farmland Protection Investigation Team (1997) *Woguo gengdi baohu mianlin de yanjun xingshi he zhengce xing jianyi* (Protection of our cultivated land faces grim circumstances and some policy recommendations). *Zhongguo tudi kexue* (*China Land Science*) 11 (1), pp. 4–5 (in Chinese).

Feng, G. C. (2004) *Guanyu Shenyang jingjiqu quyu yitihua de zongti gouxiang* (Overall thinking for regional integration in the Shenyang Economic Zone). Available online at: www.ln.xinhuanet.com/2004–06/10/content_2294908.htm (accessed 26 June 2006) (in Chinese).

Feuchtwang, S. (2004) Theorizing place. In Feuchtwang, S. (ed.) *Making Place: State Projects, Globalization and Local Responses in China.* London, Portland and Sydney: UCL Press (Cavendish), pp. 3–30.

Fisher, J. C. (1962) Planning the city of socialist man. *Journal of the American Institute of Planners* 28, pp. 251–65.

Forbes, D. and Thrift, N. (eds) (1987) *The Socialist Third World: Urban Development and Territorial Planning.* New York: Blackwell.

French, R. A. and Hamilton, F. E. I. (eds) (1979) *The Socialist City: Spatial Structure and Urban Policy.* New York: John Wiley.

Freund, P. and Martin, G. (1999) Driving south: the globalization of auto-consumption and its social organization of space. Available online at: www.chss.montclair.edu/~hadisb/drivsout.pdf (accessed 14 September 2004).

Friedmann, E. (1979) On Maoist conceptualizations of the capitalist world system. *China Quarterly* 80, pp. 806–37.

Friedmann, J. (1986) The world city hypothesis. *Development and Change* 17 (1), pp. 69–83.

—— (2005) *China's Urban Transition*. Minneapolis and London: University of Minnesota Press.

Friedmann, J. and Wolff, G. (1982) World city formation. *International Journal of Urban and Regional Research* 6 (3), pp. 309–44.

Garreau, J. (1991) *Edge City: Life on the New Frontier*. New York: Doubleday.

Gates, D. F. and Yin, J. Z. (2004) Urbanization and energy in China: issues and implications. In Chen, A., Liu, G. C. and Zhang, K. H. (eds) *Urbanization and Social Welfare in China*. Aldershot and Burlington, VT: Ashgate, pp. 351–71.

Gaubatz, P. (1995) Changing Beijing. *Geographical Review* 85 (1), pp. 79–86.

—— (1999) China's urban transformation: patterns and processes of morphological change in Beijing, Shanghai and Guangzhou. *Urban Studies* 36 (9), pp. 1495–521.

Ginsburg, N., Koppel, B. and McGee, T. G. (eds) (1991) *The Extended Metropolis: Settlement Transition in Asia*. Honolulu: University of Hawaii Press.

Goldman, M. and Perry, E. J. (eds) (2002) *Changing Meanings of Citizenship in Modern China*. Cambridge MA: Harvard University Press.

Goldstein-Gidoni, O. (2001) Hybridity and distinctions in Japanese contemporary commercial weddings. *Social Science Japan Journal* 4 (1), pp. 21–38.

Gong, H. (2002) Growth of tertiary sector in China's large cities. *Asian Geographer* 21 (1&2), pp. 85–100.

Goodman, D. S. G. (1996) The People's Republic of China: the party-state, capitalist revolution and new entrepreneurs. In Robison, R. and Goodman, D. S. G. (eds) *The New Rich in Asia: Mobile Phones, McDonald's and Middle Class Revolution*, London: Routledge, pp. 225–42.

Gottmann, J. (1961) *Megalopolis: The Urbanized Northeastern Seaboard of the United States*. Norwood MA: Plimpton Press.

Gu, C. L. and Zhao, L. X. (1998) (eds) *Zhongguo gaojishu chanye yu yuanqu* (*China's High Tech Industry and Parks*). Beijing: Zhongxing Press (in Chinese).

Gu, C. L., Zhang, Q., Cai, J. M., Niu, Y. F. and Sun, Y. (1999) *Jingji chuanqiufa yi Zhongguo chengshi fazhan* (*Economic Globalization and Chinese Urban Development*). Beijing: The Commercial Press (in Chinese).

Guangdong Population Census Office (2002) *Guangdongsheng 2000 nian renkou pucha ziliao* (*Tabulation of the 2000 Population Census of Guangdong Province,* Volumes 1–6). Beijing: State Statistical Press (in Chinese).

Guangdong Province Population Census Office (1988) *Zhongguo 1987 nian 1% renkou quyang diaocha ziliao: Guangdong fence* (*Tabulation of China's 1% Population Sample Survey of 1987: Guangdong Volume*). Beijing: State Statistical Press (in Chinese).

—— (1991) *Guangdongsheng disici Renkou pucha shougong huizong ziliao* (*Manual Processed Data for the fourth Population Census of Guangdong Province*). Guangzhou: Internal Publication (in Chinese).

Guangdong Statistical Bureau (1986), *Guangdongsheng xiaocheng zhen diaocha ziliao huibian* (*A Collection of Investigation Data on Small Towns in Guangdong Province*). Guangzhou: Internal Publication.

—— (1990–2000) *Guangdong tongji nianjian* (*Guangdong Statistical Yearbook*). Beijing: State Statistical Press (in Chinese).

Guangzhou Statistical Bureau (1999–2001) *Guangzhou tongji nianjian* (*Guangzhou Statistical Yearbook*). Beijing: State Statistical Press (in Chinese).

Gui, C. L., Zhang, Q., Cai, J. M., Niu, Y. F. and Sun, Y. (1999) *Jingji chuanqiufa yi Zhongguo chengshi fazhan* (*Economic Globalization and Chinese Urban Development*). Beijing: The Commercial Press, pp. 50–1 (in Chinese).

Guldin, G. E. (ed.) (1997) *Farewell to Peasant China: Rural Urbanization and Social Change in the Late Twentieth Century.* Armonk, NY: M. E. Sharpe.

Guthrie, D. (2000) Understanding China's transition to capitalism: the contributions of Victor Nee and Andrew Walder. *Sociological Forum* 15 (4), pp. 727–49.

Hall, P. G. (1966) *The World Cities.* London: Weidenfeld and Nicolson.

Hamer, A. M. (1994) Economic impacts of third world mega-cities: is size the issue? In Fuchs, R. J., Brennan, E., Chamie, J., Lo, F. C. and Uitto, J. (eds) *Mega-City: Growth and the Future.* Tokyo: United Nations University Press, pp. 172–91.

Han, S. (2000) Shanghai between state and market in urban transformation. *Urban Studies* 37 (11), pp. 2091–112.

Hannerz, U. (1996) *Transnational Connections: Culture, People, Places.* London and New York: Routledge.

Hardoy, J. E., Mitlin, D. and Satterwaite, D. (2001) *Environmental Problems in an Urbanizing World.* London: Earthscan.

Harvey, D. (1982) *The Limits of Capital.* Oxford: Oxford University Press.

—— (1985) *The Urbanization of Capital: Studies in the History and Theory of Capitalist Urbanization.* Baltimore, MD: Johns Hopkins University Press.

—— (1989a) From managerialism to entrepreneurialism: the transformation in urban governance in late capitalism. *Geografiska Annaler B* 71 (1), pp. 3–17.

—— (1989b) *The Condition of Postmodernity: An Enquiry into the Origins of Cultural Change.* Oxford: Blackwell.

He, S. J. and Wu, F. L. (2005) Property-led redevelopment in post-reform China: a case study of Xintiandi redevelopment project in Shanghai. *Journal of Urban Affairs* 27 (1), pp. 1–23.

Heikkila, E. J., Shen, T. Y. and Yang, K. Z. (2003) Fuzzy urban sets: theory and application to desakota regions in China. *Environment and Planning B* 30 (2), pp. 239–54.

Herod, A. and Wright, M. (2002) (eds) *Geographies of Power: Placing Scale.* Oxford: Blackwell.

Hiller, H. (2000) Mega-events, urban boosterism and growth strategies: an analysis of the objectives and legitimations of the Capetown 2004 Olympic bid. *International Journal of Urban and Regional Research* 24 (2), pp. 439–58.

Ho, P. (2001) Who owns China's land? *China Quarterly*, 23 (1), pp. 394–421.

Ho, S. P. S. (1994) *Rural China in Transition.* Oxford: Clarendon Press.

Ho, S. P. S. and Huenemann, R. W. (1984) *China's Open Door Policy.* Vancouver: University of British Columbia Press.

Ho, S. P. S. and Lin, G. C. S. (2003) Emerging land markets in rural and urban China: policies and practices. *China Quarterly* 175, pp. 681–707.

—— (2004a) Converting land to nonagricultural use in China's coastal provinces. *Modern China* 30 (1), pp. 81–112.

—— (2004b) Non-agricultural land use in post-reform China. *China Quarterly* 179, pp. 758–81.

Hong, Z. (2004) Mapping the evolution and transformation of private entrepreneurs in China. *Journal of Chinese Political Science* 9 (1), pp. 23–42.

Hong Kong Census and Statistics Department (1972) *Hong Kong Population and Housing Census (1971 Main Report)*. Hong Kong: Hong Kong Government Printing House.

—— (1996) *Hong Kong 1996 Population By-census (Summary Results)*. Hong Kong: Hong Kong Government Printing House.

Hong Kong Trade Development Council (2004) *Revitalisation of Northeast China through SOE reform: Hong Kong's position and strategy*. Economic Forum Report, 19 August 2004.

Hook, b. (ed.) (1998) *Beijing and Tianjin: Towards a Millenial Metropolis*. Hong Kong: Oxford University Press.

Hsing, Y. T. (1998) *Making Capitalism in China: The Taiwanese Connection*. New York: Oxford University Press.

—— (2006) Brokering power and property in China's townships. *Pacific Review* 19 (1), pp. 103–24.

Hsu, C. (2006) Cadres, getihu, and good businesspeople: making sense of entrepreneurs in early post socialist China. *Urban Anthropology* 35 (1), pp. 1–39.

Hu, X. W., Zhou, Y. X. and Gu, C. L. (2000) *Zhongguo yanhai chengzhen miji diqu kongjian jiju yu kuosan yanjiu* (*Studies of Agglomeration and Dispersal in China's Coastal City-Town Concentrated Areas*). Beijing: Science Press (in Chinese).

Hubbard, P. and Hall, T. (eds) (1998) *The Entrepreneurial City: Geographies of Politics, Regime and Representation*. New York: John Wiley.

Japan–China Northeast Development Association (1991) *Liaodong Peninsula and Dalian Economic Development: Present and Perspective* (translated into Chinese in 1992 by Territory Planning and Regional Economy Section, State Planning Committee).

Jessop, B. (2000) The crisis of the national spatio-temporal fix and the tendential ecological dominance of globalizing capitalism. *International Journal of Urban and Regional Research* 24 (2), pp. 323–60.

Jiangsu Statistical Bureau (1990) *Jiangsu sishinian* (*Jiangsu Forty Years 1949–89*). Beijing: State Statistical Press (in Chinese).

—— (various years) *Jiangsu tongji nianjian* (*Jiangsu Statistical Yearbook*). Beijing: State Statistical Press (in Chinese).

Jing, T. H., Chen, M. P., Chen, W., You, A. Q. and Wei, S. H. (eds) (2006) *Zhongguo quyu jingji fazhan baogao* (*The Development Report of China's Regional Economy*). Beijing: Social Sciences Academic Press (in Chinese).

Johnson, G. E. (1992) The political economy of Chinese urbanization in Guangdong and the Pearl River Delta region. In Guldin, G. E. *Urbanizing China*. Westport, CT: Greenwood, pp. 185–220.

Johnson, G. E. and Peterson, G. D. (1999) *Historical Dictionary of Guangzhou (Canton) and Guangdong*. London: Scarecrow.

Johnson, G. E. and Woon, Y. F. (1997) Rural development patterns in post-reform China: the Pearl River Delta region in the 1990s. *Development and Change* 28 (4), pp. 731–51.

Jones, G. W. (2001) Studying extended metropolitan regions in south-east Asia. Paper presented at the XXIV General Conference of the IUSSP, Salvador, Brazil, 18–24 August 2001.

Kelly, P. F. (1998) The politics of urban – rural relationships: land conversion in the Philippines. *Environment and Urbanization* 10 (1), pp. 35–54.

—— (1999) The geography and politics of globalization. *Progress in Human Geography* 23 (3), pp. 379–400.

Kenworthy, J. R. and Laube, F. B. (1996) Automobile dependence in cities: an international comparison of urban transport and land use patterns with implications for sustainability. *Environmental Impact Assessment Review* 16 (4–6), pp. 279–308.

Khan, A. R. (1996) The impact of recent macroeconomic and sectoral changes on the poor and women in China (unpublished paper). ILO Regional Office for Asia and the Pacific, Bangkok, August.

Kirkby, R. J. R. (1985) *Urbanization in China: Town and Country in a Developing Economy 1949–2000 AD*. London: Routledge.

Knox, P. L. (1996) Globalization and urban change. *Urban Geography* 17 (1), pp. 115–17.

Kornai, J. (1986) The soft budget constraint. *Kyklos* 39 (1), pp. 3–30.

—— (1992) *The Socialist System: The Political Economy of Communism*. Princeton NJ: Princeton University Press.

Kotlar, P., Haider, P. D. H. and Rein, I. (1990) *Marketing Places: Attracting Investment, Industry and Tourism to Cities, States and Nations*. New York: Free Press.

Kraas, F. (2003) Megacities as global risk areas. *Petermanns Geographische Mitteilungen* 147 (4), pp. 6–15.

Kunshan County Gazetteer Editorial Office (various years) *Kunshan xianzhi* (*Kunshan County Gazetteer*). Shanghai: Shanghai People's Publishers (in Chinese).

Kunshan Statistical Bureau (various years) *Kunshan tongji nianjian* (*Kunshan Statistical Yearbook*). Kunshan: Kunshan Statistical Publisher (in Chinese).

Kwok, R. Y. W. (1992) Urbanization under economic reform. In Guldin, G. E. (ed.) *Urbanizing China*. Westport, CT: Greenwood, pp. 65–85.

Kwok, R. Y. and Parish, W. L. (eds) (1981) *Chinese Urban Reform. What Model Now?* Armonk and London: M. E. Sharpe.

Laquian, A. A. (1989) *The Effects of National Urban Strategy and Regional Development Policy on Patterns of Urban Growth in China*. Unpublished Paper, Vancouver: Centre for Human Settlements, University of British Columbia.

—— (2005) *Beyond Metropolis: The Planning and Governance of Asia's Mega-Urban Regions*. Baltimore MD: Johns Hopkins University Press.

Lardy, N. R. (1987) *China's Entry into the World Economy*. Lanham MD: University Press of America.

Lee, Y. S. (1991) Rural non-agricultural development in the extended metropolitan region: the case of southern Jiangsu. In Ginsburg, N., Koppel, B. and McGee, T. G. (eds) *The Extended Metropolis: Settlement Transition in Asia*. Honolulu: University of Hawaii Press, pp. 137–56.

Lefebvre, H. (1991) *The Production of Space*. Nicholson-Smith, D. (trans.) Oxford and Cambridge, MA: Blackwell.

Leung, C. K. (1993) Personal contacts, subcontracting linkages, and development in the Hong Kong-Zhujiang delta region. *Annals of the Association of American Geographers* 83 (2), pp. 272–302.

Li, D. D. (1998a) Changing incentives of the Chinese bureaucracy. *American Economic Review* 88 (2), pp. 393–7.

Li, H. (1998b) *Woguo kaifaqu bujuji tudi liyong xianzhuang fensi yu yanjiu* (A study of the location and land use pattern of development zones in China). *Zhongguo tudi kexue* (*China Land Science*) 12 (3), pp. 9–12 (in Chinese).

Li, H. H. (1997) The political economy of the privatization of the land market in Shanghai. *Urban Studies* 34 (2), pp. 321–35.

Li, W. Y. (1986) Developing regional industrial systems in the Chinese People's Repub-
lic. In Hamilton, F. E. I. (ed.) *Industrialization in Developing and Peripheral Regions.*
London: Croom Helm, pp. 335–51.
—— (1990) Recent development of industrial geography in China. In Geographical
Society of China (ed.) *Recent Development of Geographical Science in China.* Beijing:
Science Press, pp. 197–203.
Li, Y. (ed.) (2000) *Zhongguo tudi ziyuan (China's Land Resources).* Beijing: China Land
Press (in Chinese).
Liang, R. C. (1992) *Lun gongyequ de xingcheng yu fazhan* (On the formation and develop-
ment of industrial regions.) *Scientia Geographica Sinica* 12 (4), pp. 336–43 (in Chinese).
Liang, Z. and Ma, Z. (2004) China's floating population: new evidence from the 2000
census. *Population and Development Review* 30 (3), pp. 467–88.
Liaoning Statistical Bureau (1985–2004) *Liaoning tongji nianjian (Liaoning Statistical
Yearbook).* Beijing: State Statistical Press (in Chinese).
Lin, G. C. S. (1993) Small town development in socialist China: a functional analysis.
Geoforum 24 (3), pp. 327–38.
—— (1994) Changing theoretical perspectives on urbanization in Asian developing
countries. *Third World Planning Review* 16 (1), pp. 1–23.
—— (1997) *Red Capitalism in South China: Growth and Development of the Pearl River
Delta.* Vancouver: University of British Columbia Press.
—— (1998) China's industrialization with controlled urbanization: anti-urbanism or
urban-biased? *Issues and Studies* 34 (6), pp. 98–116.
—— (1999) State policy and spatial restructuring in post-reform China, 1978–95.
International Journal of Urban and Regional Research 23 (4), pp. 670–96.
—— (2000) State, capital, and space in China in an age of volatile globalization.
Environment and Planning A 32 (3), pp. 455–71.
—— (2001a) Metropolitan development in a transitional socialist economy: spatial
restructuring in the Pearl River Delta, China. *Urban Studies* 38 (3), pp. 383–406.
—— (2001b) Evolving spatial form of urban – rural interaction in the Pearl River Delta,
China. *Professional Geographer* 53 (1), pp. 56–70.
—— (2002a) The growth and structural change of Chinese cities: a contextual and geographic analysis. *Cities* 19 (5), pp. 299–316.
—— (2002b) Changing discourses in China geography: a narrative evaluation. *Environment and Planning A* 34 (10), pp. 1809–31.
—— (2004a) Toward a post-socialist city? Economic tertiarization and urban reformation
in the Guangzhou metropolis, China. *Eurasian Geography and Economics* 45 (1),
pp. 18–44.
—— (2004b) The Chinese globalizing cities: national centers of globalization and urban
transformation. *Progress in Planning* 61 (3), pp. 143–57.
—— (2006) Peri-urbanism in globalizing China: a study of new urbanism in Dongguan.
Eurasian Geography and Economics 47 (1), pp. 28–53.
—— (2007) Chinese urbanism in question: state, society, and the reproduction of urban
spaces. *Urban Geography* 28 (1), pp. 7–29.
Lin, G. C. S. and Ho, S. P. S. (2003) China's land resources and land-use change: insights
from the 1996 land survey. *Land Use Policy* 20 (2), pp. 87–107.
—— (2005) The state, land system, and land development processes in contemporary
China. *Annals of the Association of American Geographers* 95 (2), pp. 411–36.
Lin, G. C. S. and Ma, L. J. C. (1994) The role of small towns in Chinese regional development. *International Regional Science Review* 17 (1), pp. 75–97.

Lin, M. X. (2004c) *Fahui Shenyang quyuxing zhongxin chengshi de gongneng he zuoyong jiakuai Liaoning zhongbu chengshi qunquyu yitihua bufa* (Promoting Shenyang city's function as regional development centre and speeding up regional integration in the urban agglomeration of the central Liaoning). Available online at: www.ln.xinhuanet.com/2004–06/10/content_2294912.htm (accessed 27 February 2007) (in Chinese).

Liu, Y. C. (ed.) (2000), *Zhongguo tudi ziyuan diaocha shujuji* (*Compilation of the Results From the Survey of China's Land Resources*). Beijing: Internal Publication (in Chinese).

Lo, C. P. (1987) Socialist ideology and urban strategies in China. *Urban Geography* 8 (5), pp. 440–58.

—— (1989) Recent spatial restructuring in the Zhujiang delta, south China: a study of socialist regional development strategy. *Annals of the Association of American Geographers* 79 (2), pp. 293–308.

—— (1992) *Hong Kong*. London: Belhaven.

—— (1994) Economic reforms and socialist city structure: a case study of Guangzhou, China. *Urban Geography* 15 (2), pp. 128–49.

Loftman, P. and Nevin, B. (1996) Going for growth: prestige projects in three British cities. *Urban Studies* 33 (6), pp. 991–1019.

Logan, J. R. (ed.) (2002) *The New Chinese City: Globalization and Market Reform*. London and New York: Blackwell.

Logan, J. R. and Molotch, H. L. (1987) *Urban Fortunes: The Political Economy of Place*. Berkeley, CA: University of California Press.

Ma, L. J. C. (1971) *Commercial Development and Urban Change in Sung China (960–1279)*. Michigan Geographical Publication No. 6. Ann Arbor, MI: Department of Geography, University of Michigan.

—— (1976) Anti-urbanism in China. *Proceedings of the Association of American Geographers* 8, pp. 114–18.

—— (1979) The Chinese approach to city planning: policy, administration, and action. *Asian Survey* 65 (9), pp. 838–55.

—— (2002) Urban transformation in China, 1949–2000: a review and research agenda. *Environment and Planning A* 33 (9), pp. 1545–69.

—— (2005) Urban administrative restructuring, changing scale relations and local economic development in China. *Political Geography* 24 (4), pp. 477–97.

Ma, L. J. C. and Cui, G. H. (1987) Administrative changes and urban population in China. *Annals of the Association of American Geographers* 77 (3), pp. 373–95.

—— (2002) Economic transition at the local level: diverse forms of town development in China. *Eurasian Geography and Economics* 43 (2), pp. 79–103.

Ma, L. J. C. and Hanten, E. W. (eds) (1981) *Urban Development in Modern China*. Boulder, CO: Westview Press.

Ma, L. J. C. and Lin, G. C. S. (1993) Development of towns in China: a case study of Guangdong Province. *Population and Development Review* 19 (3), pp. 583–606.

Ma, L. J. C. and Wu, F. L. (2005a) (eds) *Restructuring the Chinese City: Changing Society, Economy and Space*. London and New York: Routledge.

—— (2005b) Restructuring the Chinese city: diverse processes and reconstituted spaces. In Ma, L. J. C. and Wu, F. L. (eds) *Restructuring the Chinese City*. London and New York: Routledge, pp. 1–20.

Ma, L. J. C. and Xiang, B. (1998) Native place, migration and the emergence of peasant enclaves in Beijing. *China Quarterly* 155, pp. 546–81.

Macleod, S. and McGee T. G. (1996) The Singapore-Johore-Riau triangle: An emerging extended metropolitan region. In Lo, F. C. and Yeung, Y. M. (eds) *Emerging World Cities in Pacific Asia.* Tokyo: United Nations University Press, pp. 417–464.

McGee, T. G. (1964) The rural–urban continuum debate: the pre-industrial city and rural–urban migration. *Pacific Viewpoint* 5 (2), pp. 159–81.

—— (1971) *The Urbanization Process in the Third World: Explorations in Search of Theory.* London: G. Bell and Sons.

—— (1986) Domains of analysis: perspectives on the study of inequality and economic growth in Malaysia. *Pacific Affairs* 59 (4), pp. 655–64.

—— (1989) Urbanisasi or kotadesasi? Evolving patterns of urbanization in Asia. In Costa, F. J., Dutt, A. K., Ma, L. J. C. and Noble, A. G. (eds) *Urbanization in Asia.* Honolulu: University of Hawaii Press, pp. 93–108.

—— (1991a) The emergence of desakota regions in Asia: expanding a hypothesis. In Ginsburg, N., Koppel, B. and McGee, T. G. (eds) *The Extended Metropolis: Settlement Transition in Asia.* Honolulu: University of Hawaii Press, pp. 3–25.

—— (1991b) Eurocentrism in geography: the case of Asian urbanization. *Canadian Geographer* 35 (4), pp. 332–44.

—— (2002) Reconstructing the Southeast Asia city in an era of volatile globalization. *Asian Journal of Social Science* 30 (1), pp. 8–27.

McGee, T. G. and Robinson, I. M. (eds) (1995) *The Mega-urban Regions of Southeast Asia.* Vancouver: University of British Columbia Press.

McGee, T. G. and Scott, S. (eds) (2001) The poor at risk: surviving the economic crisis in Southeast Asia. *Final Report on Project on Social Safety Net Programmes in Selected Southeast Asian Countries 1997–2000.* Vancouver: Centre for Southeast Asian Studies, University of British Columbia.

McGranahan, G. and Satterthwaite, D. (2002) The environmental dimensions of sustainable development for cities. *Geography* 87 (3), pp. 213–26.

McManus, P. and Haughton, G. (2006) Planning with ecological footprints: a sympathetic critique of theory and practice. *Environment and Urbanization* 18 (1), pp. 113–28.

Marcotullio, P. J. (2003) Globalization, urban form and environmental conditions in Asia-Pacific cities. *Urban Studies* 40 (2), pp. 219–47.

Marcotullio, P. J. and Lee, Y. S. F. (2003) Environmental transitions and urban transportation systems: a comparison of the North American and Asian experiences. *International Development Planning Review* 25 (4), pp. 325–54.

Marton, A. M. (1995) Mega-urbanization in southern Jiangsu. *Chinese Environment and Development* 6 (1–2), pp. 9–42.

—— (2000) *China's Spatial Economic Development: Restless Landscapes in the lower Yangzi delta.* London and New York: Routledge.

—— (2002) Local geographies of globalisation: rural agglomeration in the Chinese countryside. *Asia Pacific Viewpoint* 43 (1), pp. 23–42.

Marton, A. M. and McGee T. G. (1998) *Yazhou dadu shiqu fazhan de xin moshi: Zhongguo de dute jingyan* (New models of metropolitan development in Asia: the Chinese experience). In Xu, X. Q., Xue, F. X. and Yan, X. P. (eds) *Zhongguo xiangcun-chengshi zhuanxing yu xietiao fazhan (China's Rural–Urban Transition and Development).* Beijing: Science Press, pp. 258–70 (in Chinese).

Marton, A. M. and Wu, W. (2006) Spaces of globalisation: institutional reforms and spatial economic development in the Pudong New Area, Shanghai. *Habitat International* 30 (2), pp. 213–29.

Midgley, P. (1994) *Urban Transport in Asia: An Operational Agenda for the 1990s.* Washington, DC: World Bank.

Mok, K. L., Wong, L. and Lee, G. O. M. (2002) The challenges of global capitalism: unemployment and state workers' reactions and responses in post-reform China. *International Journal of Human Resource Management* 13 (3), pp. 399–415.

Montgomery, M., Stren, R., Cohen, B. and Reed, H. E. (eds) (2003) *Cities Transformed: Demographic Change and its Implications in the Developing World.* Washington DC: National Academies Press.

Mumford, L. (1961) *The City in History: Its Origins, Its Transformations and its Prospects.* New York: Harcourt.

Munro, W. B. (1926) *The Government of American Cities.* New York: Macmillan.

Murphey, R. (1974) The treaty ports and China's modernization. In Elvin, M. and Skinner, G. W. (eds) *The Chinese City between Two Worlds.* Stanford, CA: Stanford University Press, pp. 17–71.

—— (1980) *The Fading of the Maoist Vision: City and Country in China's Development.* London: Methuen.

Murray, P. and Szelenyi, I. (1984) The city in the transition to socialism. *International Journal of Urban and Regional Research* 8 (1), pp. 90–107.

Naughton, B. (1995a) *Growing out of the Plan.* New York: Cambridge University Press.

—— (1995b) Cities in the Chinese economic system: changing roles and conditions for autonomy. In Davis, D. S., Kraus, R., Naughton, B. and Perry, E. J. (eds) *Urban Spaces in Contemporary China.* Washington, DC: Woodrow Wilson Center Press, pp. 61–89.

Nee, V. (1991) A theory of market transition: from redistribution to markets in state socialism. *American Sociological Review* 54 (5), pp. 663–81.

—— (1992) Organizational dynamics of market transition: hybrid forms, property rights, and mixed economy in China. *Administrative Science Quarterly* 37 (1), pp. 1–27.

Nee, V. and Cao, Y. (2000) Controversies and evidence in the market transition debate. *American Journal of Sociology* 105, pp. 1175–95.

Nee, V. and Swedburg, R. (eds) (2005) *The Economic Sociology of Capitalism.* Princeton, NJ: Princeton University Press.

Nijman, J. (2000) The paradigmatic city. *Annals of the Association of American Geographers* 90 (1), pp. 135–45.

Oakes, T. (2000) China's provincial identities: reviving regionalisms and reinventing "Chineseness." *Journal of Asian Studies* 59 (3), pp. 667–92.

Ofer, G. (1977) Economizing on urbanization in socialist countries: historical necessity or socialist strategy. In Brown, A. A. and Newberger, E. (eds) *International Migration: A Comparative Perspective.* New York: Academic Press, pp. 277–303.

Ohmae, K. (1995) *The End of the Nation State: The Rise of Regional Economies.* London: Harper Collins.

Oi, J. C. (1992) Fiscal reform and the economic foundations of local state corporatism. *World Politics* 45 (1), pp. 99–126.

—— (1999) *Rural China Takes Off: Institutional Foundations of Economic Reform.* Berkeley, CA: University of California Press.

Oi, J. C. and Walder, A. G. (1999) *Property Rights and Economic Reform in China.* Stanford, CA: Stanford University Press.

Olds, K. (1997) Globalizing Shanghai: the "global intelligence corps" and the building of Pudong. *Cities* 14 (2), pp. 109–23.

Olds, K. and Poon, J. (2002) Theories and discourses of economic geography: papers from the Singapore Conference on Economic Geography, December 2000. *Environment and Planning A* 34 (3), pp. 379–83.

Organization for Economic Co-Operation and Development (2005) *Governance in China*. Paris: Organization for Economic Co-operation and Development.

Pannell, C. W. (1977) Past and present city structure in China. *Town Planning Review* 48 (2), pp. 157–72.

—— (1990) China's urban geography. *Progress in Human Geography* 14 (2), pp. 214–36.

—— (1992) The role of great cities in China. In Guldin, G. E. (ed.) *Urbanizing China*. Westport, CT: Greenwood, pp. 11–39.

Pearson, M. M. (1997) *China's New Business Elite: The Political Consequences of Economic Reform*. Berkeley and Los Angeles: University of California Press.

People's Daily (2004a) (*Renmin ribao*) 19 April.

—— (2004b) (China making efforts to cultivate middle income class) 26 March.

Perkins, W. (1977) *Rural Small-Scale Industry in the People's Republic of China*. Report of the American Rural Small-Scale Industry Delegation. Berkeley, CA: University of California Press.

Pieterse, J. N. (1995) Globalization as hybridization. In Featherstone, M., Lash, S. and Robertson, R. (eds) *Global Modernities*. London: Sage, pp. 45–68.

—— (2001) Hybridity, so what? The anti-hybridity backlash and the riddles of recognition. *Theory, Culture and Society* 18 (2–3), pp. 219–45.

Population Census Office under the State Council (2002) *Zhongguo 2000 nian renkou pucha ziliao* (*Tabulation of the 2000 Population Census of the People's Republic of China, Volume 1*). Beijing: State Statistics Press (in Chinese).

PRNewswire (2004) Cooper Standard Automotive opens NVH control systems manufacturing facility in Kunshan. Available online at: www.prnewswire.com/cgi-bin/stories.pl (accessed 20 October 2005) (in Chinese).

Qian, Z. H. and Wong, T. C. (2000) The rising urban poverty: a dilemma of market reforms in China. *Journal of Contemporary China* 9 (23), pp. 113–25.

Qinghua University Urban–Rural Development Research Group (1995) *Suxichang diqu chengxiang kongjian huanjing fazhan guihua yanjiu* (*Suxichang Area Urban–Rural Spatial Environment Development Planning Research*). Beijing: Qinghua University (in Chinese).

Rees, W. E. (1992) Ecological footprints and appropriated carrying capacity: what urban economics leaves out. *Environment and Urbanization* 4 (2), pp. 21–30.

Rimmer, P. J. (2002) Overview: restructuring Chinese space in the new millennium. *Asia Pacific Viewpoint* 43 (1), pp. 1–8.

Roy, J. (2006) A new look in the northeast. *EuroBiz*. (November), pp. 48–53.

Santos, M. (1979) *The Shared Space: The Two Circuits of the Urban Economy in Underdeveloped Countries*. London and New York: Methuen.

Sassen, S. (1991) *The Global City: New York, London, Tokyo*. Princeton, NJ: Princeton University Press.

Satterthwaite, D. and Tacoli, C. (2003) The urban part of rural development: the role of small and intermediate urban centers in rural and regional development and poverty reduction. *Rural–Urban Working Paper* 9, International Institute for Environment and Development, London (available online at: www.iied.org/rural_urban/downloads.html#UPWPS).

Scott, A. J. (1988) *Regions and the World Economy: The Coming Shape of Global Production, Competition and the Political Order*. Oxford: Oxford University Press.

—— (1999) Global city regions and the new world system. Paper presented at the 16th Pacific Regional Science Congress, Seoul, South Korea, 12–16 July.

—— (ed.) (2001) *Global City-Regions: Trends, Theory, Policy.* Oxford and New York: Oxford University Press.

Scott, J. C. (1988) *Seeing Like A State: How Certain Schemes to Improve the Human Condition Have Failed.* New Haven, CT: Yale University Press.

Seto, K. C. and Kaufmann, R. K. (2003) Modeling the drivers of urban land use change in the Pearl River Delta, China: integrating remote sensing with socio-economic data. *Land Economics* 79 (1), pp. 106–121.

Seto, K. C., Kaufmann, R. K. and Woodcock, C. E. (2002) Monitoring land-use change in the Pearl River Delta using Landsat TM. *International Journal of Remote Sensing* 23 (10), pp. 1985–2004.

Shanghai Statistical Bureau (2000a) *Shanghai fandichan shichang 1999* (*Shanghai Land Market 1999*) Beijing: State Statistical Press (in Chinese).

—— (2000b) *Xin Shanghai wushinian guomin jingji he shehui lishe tongji ziliao 1949–1999* (*New Shanghai Fifty Years Statistics 1949–1999*). Beijing: State Statistical Press (in Chinese).

—— (1986–2006) *Shanghai tongji nianjian* (*Shanghai Statistical Yearbook*) Beijing: State Statistical Press (in Chinese).

Shen, D. Q. (1988) *Changjiang liuyu kaifade zhengtixing, jieduanxing yu leixingxing* (The periodicity, typicality and overall development of the Yangzi River valley). In Si, Y. F. (ed.) *Zhongguo kexueyuan Nanjing dili yu hupo yanjiusuo jikan* (*Memoirs of the Chinese Academy of Sciences Nanjing Institute of Geography and Limnology*, vol. 5). Nanjing: People's Press, pp. 99–100 (in Chinese).

Shen, J. (2005) Space, scale and the state: reorganizing urban space in China. In Ma, L. J. C. and Wu, F. (eds) *Restructuring the Chinese City.* London: Routledge, pp. 39–58.

Shen, J., Wong, K. and Feng, Z. (2002) State-sponsored and spontaneous urbanization in the Pearl River Delta of south China, 1980–1998. *Urban Geography* 23 (7), pp. 674–94.

Sheng, L. (1999) *Zhongguo chengshi pingkun renkou shuliang fengxi* (Estimation of China's urban poverty population), *Renkou yanjiu* (*Population Research*) 23 (6), pp. 1–8 (in Chinese).

Shi, C., Hutchinson, S., Yu, L. and Xu S. (2001) Towards a sustainable coast: an integrated coastal zone management framework for Shanghai, China. *Ocean & Coastal Management* 44 (5–6), pp. 411–27.

Simmonds, R. and Hack, G. (eds) (2000) *Global City Regions: Their Emerging Forms.* New York and London: Spon Press.

Sit, V. F. S. (1989) Hong Kong's new industrial partnership with the Pearl River Delta. *Asian Geographer* 8 (1&2), pp. 103–15.

—— (1995) *Beijing: The Nature and Planning of a Chinese Capital City.* New York: John Wiley.

—— (2001) Increasing globalization and the growth of the Hong Kong extended metropolitan region. In Lo, F. C. and Marcotullio, P. J. (eds) *Globalization and Sustainability of Cities in the Asia Pacific Region.* Tokyo: United Nations University Press, pp. 199–238.

—— (2005) China's extended metropolitan regions: formation and definition. *International Development and planning Review* 27 (3), pp. 407–41.

Sit, V. F. S. and Cai, J. M. (2003) Formation and development strategies of China's extended metropolitan regions. *Geographical Research* 22 (5), pp. 531–40.

Sit, V. F. S. and Yang, C. (1997) Foreign-investment-induced exo-urbanization in the Pearl River Delta, China. *Urban Studies* 34 (4), pp. 647–77.

Smart, A. (1998) Economic transformation and property regimes in China. In: Smith, A. and Pickles, J. (eds) *Theorizing Transition in Eastern Europe*. London: Routledge, pp. 428–49.

Smart, A. and Lee, J. (2003) Financialization and the role of real estate in Hong Kong's regime of accumulation. *Economic Geography* 79 (2), pp. 163–71.

Smart, A. and Lin, G. C. S. (2007) Local capitalisms, local citizenship and translocality: rescaling from below in the Pearl River Delta region China. *International Journal of Urban and Regional Research* 31 (2), pp. 280–302.

Smart, A. and Smart, J. (2001) Local citizenship: welfare reform urban/rural status, and exclusion in China. *Environment and Planning A* 33 (10), pp. 1709–898.

Smart, J. and Smart, A. (1991) Personal connections and divergent economies: a case study of Hong Kong investment in China. *International Journal of Urban and Regional Research* 15 (2), pp. 216–33.

Smith, N. (2000) Scale. In Johnston, R. J., Gregory, D., Pratt, G. and Watts, M. (eds) *The Dictionary of Human Geography*. Oxford: Blackwell, pp. 724–7.

Smyth, R. and Zhai, Q. G. (2003) Economic restructuring in China's large and medium-sized state-owned enterprises: evidence from Liaoning. *Journal of Contemporary China*, 12 (34), pp. 173–205.

So, A. Y. (2002) Studies of the Pearl River Delta: new findings and future research agenda. In Wong, K. Y. and Shen, J. F. (eds) *Resource Management, Urbanization and Governance in Hong Kong and the Zhujiang Delta*. Hong Kong: Chinese University Press, pp. 205–307.

Solinger, D. J. (1999) *Contesting Citizenship in Urban China*. Berkeley, CA: University of California Press.

—— (2006) The creation of a new underclass in China and its implications. *Environment and Urbanization* 18 (1), pp. 177–93.

Song, L. and Shen, Y. (1998) SOEs expect profits in Liaoning to speed up reform. *China Daily*. (2 February). Available online at: www.chinadaily.com.cn (accessed on 28 February 2007).

Song, W. (2002) *Youhua quyu kongjian jiegou yu fazhan Dalian beisanshi jingji* (Optimization of the regional spatial structure to develop the economic growth the three northern cities in Dalian). *Liaoning Shida Xuebao* (*Journal of Liaoning Normal University*) (Natural Science Edition) 25 (2), pp. 184–6 (in Chinese).

Special Zones Office of the State Council (1991) *Zhongguo yanhai chengshi jingji jishu kaifaqu* (*China's Coastal Municipal Economic and Technological Development Zones*). Beijing: State Council (in Chinese).

State Council of the PRC (2001) *The Tenth Five Year Plan of China*. Beijing: New Star Publishers.

Stoker, G. (1995) Regime theory and urban politics. In Judge, D., Stoker, G. and Wolman, H. (eds) *Theories of Urban politics*. London: Sage, pp. 54–71.

Stone, C. (1989) *Regime Politics: Governing Atlanta, 1946–1988*. Lawrence: University Press of Kansas.

Sui, D. Z. and Zeng, H. (2001) Modeling the dynamics of landscape structure in Asia's emerging desakota regions: a case study in Shenzhen. *Landscape and Urban Planning* 53 (1–4), pp. 37–52.

Sustainable Development Research Group. (2005) *China Urban Development Report 2005*. Beijing: Sustainable Development Research Group, Chinese Academy of Sciences.

Suzhou Statistical Bureau (various years) *Suzhou tongji nianjian* (*Suzhou Statistical Yearbook*). Beijing: State Statistical Press (in Chinese).

Szelenyi, I. (1996) Cities under socialism – and after. In Andrusz, G., Harloe, M. and Szelenyi, I. (eds) *Cities after Socialism: Urban and Regional Change and Conflict in Post-Socialist Societies*. Cambridge, MA: Blackwell, pp. 286–317.

Tang, W. F. and Parish, W. (2000) *Chinese Urban Life under Reform: The Changing Social Contract*. Cambridge: Cambridge University Press.

Tang, W. S. (1997) Urbanization in China: a review of its causal mechanisms and spatial relationships. *Progress in Planning* 48 (1), pp. 1–65.

—— (1998) Urbanization in Fujian, 1949–1993. In Yeung, Y. M. (ed.) *Urban Development in Asia Retrospect and Prospect*. Hong Kong: Hong Kong Institute of Asia Pacific Studies, Chinese University of Hong Kong, pp. 341–72.

Tang, W. S. and Chung, H. (2000) Urban–rural transition in China: beyond the desakota model. In Li, S. M. and Tang, W. S. (eds) *China's Regions, Polity and Economy: A Study of Spatial Transformation in the Post-reform Era*. Hong Kong: Chinese University Press, pp. 275–308.

—— (2002) Rural–urban transition in China: illegal land-use and construction. *Asia-Pacific Viewpoint* 43 (1), pp. 43–62.

Taylor, B. and Kwok, R. Y. W. (1989) From export center to world city: planning for the transformation of Hong Kong. *Journal of the American Planning Association* 55 (3), pp. 309–22.

Thoburn, J. T., Leung, H. M., Chau, E. and Tang, S. H. K. (1990) *Foreign Investment in China Under the Open Policy*. Hong Kong: Gower Publishing.

Tsai, K. S. (2002) *Back Alley Banking. Private Entrepreneurs in China*. Ithaca, NY: Cornell University Press.

UNESCAP (Economic and Social Commission for Asia and the Pacific) (2000) Urban poverty alleviation. Paper delivered to the Regional High-level Meeting in preparation for Istanbul+5 for Asia and the Pacific, 19–23 October, Hangzhou, China.

Unger, J. and Chan, A. (1999) Inheritors of the boom: private enterprise and the role of the local government in a rural south China township. *China Journal* 42, pp. 44–7.

United Nations Population Division (2002) *World Urbanization Prospects. The 2001 Revision Data Table and Highlights*. New York: United Nations.

Veeck, G. (ed.) (1991) *The Uneven Landscape: Geographical Studies in Post-Reform China*. Baton Rouge, LA: Geoscience Publication.

Vogel, E. F. (1979) Japan as number one: lessons for America. Cambridge, MA: Harvard University Press.

—— (1989) *One Step ahead in China: Guangdong under Reform*. Cambridge, MA: Harvard University Press.

Wakeman, F. (1995) The civil society and public sphere debate. Western reflections on Chinese public culture. *Modern China* 19 (2), pp. 108–38.

Walder, A. G. (1995) China's transitional economy: interpreting its significance. *China Quarterly* 144, pp. 963–79.

Wang, H. and Bai, Q. H. (2003) *Woguo sanda dushiquan fazhan yanjiu* (Study on China's three extended metropolitan regions). *Ruan kexue* (*Soft Science*) 17 (5), pp. 36–46 (in Chinese).

Wang, M. Y. L. (1995) *The Socioeconomic and Spatial Transformation in the Shenyang–Dalian Extended Metropolitan Region of China, 1978–1992*. PhD Dissertation, Department of Geography, University of British Columbia.

—— (1997a) The disappearing rural–urban boundary: rural socio-economic transformation in the Shenyang–Dalian region of China. *Third World Planning Review* 19 (3), pp. 229–50.

—— (1997b) Urban growth and the transformation of rural China: the case of southern Manchuria. *Asia Pacific Viewpoint* 38 (1), pp. 1–18.

—— (1998) *Mega Urban Regions in China.* Beijing: China Ocean Press.

—— (2002a) Small city, big solution? China's hukou system reform and its potential impacts. *DISP* 150, pp. 23–9.

—— (2004) New urban poverty in China: disadvantaged retrenched workers. *International Development Planning Review* 26 (2), pp. 117–39.

Wang, M. Y. L. and Meng, X. C. (2004) Global-local initiatives in FDI: the experience of Shenzhen, China. *Asia Pacific Viewpoint* 45 (2), pp. 181–96.

Wang, M. Y. L., Webber, M. and Zhu, Y. (2002) China's puzzle game: four spatial shifts of development. In Webber, M., Wang, M. and Zhu, Y. (eds), *China's Transition to a Global Economy.* Hampshire: Palgrave Macmillan, pp. 113–42.

Wang, Y. P. (2002b) Low income communities and urban poverty in China. Paper delivered at the Workshop on Spatial Restructuring, Urban Planning and Politics in China, University at Albany, State University of New York, 16 June.

Webber, M. J., Wang, M. Y. and Zhu, Y. (eds) (2002) *China's Transition to a Global Economy.* Hampshire: Palgrave Macmillan.

Weber, M. (1951) *The Religion of China.* New York: Free Press.

Webster, D. (2001) On the edge: shaping the future of periurban East Asia. Discussion Paper prepared for EASUR, World Bank (12 June).

—— (2002) *On the Edge: Shaping the Future of Peri-Urban East Asia.* Discussion Paper of the Asia Pacific Research Center, Stanford University.

Webster, D. and Muller, L. (2001) *Coastal Peri-Urbanization in China: New Dynamics, New Challenges, the Case of the Hangzhou – Ningbo Corridor.* Working Paper, Asia-Pacific Research Center, Stanford University.

—— (2002) *Challenges of Peri-urbanization in the Lower Yangtze region: The Case of the Hangzhou-Ningbo Corridor.* Discussion Paper of the Asia Pacific Research Center, Stanford University.

Webster, D., Cai, J., Muller, L. and Luo, B. (2003) *Emerging Third Stage Peri-Urbanization: Functional Specialization in the Hangzhou Peri-Urban Region.* Discussion Paper of the Asia Pacific Research Center, Stanford University.

Wei, H., Shen, Z. and Wang, M. Y. (2002) Structural adjustment: creating a new textile industry. In Webber, M., Wang, M. Y. and Zhu, Y. (eds), *China's Transition to a Global Economy*, Hampshire: Palgrave Macmillan, pp. 191–204.

Wei, Y. H. D. (2002) Beyond the Sunan model: trajectory and underlying factors of development in Kunshan, China. *Environment and planning A* 34 (10), pp. 1725–47.

Westbrod, R. (1999) Solving China's urban crisis: China's transportation energy future. *Journal of Urban Technology* 6 (1), pp. 89–100.

Wheatley, P. (1971) *The Pivot of the Four Quarters: A Preliminary Enquiry into the Origins and Character of the Ancient Chinese City.* Chicago, IL: Aldine.

White, L. (1981) Shanghai–suburb relations, 1949–1966. In Howe, C. (ed.) *Shanghai: Revolution and Development in an Asian Metropolis.* New York: Cambridge University Press, pp. 241–68.

Whyte, M. K. and Parish, W. L. (1984) *Urban Life in Contemporary China.* Chicago, IL: University of Chicago Press.

Wong, K. K. and Zhao, X. B. (1999) The influence of bureaucratic behavior on land apportionment in China: the informal process. *Environment and Planning C* 17 (1), pp. 113–26.

Wong, K. Y. and Shen, J. F. (eds) (2002) *Resource Management, Urbanization and Governance*. Hong Kong: Chinese University Press.

Woodside, A. (1998) Reconciling the Chinese and Western theory worlds in an era of Western development fatigue. *Modern China* 24 (2), pp. 121–34.

Wright, A. F. (1977) The cosmology of the Chinese city. In Skinner, G. W. (ed.) *The City in Late Imperial China*. Stanford, CA: Stanford University Press, pp. 33–73.

Wu, F. (2000a) The global and local dimensions of place-making: remaking Shanghai as a world city. *Urban Studies* 39 (8), pp. 1359–77.

—— (2000b) Place promotion in Shanghai, PRC. *Cities* 17 (5), pp. 349–61.

—— (2001) China's recent urban development in the process of land and housing marketisation and economic globalization. *Habitat International* 25 (2), pp. 273–9.

—— (2002a) Socio-spatial differentiation in urban China: evidence from Shanghai's real estate markets. *Environment and Planning A* 34 (9), pp. 1591–615.

—— (2003a) The (post-) socialist entrepreneurial city as state project: Shanghai's reglobalisation in question. *Urban studies* 40 (9), pp. 1673–98.

—— (2003b) Transitional cities. *Environment and Planning A* 35 (8), pp. 1331–8.

—— (2004a) Urban poverty and marginalization under market transition: the case of Chinese cities. *International Journal of Urban and Regional Research* 28 (2), pp. 401–23.

Wu, F. L. and Ma, L. J. C. (2005) The Chinese city in transition. Towards theorizing China's urban restructuring. In Ma, L. J. C. and Wu, F. L. (eds) *Restructuring the Chinese City: Changing Society, Economy and Space*. London and New York: Routledge, pp. 260–79.

Wu, F. L. and Webber, K (2004) The rise of "foreign gated communities" in Beijing: between economic globalization and local institutions. *Cities* 21 (3), pp. 203–13.

Wu, F. L. and Yeh, A. G. O. (1999) Urban spatial structure in a transitional economy: the case of Guangzhou, China. *Journal of the American Planning Association* 65 (4), pp. 377–94.

Wu, J. and Radbone, I. (2005) Global integration and intra-urban determinants of foreign direct investment in Shanghai. *Cities* 22 (4), pp. 275–86.

Wu, K. and Sun, L. J. (eds) (2003) *Jinri Kunshan (Kunshan Today)*. Beijing: Jinghua Press (in Chinese).

Wu, W. (1999a) City profile: Shanghai. *Cities* 16 (3), pp. 207–16.

—— (1999b) Reforming China's institutional environment for urban infrastructure provision. *Urban Studies* 36 (13), pp. 2263–82.

Wu, W. (1999c) Temporary migrants in China's urban settings: housing and settlement patterns. Paper presented at the International Conference on the Future of Chinese Cities, Shanghai.

—— (2002b) Temporary migrants in Shanghai: housing and settlement patterns. In Logan, J. R. (ed.) *The New Chinese City: Globalization and Market Reform*. London and New York: Blackwell, pp. 212–26.

—— (2004b) Cultural strategies in Shanghai: regenerating cosmopolitanism in an era of globalization. *Progress in Planning* 61 (3), pp. 159–80.

—— (2005) Migrant residential distribution and metropolitan spatial development in Shanghai. In Ma, L. J. C. and Wu, F. L. (eds) *Restructuring the Chinese City: Changing Society, Economy and Space*. London and New York: Routledge, pp. 222–42.

Xia, Y. and Sun, J. (2000) *Jiushiniandai Pudong chengshihua yu nongcun laodongli zhuanyi* (Pudong urbanization and rural labour transfer in the 1990s). *Nanfang renkou* (*South China Population*) 4 (15), pp. 39–44 (in Chinese).

Xie, Y., Tian, Y. and Xing, X. (2005) Socio-economic driving forces of arable land conversion: a case study of Wuxian city, China. *Global Environmental Change* 15 (3), pp. 238–52.

Xie, Y., Yu, M., Bai, Y. and Xing, X. (2006) Ecological analysis of an emerging urban landscape pattern: desakota, a case study of Suzhou, China. *Landscape Ecology* 21 (8), pp. 1297–309.

Xu, J. and Yeh, A. G. O. (2005) City repositioning and competitiveness building in regional development: new development strategies in Guangzhou China. *International Journal of Urban and Regional Research* 29 (2), pp. 283–308.

Xu, X. M. (2006) Unofficial "nanny" of Kunshan. *China Daily/Shanghai and Delta Supplement*, 31 March, p. 4.

Xu, X. Q. and Li, S. M. (1990) China's open door policy and urbanization in the Pearl River Delta region. *International Journal of Urban and Regional Research* 14 (1), pp. 49–69.

Xu, X. Y. and Zhou, T. (2001) *Taibao dui Shanghai yiwang qingshen* (Taiwanese enjoy living in Shanghai). *Jinri Zhongguo* (*China Today*), October, pp. 7–9 (in Chinese).

Yan, X. P. and Lin, P. P. (2004) The change of spatial disparities of urban development in China, 1990s. *ACTA Geographica Sinica* 59 (3), pp. 437–45.

Yang, G. and Wang, L. (2001) *Xin de shiji yu xin de pinkun: Zhongguo chengshi pinkun wenti yanjiu* (New century, new poverty: research on China's urban poverty problem). *Jingji tizhi gaige* (*Economic System Reform*) 1, pp. 5–11 (in Chinese).

Yang, W. (2000) *Shanghai chanye jiegou yu buju yanjiu* (*A Study on Shanghai Industrial Structure*). Shanghai: East China Normal University Press (in Chinese).

Yang, Y. (1998) *Wo guo de chengshi pingkong jiqi zhili jizhi chuangxin* (China's urban poverty and its new anti-poverty mechanism). *Xin dong fang* (*New Orient*) 4, pp. 10–15, 37 (in Chinese).

Yao, S. M. (1992) *Zhongguo de chengshi qun* (*The Urban Agglomerations of China*). Hefei: Science and Technology Press (in Chinese).

Yau, S. and Chen, S. (1998) Trends in urban spatial change in the Yangtze River delta. In Xu, X., Xue, F. and Yen, X. (eds) *Zhongguo xiangcun-chengshi zhuanxing yu xietiao fazhan* (*China's Rural–Urban Transition and Development*). Beijing: Science Press, pp. 271–80.

Yeh, A. G. O. (1997) Economic restructuring and land use planning in Hong Kong. *Land Use Policy* 14 (1), pp. 25–39.

—— (2005) Dual land market and internal spatial structure of Chinese cities. In Ma, L. J. C. and Wu, F. L. (eds) *Restructuring the Chinese City: Changing Society, Economy and Space*. London and New York: Routledge, pp. 59–79.

Yeh, A. G. O. and Li, X. (1997) An integrated remote sensing and GIS approach in the monitoring and evaluation of rapid urban growth for sustainable urban development in the Pearl River Delta, China. *International Planning Studies* 2 (2), pp. 195–222.

Yeh, A. G. O. and Wu, F. L. (1996) The new land development process and urban development in Chinese cities. *International Journal of Urban and Regional Research* 20 (2), pp. 330–53.

—— (1998) The urban planning system in China. *Progress in Planning* 51 (3), pp. 165–252.

—— (1999) The transformation of the urban planning system in China from a centrally planned to transitional economy. *Progress in Planning* 51 (3), pp. 167–252.

Yeh, A. G. O. and Xu, X. Q. (1996) Globalization and the urban system in China. In Lo, F. C. and Yeung, Y. M. (eds) *Emerging World Cities in Pacific Asia.* Tokyo: United Nations University Press, pp. 219–67.

Yeh, A. G. O., Lee, Y. S. F., Lee, T. and Nien, D. S. (eds) (2002) *Building a Competitive Pearl River Delta Region.* Hong Kong: Centre of Urban Planning and Environmental Management, University of Hong Kong.

Yeung, H. W. C. (2002a) Doing what kind of economic geography. *Journal of Economic Geography* 2 (2), pp. 250–2.

—— (2002b) The limits to globalization theory: a geographical perspective on global economic change. *Economic Geography* 78 (3), pp. 285–305.

Yeung, H. W. C. and Lin, G. C. S. (2003) Theorizing economic geographies of Asia. *Economic Geography* 79 (2), pp. 107–28.

Yeung, Y. M. (2005a) Emergence of the Pan-Pearl River Delta. *Geografiska Annaler B* 87 (1), pp. 75–9.

—— (2005b) *The Pearl River Mega-Urban Region: Internal Dynamics and External Linkages.* Occasional Paper No 12. Shanghai–Hong Kong Development Institute, Institute of Asia Pacific Studies, Chinese University of Hong Kong.

Yeung, Y. M. and Chu, D. (eds) (1998) *Guangdong: Survey of a Province Undergoing Rapid Change* (2nd edn). Hong Kong: Hong Kong Chinese University Press.

Yeung, Y. M. and Hu, X. W. (eds) (1992) *China's Coastal Cities.* Honolulu: University of Hawaii Press.

Yeung, Y. M. and Shen, J. (eds) (2004) *Developing China's West: A Critical Path to Balanced National Development.* Hong Kong: Hong Kong Chinese University Press.

Yeung, Y. M. and Sun, Y. W. (eds) (1996) *Shanghai: Transformation and Modernisation under China's Open Door Policy.* Hong Kong: Hong Kong Chinese University Press.

Yeung, Y. M. and Zhou, Y. (eds) (1988 and 1988–89) Urbanization in China: an inside–outside perspective. *Chinese Society and Anthropology.* Parts 1 and 2. 19 (3–4); 21 (2).

Yu, H. P., Hao, H. F. and Gou, H. (1999) *Liaoning nongcun chanye jiegou yanjiu* (Research on rural industrial structure in Liaoning). *Caijing wenti (Financial Problems)* 9, pp. 61–7 (in Chinese).

Yue, Q. F. (ed.) (1992) *Liaoning jingji zhidian (Dictionary of Liaoning Economic Affairs)*, Beijing: People's Press (in Chinese).

Yusuf, S. and Wu, W. (1997) *The Dynamics of Growth in Three Chinese Cities.* New York: Oxford University Press.

—— (2002) Pathways to a world city: Shanghai rising in an era of globalization. *Urban Studies* 39 (7), pp. 1213–40.

Zhang, J. (2005) China's urbanization puzzle. *China Business.* 1 October.

Zhang, L. and Zhao, S. X. B. (1998) Re-examining China's "urban" concept and level of urbanization. *China Quarterly* 154, pp. 330–81.

Zhang, L., Zhao, S. X. B. and Tian, J. P. (2003) Self-help in housing and *chengzhongcun* in China's urbanization. *International Journal of Urban and Regional Research* 27 (4), pp. 912–37.

Zhang, T. W. (2000) Land market forces and government's role in sprawl. *Cities* 17 (2), pp. 123–35.

—— (2002a) Decentralization, localization, and the emergence of a quasi-participatory decision-making structure in urban development in Shanghai. *International Planning Studies* 7 (4), pp. 303–23.

—— (2002b) Challenges facing Chinese planners in transitional China. *Journal of Planning, Education and Research* 22 (1), pp. 64–76.

Zhao, S. X. B. (1998) Re-examining China's "urban" concept and the level of urbanization. *China Quarterly* 154, pp. 330–81.

Zhao, S. X. B., Chan, R. C. K. and Sit, K. T. O. (2003) Globalization and the dominance of large cities in contemporary China. *Cities* 20 (4), pp. 265–78.

Zhou, X. (2000) Economic transformation and income inequality in urban China: evidence from panel data. *American Journal of Sociology* 105 (4), pp. 1135–74.

Zhou, Y. and Chao, G. (1999) The progression of China's urbanization in the two decades since economic reforms and the open door. *City Planning Review* 12, pp. 8–15.

Zhou, Y. X. (1991) The metropolitan interlocking region in China: a preliminary hypothesis. In Ginsburg, N., Koppel, B. and McGee, T. G. (eds) (1991) *The Extended Metropolis: Settlement Transition in Asia.* Honolulu: University of Hawaii Press, pp. 89–111.

—— (1998) Beijing and the development of dual central business districts. *Geographical Review* 88 (3), pp. 429–36.

Zhou, Y. X. and Ma, L. J. C. (2000) Economic restructuring and suburbanization in China. *Urban Geography* 21 (3), pp. 205–36.

—— (2003) China's urbanization levels: reconstructing a baseline from the fifth population census. *China Quarterly* 173, pp. 176–96.

Zhou, Y. X. and Yang, Q. (1995) Geographical analysis of the industrial economic return of Chinese cities. *Urban Geography* 16 (6), pp. 505–20.

Zhu, H. C. and Wang, D. Q. (2002) *Kunshan jingji huying Shanghai Pudong de zongti gouxiang* (*The Comprehensive Concept of the Mutual Kunshan Economic Echo of Shanghai Pudong*). [Excerpted from a personal communication from the first author], pp. 298–303 (in Chinese).

Zhu, Y. (1998) Formal and informal urbanization in China: trends in Fujian Province. *Third World Planning Review* 20 (3), pp. 267–84.

—— (1999) *New Paths to Urbanization in China: Seeking More Balanced Patterns*. New York: Nova Science Publishers.

—— (2000) In-situ urbanization in rural China: case studies from Fujian Province. *Development and Change* 31 (2), pp. 413–34.

—— (2002) Beyond large city-centred urbanization: in-situ transformations of rural areas in Fujian Province. *Asia Pacific Viewpoint* 43 (1), pp. 9–22.

—— (2004) Changing urbanization processes and in-situ transformation: reflections upon China's settlement definitions. In Champion, T. and Hugo, G. (eds) *New Forms of Urbanization: Beyond the Rural–Urban Dichotomy*. Aldershot and Burlington, VT: Ashgate, pp. 207–28.

Zhu, Z. G. and Yau, S. (2000) New patterns of urban development in China. *Chinese Geographical Science* 10 (1), pp. 20–9.

Index